PENGUIN CLASSICS

THE MERRY WIVES OF WINDSOR

T. J. B. SPENCER, sometime Director of the Shakespeare Institute of the University of Birmingham, was the founding editor of the New Penguin Shakespeare, for which he edited both *Romeo and Juliet* and *Hamlet*.

STANLEY WELLS is Honorary President of the Shakespeare Birthplace Trust, Emeritus Professor of Shakespeare Studies at the University of Birmingham, and General Editor of the Oxford Shakespeare. His many books include *Shakespeare: For All Time*, *Shakespeare & Co.*, *Shakespeare, Sex, and Love* and *Great Shakespeare Actors*.

G. R. HIBBARD taught at the Universities of Nottingham and Waterloo, Canada. Author of the standard biography of Thomas Nashe, he edited, among other plays, the Penguin Shakespeare editions of *Coriolanus*, *The Taming of the Shrew* and *Timon of Athens*.

CATHERINE RICHARDSON is a Reader in Renaissance Studies at the University of Kent. She studies the literature and history of early modern material culture, and has written books on *Domestic Life and Domestic Tragedy in Early Modern England* (2006), *Shakespeare and Material Culture* (2011) and, with Tara Hamling, *A Day at Home in Early Modern England: The Materiality of Domestic Life, 1500–1700* (2016).

WILLIAM SHAKESPEARE

The Merry Wives of Windsor

Edited with a Commentary by
G. R. HIBBARD
and with an Introduction by
CATHERINE RICHARDSON

PENGUIN BOOKS

PENGUIN CLASSICS

UK | USA | Canada | Ireland | Australia
India | New Zealand | South Africa

Penguin Books is part of the Penguin Random House group of companies
whose addresses can be found at global.penguinrandomhouse.com.

This edition first published in Penguin Books 1973
Reissued in the Penguin Shakespeare series 2005
Reissued in Penguin Classics 2015

001

Set in PostScript Monotype Fournier
Typeset by Palimpsest Book Production Limited, Falkirk, Stirlingshire
Printed in Great Britain by Clays Ltd, St Ives plc

ISBN: 978-0-141-39657-6

www.greenpenguin.co.uk

MIX
Paper from
responsible sources
FSC® C018179

Penguin Random House is committed to a
sustainable future for our business, our readers
and our planet. This book is made from Forest
Stewardship Council® certified paper.

Contents

General Introduction

Every play by Shakespeare is unique. This is part of his greatness. A restless and indefatigable experimenter, he moved with a rare amalgamation of artistic integrity and dedicated professionalism from one kind of drama to another. Never shackled by convention, he offered his actors the alternation between serious and comic modes from play to play, and often also within the plays themselves, that the repertory system within which he worked demanded, and which provided an invaluable stimulus to his imagination. Introductions to individual works in this series attempt to define their individuality. But there are common factors that underpin Shakespeare's career.

Nothing in his heredity offers clues to the origins of his genius. His upbringing in Stratford-upon-Avon, where he was born in 1564, was unexceptional. His mother, born Mary Arden, came from a prosperous farming family. Her father chose her as his executor over her eight sisters and his four stepchildren when she was only in her late teens, which suggests that she was of more than average practical ability. Her husband John, a glover, apparently unable to write, was nevertheless a capable businessman and loyal townsfellow, who seems to have fallen on relatively hard times in later life. He would have been brought up as a Catholic, and may have retained

Catholic sympathies, but his son subscribed publicly to Anglicanism throughout his life.

The most important formative influence on Shakespeare was his school. As the son of an alderman who became bailiff (or mayor) in 1568, he had the right to attend the town's grammar school. Here he would have received an education grounded in classical rhetoric and oratory, studying authors such as Ovid, Cicero and Quintilian, and would have been required to read, speak, write and even think in Latin from his early years. This classical education permeates Shakespeare's work from the beginning to the end of his career. It is apparent in the self-conscious classicism of plays of the early 1590s such as the tragedy of *Titus Andronicus*, *The Comedy of Errors*, and the narrative poems *Venus and Adonis* (1592–3) and *The Rape of Lucrece* (1593–4), and is still evident in his latest plays, informing the dream visions of *Pericles* and *Cymbeline* and the masque in *The Tempest*, written between 1607 and 1611. It inflects his literary style throughout his career. In his earliest writings the verse, based on the ten-syllabled, five-beat iambic pentameter, is highly patterned. Rhetorical devices deriving from classical literature, such as alliteration and antithesis, extended similes and elaborate wordplay, abound. Often, as in *Love's Labour's Lost* and *A Midsummer Night's Dream*, he uses rhyming patterns associated with lyric poetry, each line self-contained in sense, the prose as well as the verse employing elaborate figures of speech. Writing at a time of linguistic ferment, Shakespeare frequently imports Latinisms into English, coining words such as abstemious, addiction, incarnadine and adjunct. He was also heavily influenced by the eloquent translations of the Bible in both the Bishops' and the Geneva versions. As his experience grows, his verse and prose become more supple,

the patterning less apparent, more ready to accommo-
date the rhythms of ordinary speech, more colloquial in
diction, as in the speeches of the Nurse in *Romeo and
Juliet*, the characterful prose of Falstaff and Hamlet's
soliloquies. The effect is of increasing psychological
realism, reaching its greatest heights in *Hamlet*, *Othello*,
King Lear, *Macbeth* and *Antony and Cleopatra*. Gradually
he discovered ways of adapting the regular beat of the
pentameter to make it an infinitely flexible instrument for
matching thought with feeling. Towards the end of his
career, in plays such as *The Winter's Tale*, *Cymbeline* and
The Tempest, he adopts a more highly mannered style,
in keeping with the more overtly symbolical and emblem-
atical mode in which he is writing.

So far as we know, Shakespeare lived in Stratford till
after his marriage to Anne Hathaway, eight years his
senior, in 1582. They had three children: a daughter,
Susanna, born in 1583 within six months of their marriage,
and twins, Hamnet and Judith, born in 1585. The next
seven years of Shakespeare's life are virtually a blank.
Theories that he may have been, for instance, a school-
master, or a lawyer, or a soldier, or a sailor, lack evidence
to support them. The first reference to him in print, in
Robert Greene's pamphlet *Greene's Groatsworth of Wit*
of 1592, parodies a line from *Henry VI, Part III*, implying
that Shakespeare was already an established playwright.
It seems likely that at some unknown point after the birth
of his twins he joined a theatre company and gained
experience as both actor and writer in the provinces and
London. The London theatres closed because of plague
in 1593 and 1594; and during these years, perhaps recognizing the need for an alternative career, he wrote and
published the narrative poems *Venus and Adonis* and *The
Rape of Lucrece*. These are the only works we can be

certain that Shakespeare himself was responsible for putting into print. Each bears the author's dedication to Henry Wriothesley, Earl of Southampton (1573–1624), the second in warmer terms than the first. Southampton, younger than Shakespeare by ten years, is the only person to whom he personally dedicated works. The Earl may have been a close friend, perhaps even the beautiful and adored young man whom Shakespeare celebrates in his *Sonnets*.

The resumption of playing after the plague years saw the founding of the Lord Chamberlain's Men, a company to which Shakespeare was to belong for the rest of his career, as actor, shareholder and playwright. No other dramatist of the period had so stable a relationship with a single company. Shakespeare knew the actors for whom he was writing and the conditions in which they performed. The permanent company was made up of around twelve to fourteen players, but one actor often played more than one role in a play and additional actors were hired as needed. Led by the tragedian Richard Burbage (1568–1619) and, initially, the comic actor Will Kemp (d. 1603), they rapidly achieved a high reputation, and when King James I succeeded Queen Elizabeth I in 1603 they were renamed as the King's Men. All the women's parts were played by boys; there is no evidence that any female role was ever played by a male actor over the age of about eighteen. Shakespeare had enough confidence in his boys to write for them long and demanding roles such as Rosalind (who, like other heroines of the romantic comedies, is disguised as a boy for much of the action) in *As You Like It*, Lady Macbeth and Cleopatra. But there are far more fathers than mothers, sons than daughters, in his plays, few if any of which require more than the company's normal complement of three or four boys.

The company played primarily in London's public playhouses – there were almost none that we know of in the rest of the country – initially in the Theatre, built in Shoreditch in 1576, and from 1599 in the Globe, on Bankside. These were wooden, more or less circular structures, open to the air, with a thrust stage surmounted by a canopy and jutting into the area where spectators who paid one penny stood, and surrounded by galleries where it was possible to be seated on payment of an additional penny. Though properties such as cauldrons, stocks, artificial trees or beds could indicate locality, there was no representational scenery. Sound effects such as flourishes of trumpets, music both martial and amorous, and accompaniments to songs were provided by the company's musicians. Actors entered through doors in the back wall of the stage. Above it was a balconied area that could represent the walls of a town (as in *King John*), or a castle (as in *Richard II*), and indeed a balcony (as in *Romeo and Juliet*). In 1609 the company also acquired the use of the Blackfriars, a smaller, indoor theatre to which admission was more expensive, and which permitted the use of more spectacular stage effects such as the descent of Jupiter on an eagle in *Cymbeline* and of goddesses in *The Tempest*. And they would frequently perform before the court in royal residences and, on their regular tours into the provinces, in non-theatrical spaces such as inns, guildhalls and the great halls of country houses.

Early in his career Shakespeare may have worked in collaboration, perhaps with Thomas Nashe (1567–c. 1601) in *Henry VI, Part I* and with George Peele (1556–96) in *Titus Andronicus*. And towards the end he collaborated with George Wilkins (*fl.* 1604–8) in *Pericles*, and with his younger colleagues Thomas Middleton (1580–1627), in *Timon of Athens*, and John Fletcher (1579–1625), in *Henry*

xii   *General Introduction*

VIII, *The Two Noble Kinsmen* and the lost play *Cardenio*. Shakespeare's output dwindled in his last years, and he died in 1616 in Stratford, where he owned a fine house, New Place, and much land. His only son had died at the age of eleven, in 1596, and his last descendant died in 1670. New Place was destroyed in the eighteenth century but the other Stratford houses associated with his life are maintained and displayed to the public by the Shakespeare Birthplace Trust.

One of the most remarkable features of Shakespeare's plays is their intellectual and emotional scope. They span a great range from the lightest of comedies, such as *The Two Gentlemen of Verona* and *The Comedy of Errors*, to the profoundest of tragedies, such as *King Lear* and *Macbeth*. He maintained an output of around two plays a year, ringing the changes between comic and serious. All his comedies have serious elements: Shylock, in *The Merchant of Venice*, almost reaches tragic dimensions, and *Measure for Measure* is profoundly serious in its examination of moral problems. Equally, none of his tragedies is without humour: Hamlet is as witty as any of his comic heroes, *Macbeth* has its Porter, and *King Lear* its Fool. His greatest comic character, Falstaff, inhabits the history plays and *Henry V* ends with a marriage, while *Henry VI, Part III*, *Richard II* and *Richard III* culminate in the tragic deaths of their protagonists.

Although in performance Shakespeare's characters can give the impression of a superabundant reality, he is not a naturalistic dramatist. None of his plays is explicitly set in his own time. The action of few of them (except for the English histories) is set even partly in England (exceptions are *The Merry Wives of Windsor* and the Induction to *The Taming of the Shrew*). Italy is his favoured location. Most of his principal story-lines derive from printed writings; but the structuring and translation of these narratives into dramatic terms is Shakespeare's own, and he invents much additional material. Most of the plays contain elements of myth and legend, and many derive from ancient or more recent history or from romantic tales of ancient times and faraway places. All reflect his reading, often in close detail. Holinshed's *Chronicles* (1577, revised 1587), a great compendium of English, Scottish and Irish history, provided material for his English history plays. The *Lives of the Noble Grecians and Romans* by the Greek writer Plutarch, finely translated into English from the French by Sir Thomas North in 1579, provided much of the narrative material, and also a mass of verbal detail, for his plays about Roman history. Some plays are closely based on shorter individual works: *As You Like It*, for instance, on the novel *Rosalynde* (1590) by his near-contemporary Thomas Lodge (1558–1625), *The Winter's Tale* on *Pandosto* (1588) by his old rival Robert Greene (1558–92) and *Othello* on a story by the Italian Giraldi Cinthio (1504–73). And the language of his plays is permeated by the Bible, the Book of Common Prayer and the proverbial sayings of his day.

Shakespeare was popular with his contemporaries, but his commitment to the theatre and to the plays in performance is demonstrated by the fact that only about half of his plays appeared in print in his lifetime, in slim paperback volumes known as quartos, so called because they were made from printers' sheets folded twice to form four leaves (eight pages). None of them shows any sign that he was involved in their publication. For him, performance was the primary means of publication. The most frequently reprinted of his works were the non-dramatic poems – the erotic *Venus and Adonis* and the more moralistic *The Rape of Lucrece*. The *Sonnets*, which appeared in 1609, under his name but possibly without his consent, were less successful, perhaps because the vogue for sonnet sequences, which peaked in the 1590s, had passed by then. They were not reprinted until 1640, and then only in garbled form along with poems by other writers. Happily, in 1623, seven years after he died, his colleagues John Heminges (1556–1630) and Henry Condell (d. 1627) published his collected plays, including eighteen that had not previously appeared in print, in the first Folio, whose name derives from the fact that the printers' sheets were folded only once to produce two leaves (four pages). Some of the quarto editions are badly printed, and the fact that some plays exist in two, or even three, early versions creates problems for editors. These are discussed in the Account of the Text in each volume of this series.

Shakespeare's plays continued in the repertoire until the Puritans closed the theatres in 1642. When performances resumed after the Restoration of the monarchy in 1660 many of the plays were not to the taste of the times, especially because their mingling of genres and failure to meet the requirements of poetic justice offended against the dictates of neoclassicism. Some, such as *The Tempest* (changed by John Dryden and William Davenant in 1667 to suit contemporary taste), *King Lear* (to which Nahum Tate gave a happy ending in 1681) and *Richard III* (heavily adapted by Colley Cibber in 1700 as a vehicle for his own talents), were extensively rewritten; others fell into neglect. Slowly they regained their place in the repertoire, and they continued to be reprinted, but it was not until the great actor David Garrick (1717–79) organized a spectacular jubilee in Stratford in 1769 that Shakespeare began to be regarded as a transcendental genius. Garrick's idolatry prefigured the enthusiasm of critics such as Samuel Taylor Coleridge (1772–1834) and William Hazlitt (1778–1830). Gradually Shakespeare's reputation spread abroad, to Germany, America, France and to other European countries.

During the nineteenth century, though the plays were generally still performed in heavily adapted or abbreviated versions, a large body of scholarship and criticism began to amass. Partly as a result of a general swing in education away from the teaching of Greek and Roman texts and towards literature written in English, Shakespeare became the object of intensive study in schools and universities. In the theatre, important turning points were the work in England of two theatre directors, William Poel (1852–1934) and his disciple Harley Granville-Barker (1877–1946), who showed that the application of knowledge, some of it newly acquired, of early staging conditions to performance of the plays could render the original texts viable in terms of the modern theatre. During the twentieth century appreciation of Shakespeare's work, encouraged by the availability of audio, film and video versions of the plays, spread around the world to such an extent that he can now be claimed as a global author.

The influence of Shakespeare's works permeates the English language. Phrases from his plays and poems – 'a tower of strength', 'green-eyed jealousy', 'a foregone conclusion' – are on the lips of people who may never have read him. They have inspired composers of songs, orchestral music and operas; painters and sculptors; poets, novelists and film-makers. Allusions to him appear in pop songs, in advertisements and in television shows. Some of his characters – Romeo and Juliet, Falstaff, Shylock and Hamlet – have acquired mythic status. He is valued for his humanity, his psychological insight, his wit and humour, his lyricism, his mastery of language, his ability to excite, surprise, move and, in the widest sense of the word, entertain audiences. He is the greatest of poets, but he is essentially a dramatic poet. Though his plays have much to offer to readers, they exist fully only in performance. In these volumes we offer individual introductions, notes on language and on specific points of the text, suggestions for further reading and information about how each work has been edited. In addition we include accounts of the ways in which successive generations of interpreters and audiences have responded to challenges and rewards offered by the plays. The Penguin Shakespeare series aspires to remove obstacles to understanding and to make pleasurable the reading of the work of the man who has done more than most to make us understand what it is to be human.

Stanley Wells

The Chronology of Shakespeare's Works

A few of Shakespeare's writings can be fairly precisely dated. An allusion to the Earl of Essex in the chorus to Act V of *Henry V*, for instance, could only have been written in 1599. But for many of the plays we have only vague information, such as the date of publication, which may have occurred long after composition, the date of a performance, which may not have been the first, or a list in Francis Meres's book *Palladis Tamia*, published in 1598, which tells us only that the plays listed there must have been written by that year. The chronology of the early plays is particularly difficult to establish. Not everyone would agree that the first part of *Henry VI* was written after the third, for instance, or *Romeo and Juliet* before *A Midsummer Night's Dream*. The following table is based on the 'Canon and Chronology' section in *William Shakespeare: A Textual Companion*, by Stanley Wells and Gary Taylor, with John Jowett and William Montgomery (1987), where more detailed information and discussion may be found.

The Two Gentlemen of Verona	1590–91
The Taming of the Shrew	1590–91
Henry VI, Part II	1591
Henry VI, Part III	1591

Introduction

'WIVES MAY BE MERRY, AND YET HONEST TOO'

So says Mistress Page (IV.2.99), pausing to give the audience a little feminine wisdom as she and her fellow 'Windsor wife' Mistress Ford prepare to humiliate Falstaff, the lecherous old knight who is courting them both. But what did being 'merry' mean in the sixteenth century? This is a very merry play in the sense that it's a very funny play – two comical stories of wooing intertwined, and a good deal of absurd competition and jealousy between men. Mistress Ford and Mistress Page are the subjects of the play's title – the only one of Shakespeare's plays named solely for women. They're not just the wives of Windsor, they're the 'merry wives' – merry in the sense that they generate a great deal of the comedy of the play by plotting to humiliate Falstaff and teach Mistress Ford's jealous husband a lesson. They are joyous, full of mirth, and constantly lively and animated. They're merry because they can see that the kinds of punishment that will teach men not to be lecherous, or jealous, make great entertainment. In this sense they 'make merry' – they make fun of other people and turn that into sport for the audience; they recognize the power of laughter. They have a keen eye for a spectacle and for its onstage and offstage audiences. They are also, like the play over which they preside, very English – they represent Merry England, celebrating the resourcefulness and good nature of its inhabitants in Shakespeare's only English comedy.

But that statement by Mistress Page suggests a darker connection, between being merry and being 'honest', meaning of good reputation. She hints at early modern concerns about the nature of women – is it possible for women to be so lively and amusing without being too uninhibited, too open and too accessible to men? Is it possible for them to organize plots that punish men and yet remain free from the suspicion of scandal generated by private actions performed behind their husbands' backs? These questions are central to the play, as each of the different plot-lines turns upon the balance between humour and honesty. The Pages' daughter Anne is to be married with a large dowry, and almost all the single men in the play are involved in wooing her – the doctor, the parson, the courtier and the justice's nephew. One man who isn't interested in Anne is Sir John Falstaff – he is busy sending love letters to her mother and her mother's friend, wooing them in courtly style and trying to arrange a meeting in order to lay hands on their husbands' money. Falstaff, filled with anticipation, attends three trysts. The wives, filled with indignation, make sure the meetings turn into three scenes of knightly humiliation. In the process, the wildly jealous Master Ford is taught to trust his wife. Being merry women in early modern England meant exhibiting a dangerous inventiveness, liveliness and strength. These questions of the power of laughter and humiliation and the control of reputation give *The Merry Wives of Windsor* a threatening force that adds depth to the absurd circumstances and knock-about scenes of its comedy.

WHAT KIND OF PLAY IS
THE MERRY WIVES OF WINDSOR?

Although, as the General Introduction to this volume indicates, 'Every play by Shakespeare is unique', *The Merry Wives of Windsor* is more unique than most. Shakespeare's history plays are about English national identity and they present narratives of significant military and political action in a clearly located past. This play also depicts English men and women, but they are not 'all the chivalry of England' (*Henry IV, Part II*, II.3.20) – the characters of highest status are arguably the most ridiculous. In the histories, Shakespeare offers his audience an elite view of events which is sometimes also commented upon by characters from the bottom of the social scale; in this play, however, he gives us the perspective of those of middling status, looking up to the court in Windsor Castle.

The Merry Wives of Windsor shares its most prominent character with the histories: Falstaff also appears in *Henry IV, Parts I* and *II* and is mentioned in *Henry V*, plays which Shakespeare was writing just before and just after *Merry Wives*. Falstaff was so popular and well known that he could cross between genres, and he brings Mistress Quickly, his followers and even Justice Shallow with him into this play. *Merry Wives* can seem like the continuation of an old story, then, but in this comedy Falstaff acts differently. Here he converses with wives rather than princes, and those wives take his jests very seriously. He has been 'updated' to a world in which bills have to be paid and responsibility taken for actions; a world that looks exactly like the sixteenth century in which Shakespeare was writing the play. Involved in local rather than national events, domestic rather than political, Falstaff's very presence shows just how different *The Merry Wives of Windsor* is from the grand scale of the history plays.

Shakespeare's other comedies deal with the frustrations of lovers trying to woo and wed in difficult circumstances. The comedies he wrote just before and after *Merry Wives* are located in exotic places; their plots are often fantastical, dealing with mistaken identity or the pairing of twins, and therefore with recovery and restoration after periods of confusion. They treat the spontaneity of youthful love, and its triumphs over the claustrophobic protectiveness of the older generation; and they frequently do so in the form of passionate poetry. But in *The Merry Wives of Windsor* the most prominent 'lover' is a fat old knight whose passion is for *two* women, or rather for their husbands' money. And then there is the frequent use of prose rather than verse in this play, which fits its parochial English subject matter, stressing the significance of the everyday, the importance of the unmomentous and the domestic.

The play opens with a matter of just such comparative unimportance – the self-righteous fury of 'Robert Shallow, Esquire', introduced as 'justice of peace', 'a gentleman born . . . who writes himself Armigero [gentleman]'. He is not to be dissuaded by Sir Hugh the parson: he is determined to take Sir John Falstaff to the Star Chamber – the court presided over by the Queen's Privy Council – because he has been 'wronged'. The excessive rehearsal of his titles represents an attempt to compete in status with the fat knight. He claims that

Falstaff has 'beaten my men, killed my deer, and broke open my lodge' (105–6) – he has ravaged his hunting park and poached his deer, symbols of his elite status. He wishes for the days of his youth: 'O'my life, if I were young again, the sword should end it' (37–8), but is counselled by Sir Hugh towards mediation – 'friends', suggests the parson, should be the sword – they should intervene between the two men with wise counsel rather than violence.

This opening focuses upon wrongdoing, on past acts of violence and disorder, and on a whole variety of ways of achieving justice and restitution for them. There is the possibility of an edgy tension as Falstaff himself comes on to the stage and responds to the accusation: 'I have done all this' (109). He claims to have 'answered' Shallow, but he plays on the two meanings of 'answer' – to make amends and to reply. The threats of violence are, however, undercut by the pomposity of Shallow, the age of the two potential combatants and the absurdity of Shallow's nephew Slender, whose attempts to bolster his uncle's status by pointing out the heredity of his claim to sign his name 'Armigero', or gentleman, are plagued by confusions: 'All his successors gone before him hath done't; and all his ancestors that come after him may' (13–14).

Wrongdoing is rife in the play. While the Fords and the Pages have households of servants and children, Falstaff has a retinue of dishonourable rogues. Slender describes them as 'your cony-catching [thieving] rascals, Bardolph, Nym, and Pistol' (I.1.118–19). Their knightly master's poverty and the fact that he chooses associates who are always pilfering and are at any moment likely to be looking 'through the grate [prison bars], like a geminy [pair] of baboons' (II.2.8–9) produces a curious association between high and low status. Although

Falstaff is a knight who commands high poetry – 'Have I caught thee, my heavenly jewel?' he asks Mistress Page (III.3.40) – he is nevertheless pragmatic, or perhaps immoral, enough to be prepared to make money by cheating people. 'There is no remedy', he claims near the start of the play, 'I must cony-catch, I must shift.' (I.3.30–31). To cony-catch was to cheat people out of their goods and money, often through elaborate confidence tricks. It was a type of crime which developed in streetwise cities, where shrewd and hardened urban dwellers preyed upon newly arrived innocents from the country. Pistol's own brand of cony-catching has an elegantly phrased violence: 'Why then, the world's mine oyster, | Which I with sword will open' (II.2.2–3); Falstaff's cony-catching involves the fraudulent wooing of two town wives.

Misconduct and transgression generate several plotlines through which revenge is proposed, discussed and exacted. Dr Caius and Sir Hugh are humiliated by the Host of the Garter when he frustrates their attempts to settle their quarrel with a duel. The Host sends both cowards to different spots to await each other, partly to avoid bloodshed, but mainly for the entertainment of the rest of the community, who watch their increasing ill-humour with amusement. The desired 'peaceful' resolution is achieved when the two parties realize that they both want to get their own back. As Sir Hugh says, speaking in Shakespeare's imitation of Welsh dialect, 'I desire you that we may be friends, and let us knog our prains together to be revenge on this same scald, scurvy, cogging companion, the host of the Garter' (III.1.108–11). It is revenge which resolves their hostility, and which later finds fulfilment in the confusing scheme for the theft of the Host's horses.

The other revenge plots in the play are closely linked. Falstaff's men Pistol and Nym take exception to being asked by their master to deliver his love letters to the merry wives – it is a job beneath their status. Refusing point-blank, they plot vengeance instead:

NYM I have operations which be humours of revenge.
PISTOL Wilt thou revenge?
NYM   By welkin and her star! (I.3.84–5)

With an elegance typical of this play's designs, their revenge entails delivering the *intent* of the letters rather than the actual letters, and not to the wives themselves but to their husbands. The contrast between Ford's jealousy and Page's faith in his wife's chastity is revealed by this petty plan for revenge, when the husbands receive the information about their wives' potential unfaithfulness. It leads Ford to visit Falstaff disguised as a Master Brook, in order to find out about the knight's liaisons with his wife.

Pistol asks Nym whether he will take his revenge 'With wit or steel' (I.3.86). The play's revenge plots move between these two poles of cunning and violence: from Shallow's obsession with using his sword; to the doctor's and priest's efforts to avoid using theirs; via Pistol's empty boast that he will use both wit *and* steel; to the least violent and most witty of the revenge plots, that of the wives against Falstaff.

On reading his letter, Mistress Page's fury leads first to a generalized sexism – 'Why, I'll exhibit a bill in the parliament for the putting down of men' (II.1.26–7) – and then to a very particularized vengeance: 'How shall I be revenged on him? For revenged I will be, as sure as his guts are made of puddings' (27–9). Taking her oath upon the surety of his bulk, she compares letters with her neighbour. Mistress Ford shares her feelings: 'How shall I be revenged on him? I think the best way were to entertain him with hope till the wicked fire of lust have melted him' (61–3). Rather than the decisive violence of the sword, the women achieve redress through the comic violence of near drownings and bizarre beatings – through their ability to conceive of revenge as sport, as entertainment.

Both wives focus upon Falstaff's bulk, as though their plotting had been generated by a fascinated disgust at the connection between such a man and the physical lusts of wooing. But Mistress Ford's speech also hints at the less personal motivations for the wives' actions: 'What tempest, I trow, threw this whale, with so many tuns of oil in his belly, ashore at Windsor?' (59–60). Falstaff is incongruous in Windsor society – both physically outsized and morally unacceptable – and Mistress Ford's image of the accidentally beached whale underscores the impermanence of his association with the town: lodged but not settled, parasitic upon its inhabitants and offering nothing in return.

THE WINDSOR COMMUNITY

The concept of community in Windsor is central to the revenge plots and the comedy of the play. The physical and social closeness of the town's inhabitants and the threats to its morals shape the story. English communities in Shakespeare's time were undergoing huge changes. The period in which he was writing *The Merry Wives of Windsor* saw massive migration from the countryside into towns and a corresponding increase in the perceived

threat of violence and social disorder. This was a period
in which social peace and calm was understood not as
the normal state for human beings but as something which
needed to be fought for and legislated for on a daily basis,
and which could be ensured only through the rigorous
maintenance of social hierarchies. Women were subject
to men, whose responsibility it was to curb their wayward
nature, and the lower orders were subject to their super-
iors. Good citizens were those who had a reputation for
honesty and peaceable dealing, and individuals cared
deeply about their 'good name'. The several plots of *The
Merry Wives of Windsor* are all centrally concerned with
these issues of communal harmony and the maintenance
of reputation.

So what kind of community does Shakespeare depict
in Windsor? The first thing we notice about it is its diversity. There are the 'comic foreigners' – the Welsh parson
Sir Hugh and the French doctor Dr Caius, the two professional men to whom the Host refers as 'soul-curer and
body-curer' (III.1.90); there is Shallow, the Justice of the
Peace who clearly lives locally but who also has lands in
Gloucestershire; there is Fenton, the young gentleman
who is Anne Page's own choice for her hand in marriage
– a courtier blown in from the castle next door; and there
is Falstaff, himself passing through, lodging at the inn
with his rugged band of men. The Pages and the Fords
with their respective households, Mistress Quickly and
the Host of the Garter Inn represent the stable indige-
nous householders and housekeepers of the town.

The social shape of the Windsor community is
revealed in the characters' discussions about Anne Page's
marriage. She brings with her a considerable dowry –
'Seven hundred pounds, and possibilities' (I.1.59–60) –
and the opportunities which this money offers for social

advancement are borne out by the quantity of her suitors. Of all the wooers, Slender is most self-conscious about his status, at pains to stress it by unsubtly dropping what he considers to be signs of refinement into conversations. Apart from his habit of swearing, gallant-like, 'by these gloves', he also swears by his own 'great chamber' (I.1.142–4) – identifying a room only to be found in the houses of the social elite.

Anne's other high-born wooer is Fenton, who is an impoverished courtier. The Host describes him in terms which connect his youth and vitality to courtly pursuits: 'He capers, he dances, he has eyes of youth, he writes verses, he speaks holiday, he smells April and May' (III.2.60–62). But Anne's father is firmly against him as a suitor to his daughter: 'He is of too high a region, he knows too much. No, he shall not knit a knot in his fortunes with the finger of my substance' (67–9). It is the combination of his elevated status and his reduced prosperity which makes Fenton an unsuitable match.

Of the other characters of eminent status, the pompous Shallow is a gentleman and Sir John Falstaff is of course a knight. Whilst Falstaff disgraces his rank by his exploits, Shallow falls short of gentility through his quarrelsome nature and his absurdity.

Each of these characters lacks wealth, or the wit to go with it. The play satirizes early modern ways of defining rank: Fenton and Falstaff have the status; Page and Ford have the money; none of them has both; Slender and Shallow have some of each but barely a brain between them. Shakespeare depicts a community tied together by the need to strengthen or increase social position, and it is, as a result, an introspective community. No character is so secure in his own social position that he entirely rises above the specific concerns and interests of Windsor life to offer the audience a touchstone of impartial wisdom or moral absolutes.

The setting of the play is also important to the kind of community Shakespeare represents – by setting *Merry Wives* in a town situated next to a royal castle he can comment on the social pretensions of his characters. Connections between the town and the royal court are imagined physically and verbally. Dr Caius is often on his way there, advising his servant Rugby to 'Come, take-a your rapier, and come after my heel to the court' (I.4.57–8), to visit 'de earl, de knight, de lords, de gentle-men, my patients' (II.3.83–4). Even Falstaff's man Bardolph has knowledge of the comings and goings of the elite, adding to the revenge plot against the Host by volunteering the spurious information that 'The Duke himself will be tomorrow at court' (IV.3.2). But it is Falstaff and Mistress Quickly who give linguistic shape to all that is courtly and elegantly polished. The former describes his younger rivals amongst the courtiers in terms which are sensual despite his mockery: 'these lisping hawthorn-buds that come like women in men's apparel and smell like Bucklersbury in simple-time' (III.3.67–9). Mistress Quickly's evocative recollection of a time 'when the court lay at Windsor', and when Mistress Ford was wooed by courtiers, 'coach after coach, letter after letter, gift after gift', similarly focuses upon the experiential difference between the elite and non-elite, the former 'smelling so sweetly – all musk – and so rushling, I warrant you, in silk and gold, and in such alligant terms' (II.2.60–66). It is the promise of such a life that Falstaff mistakenly assumes will lure the wives into intimacy. As he says to Mistress Ford, 'Thou wouldst make an absolute courtier, and the firm fixture of thy foot would give an

excellent motion to thy gait in a semi-circled farthingale'
(III.3.57–60).

The differences between court and town life are made
manifest for the audience in these descriptions, but so is
the influence of the court – it is always just offstage,
offering a regular spectacle for townspeople like Mistress
Quickly to enjoy. These splashes of elite colour make
the community of Windsor a uniquely diverse one,
touched by greatness and yet plagued by petty crime.

The sense of Windsor as a cosmopolitan and yet
coherent society comes most strongly from the carefully
differentiated languages of its inhabitants. This play has
more references to English as a language than any of
Shakespeare's other plays, and very many of them are
negative, in the sense that they involve characters
complaining about their fellows' use and abuse of words.
Page says of Nym, 'Here's a fellow frights English out
of his wits' (II.1.129–30), and Mistress Quickly refers to
her master Caius's 'old abusing of God's patience and
the King's English' (I.4.5). Shakespeare makes great comic
capital out of the misuse of words, one memorable
example being Caius's expression of his willingness to
join the small party of neighbours going hawking: 'If
there be one or two, I shall make-a the turd' (III.3.22).
Forestalling the duel between Caius and Evans, the Host
gives orders to 'Disarm them, and let them question'.
Replacing swords with words, he advises, 'Let them keep
their limbs whole and hack our English' (III.1.70–71). In
his final humiliation, Falstaff protests against Sir Hugh
Evans with 'Have I lived to stand at the taunt of one that
makes fritters of English?' (V.5.141–2). The national
language is being hacked and slashed by foreigners.

But the community also gains variety through the
dense and cunning use of words. The language used by

Falstaff and the Host is the most complex. 'Discard, bully Hercules, cashier. Let them wag; trot, trot' (I.3.6–7), says host to guest, as Falstaff explains his inability to afford his impecunious retinue any longer. The Host's language is frequently excessive, building up anticipation of the duel he has in fact already prevented by accumulating words one upon another. He has come, he says to Caius, 'To see thee fight, to see thee foin, to see thee traverse, to see thee here, to see thee there, to see thee pass thy punto, thy stock, thy reverse, thy distance, thy montant' (II.3.21–4).

This immoderate use of words and phrases is also present in Falstaff's speech, for instance his abuse of Pistol, whom he accuses of trying to 'ensconce your rags, your cat-a-mountain looks, your red-lattice phrases, and your bold beating oaths, under the shelter of your honour!' (II.2.25–7). It is his over-indulgence in language which gives him energy – more energy than is usual for a man of his age and bulk. 'O, she did so course o'er my exteriors with such a greedy intention that the appetite of her eye did seem to scorch me up like a burning-glass' (I.3.60–62), he says of Mistress Page. Shakespeare endows him with virility through the immoderation of his language – his sheer verbal force creating energetic sexual potency: 'She is a region in Guiana, all gold and bounty . . . They shall be my East and West Indies, and I will trade to them both' (I.3.63–7).

The fat knight ascends and descends the registers of elite and popular language like an opera singer with incredible range. Within one speech he begins by addressing Robin, his page, in high courtly style, and progresses to attend to Pistol and Nym in language more appropriate for talking to an animal:

Sail like my pinnace to these golden shores.
Rogues, hence, avaunt! Vanish like hailstones, go!
Trudge, plod away o'th'hoof, seek shelter, pack!'

$$(\text{I.3.75–7})$$

As London expanded through immigration in the sixteenth century its inhabitants became used to hearing a hubbub of different dialects, and Shakespeare reflects this complex soundscape throughout the play. Falstaff's men cony-catch – they cheat people by using strange language – Bardolph's description of Slender's drunkenness on the night when they picked his pocket, for instance: 'And being fap, sir, was, as they say, cashiered. And so conclusions passed the careers.' Slender's response to this curious kind of speech is to assume he is speaking a foreign language: 'Ay, you spake in Latin then too' (I.1.164–6). Add to this some rich dialect words – Mistress Quickly describing the Fords' marriage, 'she leads a very frampold life with him' (II.2.87), or Mistress Ford herself reprimanding her servants, 'Look how you drumble!' (III.3.139), and it is clear that Shakespeare's habitual experimentation with language is not lacking in *The Merry Wives of Windsor*. He uses these distinctive discourses to define a tight-knit community made out of the dynamic of variation and diversity: one in which difference leads to shared goals but also misunderstandings; united action but also competition.

The community of Windsor is equally carefully realized in the minute details of its geography. The various locations of the duel between Caius and Evans are situated in named places around the real Windsor. The Host, as coordinator of the event, sends Page, Shallow and Slender 'through the town to Frogmore' (II.3.68), constructing a huge geography just offstage by stating that he will then 'bring the doctor about by the fields' (70–71). Waiting in Frogmore with the other combatant, Simple sets out the range of places in which he has searched for Caius: 'Marry, sir, the pittie-ward, the park-ward, every way; Old Windsor way, and every way but the town way' (III.1.5–7). He then locates the stage within a wide landscape through which he can perceive others at a distance. 'There comes my master, Master Shallow,' he points out, 'and another gentleman, from Frogmore, over the stile, this way' (30–32). The town of Windsor is represented on the stage through these simple but specific details of places and spaces.

The sharp image of local life that the play offers its audiences led generations of scholars to look for parallels between the characters of _The Merry Wives of Windsor_ and people or stories known to Shakespeare. His Windsor seemed so real, they thought, it must have been based on real people. The opening accusation that Falstaff has poached deer, for instance, has been seen as an allusion to the legend that Shakespeare had to leave his home in Stratford-upon-Avon when he stole deer from the park of the Lucy family of Charlecote. Then there is the name taken by Master Ford when he disguises himself for his visits to Falstaff – Master Brook. This is seen as a gibe at William Brooke, Lord Cobham. The 'real' Brooke was offended when Shakespeare called his original old knight 'Oldcastle' after one of Cobham's relatives, and this led Shakespeare to rechristen him Falstaff. These and other allusions work by identifying important people who would have been familiar to Shakespeare's audience by name. For the families picked out in such a way, name was closely linked to reputation – connecting powerful landowners to bungling old justices offered a simple

but powerful form of mockery. Other critics have seen
allusions to more humble contemporary individuals. For
instance, the character of Page could be seen as a reference to a notorious contemporary murder, dramatized in
a lost play of 1599 by Ben Jonson and Thomas Dekker
called *Page of Plymouth*, in which a husband is murdered
by men bribed by his wife and her lover. Such topical
allusions would give the humorous treatment of jealousy
and the threat of betrayal a rather bitter edge. They
enlarge the themes of revenge and justice, suggesting
connections between the play and the genre of revenge
tragedy which later influenced *Hamlet*. If the play's first
audiences made connections like these, they would have
been amused by the disparities between wives who plot
murder by poisoning food and bribing servants and wives
who order their households impeccably. Such connections also take account of the socially very diverse
commercial theatre audience for this play, who would
perhaps be more familiar with the cheap pamphlets and
ballads which peddled contemporary crimes than they
would with references to the aristocracy.

Shakespeare constructs his illusion of a real Windsor
partly through small pieces of information which the
characters give away about shared experiences outside
the action of the play. Asked what he lost when he was
robbed by Pistol, Bardolph and Nym, Slender answers,
'two Edward shovel-boards [coins], that cost me two
shillings and twopence apiece of Yed Miller' (I.1.144–6).
The extraneous detail of the purchase of the coins from
Yed Miller is meant to emphasize the point that Slender
rarely understands the difference between pertinent and
impertinent information, but it also gives a suggestion of
his life prior to this point in the play. His man humours
him, in tones which could be mocking, when he searches

for his Book of Riddles: 'Book of Riddles? Why, did you not lend it to Alice Shortcake upon Allhallowmas last, a fortnight afore Michaelmas?' (I.1.188–90). The information is very silly, but these small details never-theless give a sense of a past to the characters – one which extends the notion of community and festive occasions backwards in time.

The much smarter Falstaff also tells similar tales of his men, ones which indicate shared memories of earlier adventures. He claims that he has obtained three reprieves for Pistol and his 'coach-fellow Nym', each achieved by trading on his own reputation. 'And when Mistress Bridget lost the handle of her fan,' he continues, 'I took't upon mine honour thou hadst it not' (II.2.8–13). To Brook, following his beating by Brook's alter ego Ford, he says, 'Since I plucked geese, played truant and whipped top, I knew not what 'twas to be beaten till lately' (V.1.23–4). And in doing so he gives the audience pause for thought about a young Falstaff, failing to learn right from wrong even at that age. Such particulars are true to the way real communities function – through memo-ries accumulated over time and through everyone's famil-iarity with often-told stories.

HOUSEHOLD AND THE COMEDY OF EVERYDAY LIFE

The Merry Wives of Windsor is a play about daily life – about eating and drinking, washing and going to school, wooing, loving and marrying, watching greyhounds racing and hawks hunting. And it is a play set within a very carefully realized domestic world. We have a clear sense of the Fords' house and Caius's, and of Falstaff's lodgings at the Garter Inn, just from reading the words on the page. The stage for which Shakespeare was writing had no elaborate sets with which to represent different houses. Instead, playwrights used the area above the stage (the one which also served as Juliet's balcony in *Romeo and Juliet*) and the doors at the back of it to indicate inside and outside, upstairs and downstairs: 'Run in here, good young man; go into this closet' (I.4.36–7), says Mistress Quickly to Simple as she tries to hide him from her master, sending him through one of the upstage doors. As Fenton calls from offstage, 'Who's within there, ho?', later in the scene, she answers, 'Who's there, I trow? Come near the house, I pray you' (127–9), and he enters through another one of the doors. Falstaff, ensconced within 'his chamber, his house, his castle . . . painted about with the story of the Prodigal, fresh and new', as the Host describes it (IV.5.5–7), calls to him from above, 'How now, mine host?' (17), and invites Mistress Quickly to 'Come up into my chamber' (118) with her final invitation from the wives.

These clear indications in the dialogue give the audience a strong sense of both the physical household within which the characters of the play go about their business and a world offstage which might be inhabited before the play starts and after it finishes, giving it an everyday life-likeness which comes close to soap opera. But they also indicate the very real possibility of being able to hide people just out of sight. During both of Falstaff's trips into Mistress Ford's house he hides himself: once, in a move which anticipates *Hamlet* in comic mode, 'behind the arras' (III.3.84–5); and then again, in response to his hostess's quick-thinking invitation: 'Step into the chamber, Sir John' (IV.2.9). Although the audience know that Falstaff's presence is innocent, the ease with which the wives achieve just what Ford fears – the concealment of even the fattest of lovers within the confines of the house – makes his jealousy troublingly less than ridiculous. The *only* thing which guarantees that early modern husbands are not being betrayed in their absence is the honesty of their wives; the deeds which they so dread are logistically entirely possible.

So Ford's jealousy is a very serious issue, despite its comic context. The irrational jealousy of husbands over their wives' relationships with other men is a theme which Shakespeare was to go on to explore to great tragic effect in both *Othello* (1603–4) and *The Winter's Tale* (1609). In these plays he considers how little it takes to make men jealous in a society where their reputation was inextricably linked to their wives' chastity. In both of these later plays the grounds for suspicion are very slight indeed, and the dramatic interest lies in the way emotion intensifies and is manipulated – Othello is persuaded by Iago across the course of the play to believe in an infidelity which he knew to be impossible, and Leontes' irrational and vehement distrust of his wife as *Winter's Tale* begins is eventually transformed into love by Paulina. In *Merry Wives* Shakespeare's concern is not to investigate the development of emotion, but rather to display its disturbing effects within the family and the community. The gravity of those effects balances the farcical humour of the comic mode in which he deals with them.

When Shakespeare was writing this play, the English house was undergoing a period of transformation. Over only a generation or so, houses had changed shape as families felt the need for different kinds of living space. The medieval halls – large rooms for general communal living which reached from floor to roof – had a ceiling added, halving their height and adding a second storey. With larger numbers of upstairs rooms there were more smaller spaces, and a higher level of privacy was possible. And there were many more things kept in these houses. This was the beginning of a consumer revolution – Shakespeare's contemporaries owned more chairs, more tables, more chests, more beds and more cupboards than their parents. They also owned more of the smaller items which make it possible to display your status to guests: they owned more cushions to soften the hard oak seating and more curtains to give privacy from the gaze of neighbours. And the numbers and quality of the objects they used for dining increased – more tablecloths and napkins for special occasions, more pewter vessels to eat from when guests came, and in some cases even silver ones. They had greater amounts of clothes and more sets of sheets, so that they could change them more frequently. A much larger proportion of everyone's wealth was being invested in these kinds of goods, but although people of every social group had more of some of these items, the expensive linens and pewter were being purchased by people of middling status – prosperous tradesmen and merchants, reasonably important people like the Pages and Fords, Slenders and Shallows, in small towns like Windsor.

Running a house was much more complicated now, and that made the role of women like Mistress Page and Mistress Ford more important. Household manuals – 'how to' guides – were published to explain how these new goods should be marshalled, and to set out the relative roles of men and women when it came to household management. When Master Ford tries to stop the buck-basket leaving the house, his wife reprimands him sharply and with deep sarcasm: 'Why, what have you to do

whither they bear it? You were best meddle with buck-
washing' (III.3.146–7). The success of her jest relies
upon the agreement between her statement and the advice
literature: on the surface of it she was absolutely right –
men were to leave domestic issues to women to deal with,
and to concentrate on their own affairs outside the house.
Mistress Quickly has a wry, comic take on all this extra
work, which she has to perform for Dr Caius: 'I keep his
house; and I wash, wring, brew, bake, scour, dress meat
and drink, make the beds, and do all myself' (I.4.93–5).
It is this division between male roles outside the house
and female roles inside, new and exciting for
Shakespeare's audience, which makes it possible for the
wives to hide their activities, and their knight, within the
household which they control for their husbands.

The contest between the wives' superior domestic
knowledge and authority and Ford's obsessive need to
keep ultimate control over his house generates the humour
in the two scenes in which Falstaff is caught there. In
response to the suggestion that he hide himself in the
kiln-hole, Mistress Ford asserts, 'He will seek there, on
my word. Neither press, coffer, chest, trunk, well, vault,
but he hath an abstract for the remembrance of such
places, and goes to them by his note. There is no hiding
you in the house' (IV.2.56–60). The household valuables
were stored in the presses, coffers, chests and trunks –
all the new goods which made up Master Ford's wealth
would be safely put away in these ideal hiding places.
Falstaff is wooing these women in order to steal their
husbands' money – as he says of Mistress Ford, 'she has
all the rule of her husband's purse' (I.3.48–9) – and imagining him in the coffers of money and amongst the household valuables provides an image of his potential plunder,
riffling through the well-ordered storage, substituting his

considerable person for the magnitude of the household goods.

Having learned of the knight's latest invitation whilst disguised as Brook, Ford speaks a soliloquy of desperate jealousy focused on his household spaces: 'He cannot creep into a halfpenny purse, nor into a pepperbox. But, lest the devil that guides him should aid him, I will search impossible places' (III.5.134–7). 'I'll creep into the chimney', says a frantic Falstaff as Ford approaches the house; 'Creep into the kiln-hole', advises Mistress Page (IV.2.50–54). With these suggestions, Falstaff does indeed enter the tiny spaces of the house in the audience's imagination. He tries to seep out of its walls like smoke, or be translated into bread, anything to melt what Hamlet calls his 'too, too solid flesh' and make himself invisible. In doing so he becomes the stuff of household chores – made potentially malleable in the hands of the wives who are expert in baking and the maintenance of fires, as a cruel contrast to his resolute physical solidity.

When Falstaff leaves the house in the buck- (or dirty-linen) basket – 'By the Lord, a buck-basket! Rammed me in' (III.5.81), as he complains to Brook – he is metaphorically associated with the dross of the house – linked to its dirt and equally in need of cleansing. Covered 'with foul shirts and smocks, socks, foul stockings, greasy napkins', and accompanied by 'the rankest compound of villainous smell that ever offended nostril' (82–5), his absorption in the brisk pace of domestic routine ensures that he receives the fitting treatment for his moral 'foulness'. In a parody of efficient practice the wives prove their domestic skills by treating him appropriately.

Falstaff's appetites make him perhaps the ultimate consumer, and the terms in which the wives discuss his bulk connect him closely to the way things are produced and consumed in the household. Mistress Ford bases her plan for revenge on entertaining him with hope until he has melted 'in his own grease' (II.1.63), and suggests that they 'use this unwholesome humidity, this gross watery pumpion [pumpkin]' (III.3.37–8). Falstaff also associates himself with cookery, describing his experiences in the basket to Ford, as a man 'as subject to heat as butter': 'when I was more than half stewed in grease, like a Dutch dish, to be thrown into the Thames, and cooled' (III.5.105–10). His excessively physical descriptions represent the play's only expressions of things bodily – they conjure up the actual parts of men and women to which lust directs the attention – and their interest in ravenous consumption and juiciness are almost sexual in themselves. Describing himself in these terms to Ford-disguised-as-Brook forces the latter to imagine the physicality of his wife's potential lover.

The wives' plots for shaming Falstaff provide three climaxes of energy and comedy. The first two meetings – when Falstaff leaves the Ford house in the buck-basket, and then in the costume of the fat woman of Brainford – generate a great deal of their humour from the fermented speed at which they work. 'Be not amazed,' Mistress Page advises her neighbour, having delivered the news that her husband is approaching, 'call all your senses to you, defend your reputation, or bid farewell to your good life for ever' (III.3.110–12). Given the stakes for reputation, the wives must act quickly – in the first scheme Mistress Page suggests Falstaff gets into the basket to be taken out to wash, but immediately she revises the plan: 'Or – it is whiting-time – send him by your two men to Datchet Mead' (III.3.123–4). The plot develops and extends swiftly, with a dextrous improvisation and inventiveness. In preparation for their last plot Mistress

Page says, 'Come, to the forge with it, then. Shape it. I would not have things cool' (IV.2.210–11). Plotting requires pace, and the wives' energies of manufacture and labour can be seen in both domestic tasks and the entertaining defeat of Falstaff's intentions.

There is a similar economy and thrift in the plots themselves, to which the wives draw the audience's attention. 'Is there not a double excellency in this?' Mistress Page asks, during Ford's search of the house. 'I know not which pleases me better – that my husband is deceived, or Sir John' (III.3.165–7), her friend replies. The two birds, of outsiders' lust and domestic jealousy, are killed with the single stone of the wives' shaming of Falstaff. The first time Ford is cheated as the knight slips past him in the basket, and Falstaff is humiliated by being disposed of in the cold waters of the Thames. The second time Ford once more misses his quarry but, with even greater efficiency, the wives use him to administer the physical punishment they desire for Falstaff – beating the knight in disguise to vent Ford's frustration at his inability to find Falstaff in his own person.

'As every man's house is his castle', said Richard Braithwaite in his 1630 *The English Gentleman*, 'so is his family a private commonwealth, wherein if due government be not observed, nothing but confusion is to be expected.' This was the period in which the connection between houses and castles became proverbial. Men delegated the responsibility of running domestic routines to their wives, but they remained in overall control. The husband's role within the house was a necessary training for his public duties because the failure of household government threatened national government: as John Dod and John Cleaver stated in their 1598 *Godlie Form of Household Government*, 'it is impossible for a man to understand to govern the common wealth, that doth not know to rule his own house'.

And this relationship between the domestic and the political gave the action of *The Merry Wives of Windsor* a further significance for early modern audiences. If domestic kings could not rule their castles, then what hope was there for order in the country as a whole? Women's behaviour, both within and without the household, had a direct influence on their husbands' reputation and honour. Wives who showed their husbands the ultimate disobedience of having them murdered, as tragedies based on these themes made clear to theatre audiences, were burnt at the stake for petty treason – this crime was the domestic equivalent of taking the life of a monarch. So Mistress Page's comment about being merry *and* honest was absolutely crucial the wives were playing a potentially very dangerous game by making a jest out of the possibility of disobeying male authority within their homes and damaging the wider reputation of the house.

Along with the financial importance of household order came the moral significance of domestic skill – the morality of doing things right, the 'honesty' of washing well and of running the household smoothly. Pistol, disguised as Hobgoblin at the end of the play, encourages the fairies in verse which promulgates exactly this notion of the moral importance of domestic tasks:

> Cricket, to Windsor chimneys shalt thou leap.
> Where fires thou findest unraked and hearths unswept,
> There pinch the maids as blue as bilberry.
> Our radiant Queen hates sluts and sluttery. (V.5.43–6)

Sluttery – the immorality of an unclean house – links women's household skills and their reputations, their routines of cleaning and the cleanliness of their bodies. And *The Merry Wives of Windsor* generates a bitter comedy from this connection too. In one of his flights of fantasy in conversation with Ford-disguised-as-Brook, Falstaff explains how he will take advantage of the man's wife: 'I will use her as the key of the cuckoldy rogue's coffer – and there's my harvest-home' (II.2.260–62). As his method of gaining entry to all Ford owns, she becomes herself one of his possessions – possessing her body becomes a strange kind of key to everything in the house.

This connection between women's bodies and their husbands' wealth casts a long shadow over the play. Suddenly, Ford's obsession with searching the smallest of hiding places takes on a sexual angle. Is it possible to imagine, in the peculiar circumstances in which he is paying Falstaff to seduce his own wife, a psychoanalytical reading of the way he searches the house for the fat knight? Is the 'really small' intimate female space, which this is *really* all about, being alluded to here in the productive openings of chimneys, chests and ovens – spaces which nourish and sustain family life?

A reading of *The Merry Wives of Windsor* in which the household is paired with the body of the woman who controls it helps to explain the disgust felt by Ford's neighbours about his insistence that they are present when he searches the house for his wife's lover. 'Here, here, here be my keys. Ascend my chambers. Search, seek, find out. I'll warrant we'll unkennel the fox' (III.3.152–4), he says. He is displaying all, opening up the inner recesses of his house in an inappropriate way and insisting that his neighbours view the whole: 'If there be anypody in the house,' says Sir Hugh Evans, 'and in the chambers, and in the coffers, and in the presses, heaven forgive my sins at the day of judgement' (198–200). One by one, Ford's onstage audience for his second attempt to find Falstaff in his house express their disapproval of this kind of display. 'Why, this passes, Master Ford', says his neighbour Page (IV.2.115), and 'this is not well, Master Ford. This wrongs you' (144–5), adds Shallow. 'Why, this is lunatics. This is mad as a mad dog', Evans begins (117), and later adds, '′Tis unreasonable. Will you take up your wife's clothes?' (132–3). To take up a woman's clothes was to pull up her skirts – to reveal the naked body underneath. The double entendre of Evans's strange English here shows the nakedness of Mistress Ford's reputation. Her husband is metaphorically displaying her body before the whole community in a mistaken attempt to preserve his family's good name.

PERSONAL REPUTATION
AND PUBLIC SPECTACLE

Ford's wild jealousy demonstrates the tight connection between male and female honesty felt by Shakespeare's audience, the former so often dependent upon the latter. The name 'cuckold', given to the husband of an unfaithful wife, shows how a woman's behaviour had the power to give her husband a dishonest name. The play's concern with male honour and reputation begins at the very beginning, with Shallow's determination to bring Falstaff to book for crimes against his property: 'Robert Shallow, Esquire, saith he is wronged' (I.1.100–101), the justice rather pompously says of himself. But on his entry Falstaff quickly points out the problem with achieving fitting redress for such crimes: "Twere better for you if it were known in counsel [private]. You'll be laughed at' (112–13). Although Shallow is determined to have amends made, the more people know about his loss, the larger the audience for Falstaff's mockery of his honour.

Falstaff's battery of Ford's honour, however, is a much larger project which spreads its pitiless humour through the scenes in which the latter meets him as Brook. In Act II, scene 2 he treats the hapless Brook to some of his most inventively abusive language as he pours scorn on Ford, calling him 'poor cuckoldy knave! . . . jealous wittolly knave' (257–9) and 'mechanical salt-butter rogue!' (265). 'Hang him,' he begins each time, going on to state, 'I will stare him out of his wits. I will awe him with my cudgel; it shall hang like a meteor o'er the cuckold's horns' (65–7). As Falstaff aggrandizes himself physically, imagining through the sheer force of his inventive rhetoric the power of a sexual prowess he is far from possessing, so Ford is diminished – eventually, in Act III, scene 5, plumbing the depths of the knight's descriptive powers as 'the peaking cornuto [cuckold] her husband' (65–6).

Ford's concerns are not expressed in the tragic terms of Othello's jealousy – as the heartrending loss of the purity of a beloved's love. Rather, in addition to the threat to his property, he sees the effect of his wife's imagined infidelity on his own identity: 'See the hell of having a false woman! . . . my reputation gnawn at' (II.2.277–9). What concerns him is the names he will be called: 'Terms! Names! . . . Cuckold! Wittol! – Cuckold! The devil himself hath not such a name' (282–5).

When dealing with these slights, Ford's speech becomes obsessively repetitive, his own reiteration of the names that he imagines others calling him offering an

almost physically painful barrage of insults. 'Buck?' he
begins, hearing the word for washing linen and immediately making the (ironically not so far off the mark)
connection to the cuckold's horns: 'I would I could wash
myself of the buck! Buck, buck, buck! Ay, buck! I warrant
you, buck – and of the season too, it shall appear'
(III.3.148–50). Always, Ford tries to get revelation in first
– attempting to forestall the public mockery which follows
discovery of a neighbour's most painful secret by openly
advertising his problems to the community at large.
Mistress Page, describing his behaviour to his wife,
explains how he 'so buffets himself on the forehead,
crying "Peer out, peer out!" [to his cuckold's horns], that
any madness I ever yet beheld seemed but tameness,
civility, and patience, to this his distemper' (IV.2.22–5).

The wives themselves are, of course, very careful
about their honest reputations – they guard them vigor-
ously – but they have a quiet confidence in their own
natures and abilities which contrasts sharply with Ford's
obsessions. It is only this unimpeachable honesty, never
seriously doubted at any point by any but the most unreasonable character in the play, which gives the wives
licence to scheme as they do. Their reputations both
legitimize and necessitate the punishment of Falstaff.
'Nay,' says Mistress Ford, 'I will consent to act any villainy
against him that may not sully the chariness of our
honesty' (II.1.91–3), and then, in advance of the final
humiliation, 'May we, with the warrant of womanhood
and the witness of a good conscience, pursue him with
any further revenge?' (IV.2.194–6). The wives weigh
every action in advance to ensure that it will strengthen,
rather than undermine, communal standards of decent
behaviour.

While Falstaff is hidden within Mistress Ford's

house, the wives act out the scenes of moral disgrace that haunt the play. In bold, stark language, Mistress Page outlines the pragmatics of the situation to her friend: 'Your husband's coming hither, woman, with all the officers in Windsor, to search for a gentleman that he says is here now in the house, by your consent, to take an ill advantage of his absence. You are undone' (III.3.100–103). The buzz words of lost reputation ring around the stage: 'You're shamed, you're overthrown, you're undone for ever' (III.3.90–91), and, establishing that Falstaff is indeed present a second time: 'Why, then, you are utterly shamed' (IV.2.39).

This is a play full of violence, but it is a violence which is by and large confined to the realm of the verbal. When Falstaff makes the rhetorically enormous yet emotionally empty claim to Mistress Ford, 'I would thy husband were dead' (III.3.45–6), he opens a door in the audience's imagination to the potentially tragic ramifications of his wooing plot. Would success require the death of the Windsor husbands? It is a reference to tragedies based on very similar plots, but one which this play does not explore. Similarly, the revenge plots culminate in the testing of linguistic strengths. The energy of Caius's fury gives a pent-up tension to the mock duel: 'I will cut his troat in de park . . . By gar, I will cut all his two stones. By gar, he shall not have a stone to throw at his dog' (I.4.106–10), he says of Sir Hugh, the threats moving between bestialization and castration – 'Scurvy jack-dog priest! By gar, me vill cut his ears' (II.3.57–8) and, with some finality, 'By gar, de herring is no dead so as I vill kill him' (II.3.11). Sir Hugh's response is an equally comic combination of the extreme violence of sexualized dismemberment and a total disregard for the niceties of English syntax: 'I will knog his urinals about his knave's costard when I have good opportunities for the [w]ork. Pless my soul!' (III.1.13–15). And to the Host who has so cunningly kept them apart – 'Well, I will smite his noddles' (III.1.114). The intense passions excited by male honour and reputation are expressed in a language of physical threat.

Master Ford, however, does exercise physical violence, in what is simultaneously a very funny and a rather menacing climax to the second tryst. He personally expels Falstaff this time, doing just as a husband whose authority has been threatened should – he shouts at his arch-rival and beats him from his doors. Ironically, of course, he thinks he is beating a large old woman rather than a fat old knight. His excessive language gives vent to some of the wounded pride he feels, and his physical prowess at this point offers a model of behaviour which might not only be appropriate, but also effective, in a different situation: 'Out of my door, you witch, you rag, you baggage, you polecat, you ronyon! Out, out! I'll conjure you, I'll fortune-tell you' (IV.2.173–5). It is satisfying for an audience because it serves the knight right, and the appropriateness of the brutality offered to him is simultaneously stressed and undercut by the cruelty of its supposed application to an old woman.

The violence of language, and occasionally action, in *The Merry Wives of Windsor* is linked to the restoration of communal moral values. Violence is embodied in the passionate words which accompany the display of social contest. If we return to Falstaff's initial advice to Shallow, ''Twere better for you if it were known in counsel' (I.1.112–13), we can trace clear links through the play from their contest over the poached deer, to Caius's and Evans's competition over Anne Page, to the final scene in which the community shames Falstaff in the person of

Herne the Hunter. In each case masculine honour is tried in public, and in each instance it has the entertainment value of the display of unduly exaggerated emotion.

Falstaff, of course, continues condescending to Shallow: 'You'll be laughed at' (I.1.113). But it is the Justice of the Peace himself who says to Master Page, 'We have sport in hand' (II.1.184), as they go to witness the duel, and the Host stage-manages a show which displays the absurdity of Caius's and Evans's pomposity to the community at large. Similarly, when the wives are considering the final fate of Falstaff, Mistress Ford predicts their husbands' response to the revelation of past events: 'I'll warrant they'll have him publicly shamed, and methinks there would be no period to the jest, should he not be publicly shamed' (IV.2.207–9). It is only the *public* nature of Falstaff's final shaming which will bring his misconduct to an end; it is only its public nature which will ensure that the wives' own unique brand of 'lechery management' can be concluded. Page underlines the sentiment in verse:

> Let our wives
> Yet once again, to make us public sport,
> Appoint a meeting with this old fat fellow,
> Where we may take him and disgrace him for it.
> (IV.4.12–15)

Falstaff's shamings develop a notion of public jest with a moral purpose. However, the play's main employer of the word 'sport' in this context is Master Ford. In Act III, confident for the first time of catching his wife in the act of dishonesty, he imposes upon his friends: 'I beseech you heartily, some of you go home with me to dinner. Besides your cheer, you shall have sport – I will show you a monster' (III.2.72–4). 'If I suspect without cause,' he says later, 'why then make sport at me; then let me be your jest; I deserve it' (III.3.141–3), showing he understands that he might *become* the spectacle himself. Once inside his house he instructs his audience, 'Up, gentlemen, you shall see sport anon. Follow me, gentlemen' (III.3.158–9). This behaviour continues at their second meeting. As Mistress Page explains, he 'hath drawn [her husband] and the rest of the company from their sport, to make another experiment of his suspicion' (IV.2.30 32). The neighbours were to have gone hawking, but Ford is determined to exchange the carefree leisure of hunting with birds for the tense display of hunting his own pair of horns. If they do not find the spectacle of his wife's adultery which he so perversely desires this time, he assures them, 'Let me for ever be your table sport. Let them say of me "As jealous as Ford, that searched a hollow walnut for his wife's leman"' (IV.2.151–4).

In one way then, Ford is alive to the capacity of such spectacles to rebound upon their makers – he understands that if there is no knight in hiding he will himself be the show; he knows he will become proverbial as an epitome of the unpleasant character trait of jealousy. What he *doesn't* seem aware of, however, is the fact that either the success *or* failure of his search for the kernel of his wife's dishonesty will make the jest rebound upon him – either a cuckold or an unreasonably jealous man. He appears perversely unable to see the proper distinction between appropriately concealing or revealing his domestic problems.

When the accepted standards of moral behaviour were transgressed in early modern England, the men and women of the community turned upon their misbehaving neighbours and subjected them to violent public ridicule. These ritual acts of public shaming and humiliation were often called charivaris, or skimmingtons, and they involved cuckolded husbands, husbands who were beaten by their wives, old men with young wives and others whose relationships were 'different' being paraded through the town sitting backwards on a donkey, or balanced on a thick staff or pole. They were accompanied by 'rough music' – the banging of pots and pans – and the taunts and shouts of those with whom they lived and worked. These domestic 'offences' were punished through the moral and satirical power of laughter, harsh language and visual mockery. It is just this kind of rough justice, administered by a community, that the play gestures towards. Shakespeare puts the early modern propensity to see publicity as *in itself* a punishment at the heart of his plotting.

THE FINAL JEST IN THE WOOD

Up until the point when Ford's jealousy comes to an end in his potentially very moving speech of penitence in Act IV, scene 4, the men and women in the play have been operating more or less independently of one another. There are very few scenes in which they even share dialogue, and when they do conversation often takes place as the two groups are moving in different directions – as at the beginning of the play when the men start to discuss marriage and the women go to prepare food; or when the men go to search the Ford household and the women dispose of Falstaff and share their joke with the audience. As soon as Ford has repented, however, the various plots of the play begin to come together: preparations for the final scene with the masque are not divided along gender lines; they show Windsor working in the kind of productive union which comes from mutual trust.

Just like the wives' other schemes with the buck basket and the witch, this performance also resolves several issues simultaneously. Reprising the two themes with which the play opened – revenge and marriage – Mistress Page outlines the double outcome she expects: 'My husband will not rejoice so much at the abuse of Falstaff as he will chafe at the doctor's marrying my daughter' (V.3.7–9).

While Caius and Slender are stealing away their fairies, Fenton is taking the real Anne from amongst the masked children, 'While other sports are tasking of their minds' (IV.6.30). Like the wives' previous plots, this too will be a magic trick – a sleight of hand which misdirects the attention of a part of its audience – although here Mistress Page is herself a victim of these distracting performances. In the Windsor woods at night, it is the confusion between costumes and the bodies underneath them, between illusion and reality, which allows the real Anne to follow her heart.

But the careful scripting of this final scene of knightly humiliation makes it both like and unlike the wives' other schemes. They pay particular attention to the effect of its parts upon an audience – as Fenton says to the Host, 'Fat Falstaff | Hath a great scene. The image of the jest | I'll show you here at large' (IV.6.16–18). But it is much more thoroughly planned this time – gone is the cumulative pragmatism of quickly born ideas. Instead, like Quince in *A Midsummer Night's Dream*, they proceed to give out the parts: Falstaff will be 'Disguised like Herne, with huge horns on his head' and the others, Mistress Page says, will dress 'Like urchins, ouphes, and fairies,

green and white' (IV.4.41, 48). She orders the men to 'Go
get us properties | And tricking for our fairies' (76–7).
Mistress Quickly offers to help Falstaff with his, rather
more taxing, property needs: 'I'll provide you a chain,
and I'll do what I can to get you a pair of horns' (V.1.5–6).
Anne Page's wooers have their cues: 'I come to her in
white,' Slender reiterates, 'and cry "mum"; she cries
"budget"; and by that we know one another' (V.2.5–7),
while Doctor Caius 'hath appointed | That he shall like-
wise shuffle her away', choosing the fairy dressed 'quaint
in green . . . loose enrobed, | With ribands pendent,
flaring 'bout her head' (IV.6.28–9, 41–2). This is to be
a play within a play – not just dramatic, but theatrical.

When the entertainment begins, it is immediately clear
that something totally different is happening. Mistress
Quickly, transformed into the Queen of Fairies, addresses
her court:

> Fairies black, grey, green, and white,
> You moonshine revellers, and shades of night,
> You orphan heirs of fixèd destiny,
> Attend your office and your quality. (V.5.37–40)

The switch to verse signals a different kind of drama.
The play has at this point become a masque – a stylized,
courtly form of entertainment involving elaborate sets,
declamatory poetry and courtly audience participation
for complex and lengthy dances. In masques, the identity of the actors was often just as important as their roles.
Shakespeare's company performed in both kinds of spectacle – in the public theatres and the shows put on to
entertain royalty. *The Merry Wives of Windsor* itself may
well have been performed before Elizabeth and her
knights on St George's Day 1597, as a celebration of the

annual feast of the Order of the Garter, as well as being staged in the public theatre for a completely different audience.

The stately show in Windsor is performed by very ordinary actors, but it is staged literally on the border between royal and urban spaces, in the deer park of the castle itself. And like the location, the verse too points up the contrasts between the royal and the everyday, the high and the low. The connection between the urban community of Windsor and the royal one which lived 'next door' is a very concrete one. Mistress Quickly likens the 'fairy rings' found in the grass in the wood to the shape and vividness of the insignia worn by members of the Order of the Garter. She instructs her court to write the garter motto, *'Honi soit qui mal y pense'* ('Evil be to those who think evil'), 'In emerald tufts, flowers purple, blue, and white, | Like sapphire, pearl, and rich embroidery, | Buckled below fair knighthood's bending knee' (V.5.70–72): the fairy emblem embellished with flowers, the knightly one with precious jewels. The fairies are to make their equivalent of the knights' garter and they are to strew good luck in the palace and encourage cleanliness in Windsor houses. They are concerned, in other words, with different kinds of housework.

As the form of the drama moves from commercial play to elite masque, so the concerns of the Order of the Garter become associated with those of the wives: *'Honi soit qui mal y pense'* and the wives' own motto 'Wives may be merry and yet honest too' – only in doubt for the pathologically jealous – are brought into connection with one another.

Within the form of the masque, a riot of different styles of language and textual references are interwoven. Entering *'disguised as Herne'* the pagan hunter, from what

Mistress Page describes as 'an old tale' told by the 'superstitious idle-headed eld' (IV.4.26, 34), Falstaff alludes to
classical tales of love's beastly transformation from
Ovid's *Metamorphoses*: 'O powerful love, that in some
respects makes a beast a man, in some other a man a
beast.' He refers to the stories in which Jove turned
himself into a bull and a swan to get his way with women;
'O omnipotent love, how near the god drew to the
complexion of a goose! A fault done first in the form of
a beast – O Jove, a beastly fault – and then another fault
in the semblance of a fowl – think on't, Jove, a foul fault!'
(V.5.4–10). The scene not only takes place outside
Windsor, it also suddenly steps outside early modern life,
and into a world of classical myths and stories.

Ovid's *Metamorphoses*, translated into English by
Arthur Golding in 1567, had provided Shakespeare with
inspiration many times before, most obviously in *A
Midsummer Night's Dream*, where another unlikely lover
puts on a beastly head and is 'translated' (III.1.112–13).
With its focus upon the confusions wrought and transformations enabled by passion, the whole play was clearly
inspired by Ovidian themes. In *The Merry Wives of
Windsor*, however, a play without a single major source
but with plenty of minor ones, the stories form part of
the drama's insistent evocation of different kinds of tale
and different literary and theatrical genres. The interest
in finding hiding places within the house in the first part
of the play – the mention of chests, trunks and piles of
linen – strikes a chord with other comic tales of cuckoldry. Stories of the ingenious schemes of wives and
their lovers – the disguises and the ruses with which they
tricked jealous husbands – were familiar to audiences
from French fabliaux and Italian novellas. From Geoffrey
Chaucer's late-fourteenth-century *Miller's Tale* and

Merchant's Tale, in which lovers from within the
husband's household snatch privacy with their wives in
boats and up trees, to Ser Giovanni Fiorentino's 1558 *Il
Pecorone* where the professor's wife slides a student under
her laundry, lovers had been secreted in an ingenious
variety of places.

But this play has consistently worked against the
conventions of such literature. When Giovanni's student
Bucciuolo is retrieved from the washing pile he is warmed,
fed and seduced – he is young and attractive and his
lover is eager to spend the night with him: 'after much
feasting and gaiety', we are told, 'the lady took his hand
and led him into the bedchamber, where with great joy
they went to bed, and all that night they gave each other
delight and peace'. Although Falstaff *thinks* he is in such
a story, as indeed does Ford, they are both mistaken about
their roles.

Here in the masque, Falstaff, *'with a buck's head upon
him'*, parodies Ovid's story of Actaeon, the young hunter
punished for peeping at the naked goddess and changed
into a stag only to be torn to death by his own hounds.
His physical form simultaneously resembles that of the
man to whom the goddess gave 'A pair of lively old
Hart's horns' (in Golding's translation), the cuckolded
man of Ford's nightmares, and Herne the Hunter. He is
both the potent stag and the butt of communal mockery,
and his presence simultaneously recalls narratives of elite
classical learning and tales of native folklore.

Falstaff's own language of love is similarly chequered
– excessive and grandiose, but with a very prosaic vocab-
ulary of images. 'My doe with the black scut!' he crudely
addresses Mistress Ford, 'Let the sky rain potatoes. Let
it thunder to the tune of "Greensleeves", hail kissing-
comfits, and snow eringoes. Let there come a tempest

of provocation, I will shelter me here' (V.5.18–21).
Compared to Cesario's 'Most excellent, accomplished
lady, the heavens rain odours on you!' in *Twelfth Night*
(III.1.81–2), a torrent of potatoes is considerably less
courtly in tone and more robustly physical.

So the play moves between the fantastical and the real,
the elite and the prosaic. The inhabitants of Windsor
puncture Falstaff's illusion of himself as a lover of Jove-
like importance:

FORD What, a hodge-pudding? A bag of flax?
MISTRESS PAGE A puffed man?
PAGE Old, cold, withered, and of intolerable entrails?
FORD And one that is as slanderous as Satan? (V.5.150–53)

How could such a man have imagined that he possessed
the physical attractiveness necessary for his plans to
succeed?

Caius' and Slender's illusions are also punctured. The
former returns to the scene of magical translation in the
wood complaining, 'By gar, I am cozened. I ha' married
un garçon, a boy; *un paysan*, by gar, a boy' (V.5.199–200).
The latter too has a fairy wife who in better light turns
out to be 'a great lubberly boy . . . 'tis a postmaster's
boy' (V.5.181–5).

The moral probity of this final scene of punishment
and restitution is constantly stressed. From Mistress
Page's serious adage, 'Against such lewdsters and their
lechery, | Those that betray them do no treachery'
(V.3.21–2), to the fairy song, 'Fie on sinful fantasy! | Fie
on lust and luxury! (V.5.93–4), to Master Page's comic
rendition of their moral high ground: 'Heaven prosper
our sport! No man means evil but the devil, and we shall
know him by his horns' (V.2.12–13), the focus upon the

rightness and morality of their actions is insistent.

Fenton caps this theme when he returns with his bride. He does so by drawing attention to the theatrical form which the night's events have taken. Explaining and excusing his triple-bluff, he reminds them, 'You would have married her most shamefully | Where there was no proportion held in love.' He sets the 'offence' which they have committed against 'A thousand irreligious cursèd hours | Which forcèd marriage would have brought upon her' to show how high the stakes were. Therefore, he claims, 'this deceit [of theatrically switching brides for boys] loses the name of craft [dishonesty or cunning]' (V.5.213–22). His assertion seems to prove the effectiveness of performance, the significance of dealing with the 'real' world through the unreal one of theatre.

At the end of the play, then, there is a realignment towards ideals which had become confused in the plotting and sub-plotting, and the performances of ritual shaming. Honesty and love, the play concludes, *do* stand outside the petty jealousies of small-town life as moral absolutes, but sometimes the transformations of drama are necessary in order to see real life clearly again.

This final revenging jest in the wood ends as the opening quarrel between Shallow and Falstaff did. The solution to the initial problem with deer poaching was neither violence nor the law; instead, the characters were tempted away from confrontation by the offer of wine and 'a hot venison pasty to dinner' at the Pages' house, during the course of which their host hoped they would 'drink down all unkindness' (I.1.181–2). Falstaff's humiliation as a deer comes to an end in similar fashion when Page extends hospitality and friendship to him: 'Yet be cheerful, knight. Thou shalt eat a posset tonight at my house' (V.5.168–9). Mention of the communally binding

meal suggests that the breaches in Windsor society have
been healed by this final action in the wood, making
possible a return to the household, and Mistress Page
suggests the final move back to Windsor town with a
purposefully inclusive invitation:

> Good husband, let us every one go home,
> And laugh this sport o'er by a country fire;
> Sir John and all. (233–5)

Although both Pages have fallen foul of their own
schemes to secure their daughter's marriage, they are
eventually forced to be content with her choice of
husband. It is this union between Anne and Fenton which
will ensure the continuation of the community, and
Mistress Page, perhaps punning on the very many meanings of the word which have echoed through the play,
signals the possibilities for the couple's future: 'Heaven
give you many, many merry days' (V.5.232).

Catherine Richardson

The Play in Performance

The Merry Wives of Windsor, like many of Shakespeare's other plays, was staged 'divers times . . . both before her majesty and elsewhere' in his own time, as the title page of the earliest edition states – at the court and in the public theatre. In recent decades, professional companies like the Royal Shakespeare Company have staged it regularly, and its large range of diverse parts, every one of them full of comic potential, has ensured its popularity with amateur groups across the world. It is supremely successful in summer festivals of 'open-air Shakespeare', lending itself well to outdoor settings from municipal parks to castle grounds. Since its first performances it has been rewritten with the introduction of even more complex plot lines; it has been turned into operas in English, French, German and Italian; and even interpreted within the conventions of Japanese theatre. In 1929 Ralph Vaughan Williams wrote *Sir John in Love*, an opera which celebrated the Englishness of *The Merry Wives*. He employed twenty folk tunes to stress the centrality of Shakespeare's English comedy to national vernacular traditions, and in doing so confirmed an enduring connection between the play and the idealized golden age of a now lost 'Merry England'.

It plays to monarchs at court and picnickers in parks;

it has comic force as both drama and opera; it is archetypally English, but has worldwide popularity. The most fundamental issue to arise out of the stage history of *The Merry Wives* might well be its flexibility – it has been successfully transferred to different places, media, audiences and periods. Curiously, it is the play's social specificity which ensures that it transfers so effectively. It is because it satirizes Elizabethan England so well – the social pretensions of characters like Slender, the role of wives, the relationship between money and status – that setting the play in different places and periods turns its comic mockery on those contexts too, commenting on both play and setting.

For any production of *The Merry Wives of Windsor* then, perhaps the first decision to be made is when to set the play. Many directors have tried to clarify the social dynamics of status and gender which Shakespeare's audience would have understood by painstakingly reproducing authentic props, costumes and scenery. Henry Ayliff's 1937 Stratford production created a whole half-timbered street, and doubleted characters inhabited Trevor Nunn's 1979 oak-beamed interiors, where shades of brown and orange aimed to conjure up a far-distant world.

On the other hand, several notable productions have set the play in the twentieth century. Bill Alexander's 1985 Stratford *Merry Wives* was set in the 1950s. The programme included a cartoon of Harold Macmillan saying 'You've never had it so good', and everything about the production smacked of post-war materialism. The wives were gossips, and the energies they expended in plotting provided relief from the monotony of domestic routines – they compared love letters while sitting under beehive-shaped driers in the hairdresser's.

Rachael Kavanaugh's 2002 RSC production was set in a post-war 1940s. The domestic interests of the play were reinterpreted in a period in which, as the programme note stated, 'New clothes, cars, currency for foreign travel, luxuries of all kinds were in desperately short supply'. In such a context, the role of the housewife became one of making ends meet, and the financial concerns of a good marriage seemed to be more about supporting a family than sustaining a title. 'Teenage girls,' the programme continued, 'deprived of perfume or nylons, would go to their local Gaumont, Odeon, Ritz or Regal three or four times a week', and the silver screen dreaminess of a proposition from a courtly knight took on a totally different kind of unreality.

In settings such as these, the play's sensitivity to the everyday consequences of social division and competition can be very effectively addressed. Invocation of the 'make do and mend' generation makes a live issue of the notion of community, and of the significance of the collective good at the expense of personal gains and aspirations.

The set will be crucial in conveying a sense of period, and productions need to decide how fully to represent Windsor homes. It is possible to stage the play with a minimum of scenery (a door or chest to signal an interior), but props will be particularly important in productions which set the play in a very specific period, clarifying the type of household represented and the significance of the objects within it. Reviews of Bill Alexander's interpretation show how interested audiences were in reading the clues to the Fords' status: a record player, a bay window with period curtains and a very specific kind of front door identified, for Michael Billington, 'mock Tudor suburbia where the cocktail cabinet is a prize feature' (*Guardian*, 4 April 1985). It was the careful choice of period-specific and class-precise props which made the social satire so effective in this production.

The portrayal of Windsor society depends on the weight given to the distinctions between the characters. Unusual recent ideas have included the Pages' resistance to Fenton as a prospective son-in-law in Kavanaugh's production, where Chuk Iwuji played him as a black GI who stood out in Windsor, but not as a courtier in a provincial town. Michael Bogdanov drew attention to Shakespeare's use of foreign characters for his 2002 Ludlow Festival production: by assembling an all-Welsh cast, he changed the dynamic between the Windsorites. Ensuring that all the characters had the same accent as Evans critiqued the play's insistence on 'otherness' — only Caius stood out as a comic outsider.

But the most obvious way of pointing up social difference is through the characters' clothing. Early modern stage costumes distinguished with infinite care between characters of different social status, and productions which want to stress the competitiveness of Windsor society need to find ways of appealing to the social coding which clothing still carries, now perhaps in designer labels rather than fine lace, rich cloths and furs. If *The Merry Wives* is at least partly a play about the relationship between money and status, then costume offers a useful shorthand for those connections.

Shakespeare delineates his characters sharply here then — by nationality, status and manner of speaking. The earliest edition of the play spots the money-making potential of the diversity of its distinctive roles by mentioning not only 'Sir John Falstaff and the Merry Wives of Windsor' but also 'the sundry variable and pleasing humours of Sir Hugh the Welsh knight, Justice Shallow, and his wise cousin Master Slender, with the swaggering vein of Ancient Pistol, and Corporal Nym.' The different plots in which these characters are involved ensure that each has their own comic set pieces – Ford's and Falstaff's long soliloquies in Act III, scene 5, for instance; Caius's and Evans's individual scenes while waiting for the duel; or Mistress Quickly's conversation with Falstaff in Act II, scene 2. Several scenes, however, offer the opportunity for the play to cohere into an ensemble piece – at the end of Act III, scene 1 when the community arrives to laugh at the duellers, and for Falstaff's punishments in Act III, scene 3, Act IV, scene 2 and Act V, scene 5. Productions need to consider the relative pacing of these different kinds of drama – to strike a balance between the development of the individual comic set pieces and the communal scenes of physical comedy.

The pace of the play will also be affected by the balance between the lightness of the comedy and the extremity of the emotion which generates it. Along with recent interest in the competitive social dynamics of the play has come a tendency to alter the pace in order to give space to its more negative aspects. Just how excessive is Master Ford's jealousy? How do the other characters react to him when he begins to rave – do they try to restrain him, or do they just look away in embarrassment? Is his penitence similarly excessive in a comic mode, or should the moving effect of a true transformation be stressed, as it was by Ian Richardson for Terry Hands in 1975?

Is Master Page more relaxed and at ease than his neighbour, or could he simply not care less? The Fords' marriage is characterized by the dynamic of jealousy, but directors have to decide whether the Pages' situation offers a contrast to this dysfunctionality, or whether in fact they have their own problems. When Mistress Page says her husband is 'as far from jealousy as I am from giving him cause' (II.1.96–7), is she describing a relationship of mutual trust and affection, or one from which the spark has gone – shared by two people who are no longer interested in one another or anybody else either? When Page says he would turn his wife loose to Falstaff, 'and what he gets more of her than sharp words, let it lie on my head' (II.1.170–72), does he have total faith in his wife's honesty, or does he know from experience that any advance made to her is likely to result in a short sharp rejection?

These decisions will be affected by the age of the wives. Playing them as older women will accentuate the competence and confidence of two characters who are old enough to understand how the world works, and how to manipulate it to their own ends. But there is also scope for much younger wives – Mistress Page does after all have a young son William, even though she is past 'the holiday time' of her beauty, and there is no firm indication of Mistress Ford's age. If they are played as younger women, Falstaff's advances might appear less cynical. Whatever age they are, decisions need to be made about whether they are provocatively sexy women likely to attract advances, or frumpy middle-aged ladies shocked by the very prospect. What is their attitude towards sexuality – do they laugh at their own bawdy puns, or are they the only ones who don't notice? John Barber's *Daily Telegraph* review of Bill Alexander's production (6 April 1985) described Janet Dale's and Lindsay Duncan's wives as 'brassy, fag-sucking, gin-slugging jokesters' – they made it clear that revenge was a great deal of fun for them, and certainly not a morally self-righteous act.

Productions must also work out how to characterize

the bond between the two women. In recent years the play has provided ample scope for a feminist interpretation of sisterhood – 'girl power' working as a force for good in a sleazy world of male jealousy and aggressively predatory sexuality – making the play into what David Adams called 'a proto-feminist critique of male lechery, incompetence, mistrust, vanity and general waste-of-space uselessness' (*The British Theatre Guide*, http://www.britishtheatreguide.info/index.htm). How do they behave towards one another? The play strongly indicates similarities between them by stressing their closeness – 'I think, if your husbands were dead, you two would marry' (III.2.13–14), as Master Ford says – but just how similar are they? Stressing their solidarity by making them appear alike risks denying their independent wit and resourcefulness by making them seem almost interchangeable, but it does underline the aspect of 'gender war' in the play. Productions can vary the similarities and differences between them – to what extent do they talk alike, dress alike, share speeches and gestures?

The success of the play depends upon invoking the audience's sympathy for the characters without giving them such depth of emotion and motivation that their function as comic stereotypes is lost. The love between Fenton and Anne is an issue with which the dialogue of the play is little concerned, but in which modern audiences have considerable interest. Just how serious is he? Does he *really* love her, or is her father's guess that he is only after her dowry not so far off the mark? Textually, the evidence hangs on just the one speech (in Act III, scene 4), but in performance their physical response to one another when they are onstage together, in gesture and eye contact, will help to determine the audience's sense of either a contrast between their genuine love and

Falstaff's masquerade, or the complete triumph of finance over romance in Windsor.

But of all the characters in this play, one in particular has traditionally been seen as central to making it work in performance. Falstaff has been the focus of audiences' attention, and the role a favourite amongst actors of an appropriate stature. His sheer physical bulk gives the play an enormous comic energy, even before he begins to speak. Productions can exploit his visual power by casting smaller actors in the other male roles, particularly perhaps Master Ford, and letting Falstaff overwhelm the stage. Orson Welles's 1966 film *The Chimes at Midnight* offered a homage to him, synthesizing his appearances in the history plays and *The Merry Wives* into a coherent character study of the fat knight. Terry Hands's 1975 Stratford production of *Merry Wives* was staged as the end point of the exploits of Falstaff, after the three history plays in which he appears. Both built upon audiences' fascination with Falstaff as a character who transcends individual plays and genres. Seen in the context of these other plays, his dubious morality, poised just on the edge of acceptable behaviour and audience sympathy, and his interest in jest and performance, are as recognizable in *Merry Wives* as his distinctive bulk.

Interpretation of the role of Falstaff can set the tone for a whole production, but its legendary status does not make for simple decisions. His size is a given, but what about his sex appeal? Is it conceivable, even for a moment, that the wives might take him seriously? The more repulsive he is as a potential lover, the more amusing his suit to the wives becomes, but he is simultaneously diminished as a force in the drama, and moves ever further from the persuasive and wily trickster who was friends

with Prince Hal in his previous incarnation in *Henry IV,
Parts I* and *II*.

He is also perhaps the hardest character to transpose
into a different period setting. Whereas the comedy of
bourgeois concerns transfers with pretension-puncturing
sharpness to subsequent historical periods, Falstaff's
authority comes mainly from his rank, and the deference
due to a knight even when he behaves like a knave does
not transfer so easily. In his review, John Barber found
it hard to credit Peter Jeffrey's 'military golf-club cad in
yellow weskit and outsize moustache and plus fours' in
Bill Alexander's production with the innate dignity of
social power which the character needs; Page and Ford,
imagined as suburban bank clerks, were unlikely to have
had anything to do with a member of the aristocracy.
Falstaff has to retain his stature if the play is to succeed,
and this Elizabethan one-off is hard to constrain within
modern social stereotypes.

The way the final scene is played is crucial here. If it
is a simple masquerade in which there is no possibility
of magical transformation, Falstaff's commanding wit is
diminished and he is truly made to look a fool. If,
however, the supernatural overtones of the scene are
exploited, then Falstaff may be given the benefit of the
doubt. The set can create or hinder belief in the magical.
Beerbohm Tree's 1902 production included moonlight
and mossy trees in front of an outline of Windsor Castle,
with 'a thick growth of bracken and fern, amid which
the glow-worms glint' (Peter Evans, in '"To the Oak, to
the Oak!"'). The mighty oak has been created in loving
detail for Byam Shaw in 1955, but it featured as a mere
stump with a hatchet stuck in it for Bill Alexander thirty
years later. These choices show how seriously the directors want their audiences to take the legend of Herne the

Hunter. Where an atmosphere of the uncanny is required, lighting and music are also very important – a significant shift just as Mistress Quickly switches to verse prepares the audience for the unexpected.

As the climax of the punishment of Falstaff's lust, this scene offers scope for mocking him in many different ways. His horns have been everything from a fully fashioned set of antlers of enormous proportions to bicycle handlebars on a colander in the Northern Broadsides production of 1993. His dignity is lost in both cases, but his status is more obviously damaged in the latter. Productions need to decide when he understands what is happening to him – with what level of knowing, for instance, does he deliver the line 'Heavens defend me from that Welsh fairy, lest he transform me to a piece of cheese' (V.5.81–2)? He draws comic attention both to the fact that fairies with Welsh accents are unusual, and to the stereotypical Welsh obsession with cheese – can Falstaff *really* think Evans is a genuine fairy? When the jest is over, does he retain either the authority of his rank or the energy of his wit – is he angry, broken, or resigned as he delivers the speech 'Well, I am your theme . . .' (159)?

But the scene needs an edge of menace if the middle-class moral concerns which the play takes so seriously are to be given due weight. The kind of punishment meted out by delicate fairies will be lighter than that administered by representatives of the more sinister side of the supernatural. Trevor Nunn and John Caird staged the oak scene on All Hallow's Eve in their 1979 production, and Bill Alexander's was also set in October. Pumpkin lanterns and children dressed as skeletons offered a cleverly updated interpretation of uncanny folk ritual – Hallowe'en remains the small remnant of the bizarre let into the majority of middle-class homes – and Falstaff was much more convincingly morally transformed as a result.

Finally, the tone of the ending has to be decided upon. Falstaff has been punished; the Pages, Caius and Slender have been tricked; Fenton has effectively rebuked Windsor's obsession with money over love. There is scope for accentuating the positive side of some of the trickery: Christopher Luscombe's Slender, in Ian Judge's 1997 RSC production, was quite delighted to have married a postmaster's boy rather than Anne Page. Nevertheless, the transition from the more negative conclusions of the play's several plots to a sense of communal harmony can be hard to effect. Productions have traditionally turned to a dance to signal the end of hostilities – it would be hard, although perhaps not impossible, to sustain a more downbeat ending to the play. The energies of the dance rekindle the pace of the wives' schemes, lulled for a while in the wood. They break the concentration on punishment and allow the audience the relief of a relaxed atmosphere of reconciliation. In the end, they permit *The Merry Wives* to move past the point where it began – in the comic concern about 'abuses' – past the semi-serious enactment of revenge, to do what comedies have to do: signal a more positive future.

Catherine Richardson

Further Reading

The Merry Wives of Windsor exists in two very different versions – the shorter Quarto and the longer Folio, on which the text of this edition is based. Both texts are available as facsimiles, the Quarto in *The Merry Wives of Windsor 1602*, ed. W. W. Greg (1957) and the Folio in *The Norton Facsimile: The First Folio of Shakespeare*, ed. Charlton Hinman (1968). Giorgio Melchiori's Arden edition of 2000 discusses the relationship between the two texts and offers an illustrated chronological stage history. If you want to know more about the reasons for the differences between the texts, Gerald D. Johnson in '*The Merry Wives of Windsor*, Q1: Provincial Touring and Adapted Texts' reviews the arguments for this shorter text as a reconstruction from the memory of the actor who played the Host. He provides extensive comparison between the versions and includes a casting plan for the Quarto, but argues that it was unlikely to have been used for touring productions (*Shakespeare Quarterly* 38, 1987, pp. 154–65). Leah Marcus in *Unediting the Renaissance* (1996) writes about the way editors have dealt with the two versions over the years, and revalues the little-used Quarto text.

Marcus also considers the arguments about topicality made in relation to the play, and retells the various stories to which it has been said to allude. There is information here about the Garter ceremonies of 1597 to which the first production has been linked. For a different perspective on these events, see Leslie Katz's article '*The Merry Wives of Windsor*: Sharing the Queen's Holiday' (*Representations* 51, summer 1995), which uses the cultural significance of the Garter feast as the starting point for an argument about the way Falstaff 'moves' between histories and comedy, and the effect this has on audiences. Peter Erickson in 'The Order of the Garter, the Cult of Elizabeth, and Class–Gender Tension in *The Merry Wives of Windsor*' examines the relationship between the play's knightly references and the prominent role of the Windsor wives (in Jean Howard and Marion O'Connor (eds.), *Shakespeare Reproduced: The Text in History and Ideology*, 1987).

For information about the play's connections to different types of early modern event, see Philip D. Collington in '"I Would Thy Husband Were Dead": *The Merry Wives of Windsor* as Mock Domestic Tragedy' (*English Literary Renaissance* 30: 2, spring 2000), where he explores the connections between the play and the 'inhumaine murther' of Master Page of Plymouth, arguing that there are important elements of domestic tragedy in Shakespeare's comedy. There is a translation of the tale from Ser Giovanni Fiorentino's *Il Pecorone* involving the student and the pile of washing (see Introduction, 'The Final Jest in the Wood'), and the section of Ovid's *Metamorphoses* on which Shakespeare draws for Falstaff's appearance in deer horns, in Geoffrey Bullough, *Narrative and Dramatic Sources of Shakespeare*, vol. II (1958).

Three articles explore in detail the relationship between Shakespeare's play and women's work within

the household. Natasha Korda, in '"Judicious oeillades":
Supervising Marital Property in *The Merry Wives of
Windsor*' (in Jean E. Howard (ed.), *Marxist Shakespeares*,
2001), outlines the advice given to men and women in
contemporary conduct books about household matters,
and its connections to female morality. Wendy Wall in
'Why Does Puck Sweep?: Fairylore, Merry Wives, and
Social Struggle' (*Shakespeare Quarterly* 52, 2001, pp.
67–106), looks at the connection between domestic chores
and the magical work of fairies in Shakespeare's England.
And Richard Helgerson, in 'The Buck Basket, the Witch,
and the Queen of Fairies: The Women's World of
Shakespeare's Windsor' (in Patricia Fumerton and Simon
Hunt (eds.), *Renaissance Culture and the Everyday*, 1999),
explores the significance of the local setting of the play.
He examines Falstaff's punishments in relation to women's
work within the home, and explains both the literal and
metaphorical significance of dirty laundry. If you want
to know more about the conduct books which these
authors draw upon (see Introduction, 'Household and
the Comedy of Everyday Life), extracts from these and
many other texts about women's lives can be found in
Kate Aughterson's *Renaissance Woman: A Sourcebook.
Constructions of Femininity in England* (1995) and her *The
English Renaissance: An Anthology of Sources and
Documents* (1998).

Ina Habermann's work on the play explores the significance of female honour, and the role which slander
played in its construction and negotiation. Whilst picking
up on the connection between women and property, her
primary interest is in the relationship between the play
and legal concepts of punishment in society (*Staging
Slander and Gender in Early Modern England*, 2003). In
her book about women and early modern jest books,

Pamela Allen Brown considers the gendered aspects of the comedy and explores its connections to different stories of lovers hidden in baskets (*Better a Shrew Than a Sheep: Women, Drama, and the Culture of Jest in Early Modern England*, 2002). Edward Berry's focus is on the masculine world of the play. In Chapter 5 of his *Shakespeare and the Hunt: A Cultural and Social Study* (2001), he considers the images of stags and hunting which follow Falstaff through the Henry plays and into this one. He examines the social significance of deer as an important part of elite feasts and hospitality, and traces the many meanings of the horned man in the final scene. Peter Evans in '"To the Oak, to the Oak!" The Finale of *The Merry Wives of Windsor*' (*Theatre Notebook* 40, 1986) examines changing fashions in staging the scene, and explores the problems encountered in the relationship between the naturalistic setting of the rest of the play and the supernatural beliefs towards which this scene gestures.

Several critics have looked at aspects of the structure of the play. Robert Miola has examined its connections to classical comedies in an effort to explain how Shakespeare draws on and alters these sources ('*The Merry Wives of Windsor*: Classical and Italian Intertexts', in *Comparative Drama* 27:3, Fall 1993). Katharine Maus is interested in what is seen and unseen in the play. She examines the theme of male jealousy, connecting Master Ford to Othello, and both of them to the early modern theatre's preoccupation with visualizing sexuality ('Horns of Dilemma: Jealousy, Gender and Spectatorship in English Renaissance Drama', *ELH* 54, 1987, pp. 561–83).

Finally, several critics have explored the rich language of the play. Leo Salingar in 'The Englishness of *The Merry Wives of Windsor*' (*Cahiers Élisabéthains* 59, 2001, pp. 9–25) looks at the relationships between social pretensions and the use and abuse of language. In '"The Adoption of Abominable Terms": The Insults That Shape Windsor's Middle Class' (*ELH* 61, 1994, pp. 253–78), Rosemary Kegl explores the connection between middle-class mentalities and the outrageous and abusive language of the play. Patricia Parker in '*The Merry Wives of Windsor* and Shakespearean Translation' (*Modern Language Quarterly* 52:3, September 1991), focuses on the language of the play as a whole. She begins with the scene of the Latin lesson, arguing for its centrality to metaphors of 'translation' in the play – for instance Pistol's sharp comment that Falstaff has 'translated' Mistress Ford's will 'out of honesty into English' (I.3.45–6). In doing so Parker uncovers fascinating networks of wordplay in the text, taking the reader from the 'outrageous Englishings' of the grammar lesson, through the 'mistaken erections' which link language to sexuality, into a riot of double meanings and linguistic dexterity which amply demonstrates the complexity of this play's comedy.

THE MERRY WIVES
OF WINDSOR

The Characters in the Play

George PAGE, a citizen of Windsor
MISTRESS PAGE, his wife
ANNE Page, their daughter
WILLIAM Page, their son, a schoolboy
Frank FORD, another citizen of Windsor
MISTRESS FORD, his wife
JOHN
ROBERT } Ford's servants
Sir Hugh EVANS, a Welsh parson
Doctor CAIUS, a French physician and suitor for the hand
of Anne Page
MISTRESS QUICKLY, Doctor Caius's housekeeper
John RUGBY, Doctor Caius's servant
The HOST of the Garter Inn
Several children of Windsor

FENTON, a young gentleman and suitor for the hand of
Anne Page

Sir John FALSTAFF
ROBIN, Falstaff's page
BARDOLPH
PISTOL } Falstaff's followers
NYM

Robert SHALLOW, a country justice of the peace

Abraham SLENDER, Shallow's nephew and suitor for the hand of Anne Page

Peter SIMPLE, Slender's servant

SHALLOW Sir Hugh, persuade me not. I will make
a Star-Chamber matter of it. If he were twenty Sir
John Falstaffs, he shall not abuse Robert Shallow,
Esquire.

SLENDER In the county of Gloucester, justice of peace and
Coram.

SHALLOW Ay, cousin Slender, and Custalorum.

SLENDER Ay, and Ratolorum too. And a gentleman born,
master parson, who writes himself Armigero – in any
bill, warrant, quittance, or obligation, Armigero.   10

SHALLOW Ay, that I do, and have done any time these
three hundred years.

SLENDER All his successors gone before him hath done't;
and all his ancestors that come after him may. They may
give the dozen white luces in their coat.

SHALLOW It is an old coat.

EVANS The dozen white louses do become an old coat well.
It agrees well, passant. It is a familiar beast to man, and
signifies love.

SHALLOW The luce is the fresh fish. The salt fish is an   20
old coat.

SLENDER I may quarter, coz?

SHALLOW You may, by marrying.

EVANS It is marring indeed, if he quarter it.

SHALLOW Not a whit.

EVANS Yes, py'r lady. If he has a quarter of your coat, there is but three skirts for yourself, in my simple conjectures. But that is all one. If Sir John Falstaff have committed disparagements unto you, I am of the Church, and will be glad to do my benevolence, to make atonements and compromises between you.

SHALLOW The Council shall hear it. It is a riot.

EVANS It is not meet the Council hear a riot. There is no fear of Got in a riot. The Council, look you, shall desire to hear the fear of Got, and not to hear a riot. Take your vizaments in that.

SHALLOW Ha! O'my life, if I were young again, the sword should end it.

EVANS It is petter that friends is the swort, and end it. And there is also another device in my prain, which peradventure prings goot discretions with it. There is Anne Page, which is daughter to Master George Page, which is pretty virginity.

SLENDER Mistress Anne Page? She has brown hair, and speaks small like a woman?

EVANS It is that fery person for all the 'orld, as just as you will desire. And seven hundred pounds of moneys, and gold, and silver, is her grandsire upon his death's-bed — Got deliver to a joyful resurrections! — give, when she is able to overtake seventeen years old. It were a goot motion if we leave our pribbles and prabbles, and desire a marriage between Master Abraham and Mistress Anne Page.

SHALLOW Did her grandsire leave her seven hundred pound?

EVANS Ay, and her father is make her a petter penny.

SHALLOW I know the young gentlewoman. She has good
    gifts.
EVANS Seven hundred pounds, and possibilities, is goot
    gifts.   60
SHALLOW Well, let us see honest Master Page. Is
    Falstaff there?
EVANS Shall I tell you a lie? I do despise a liar as I do
    despise one that is false, or as I despise one that is not
    true. The knight Sir John is there. And I beseech you be
    ruled by your well-willers. I will peat the door for
    Master Page. (*He knocks*) What, ho! Got pless your
    house here!
PAGE (*within*) Who's there?
EVANS Here is Got's plessing, and your friend, and   70
    Justice Shallow; and here young Master Slender, that
    peradventures shall tell you another tale, if matters grow
    to your likings.
    Enter Page
PAGE I am glad to see your worships well. I thank you
    for my venison, Master Shallow.
SHALLOW Master Page, I am glad to see you. Much good
    do it your good heart! I wished your venison better – it
    was ill killed. How doth good Mistress Page? – And I
    thank you always with my heart, la! With my heart.
PAGE Sir, I thank you.   80
SHALLOW Sir, I thank you. By yea and no, I do.
PAGE I am glad to see you, good Master Slender.
SLENDER How does your fallow greyhound, sir? I heard
    say he was outrun on Cotsall.
PAGE It could not be judged, sir.
SLENDER You'll not confess. You'll not confess.
SHALLOW That he will not. 'Tis your fault, 'tis your
    fault. 'Tis a good dog.

PAGE A cur, sir.

90 SHALLOW Sir, he's a good dog and a fair dog. Can there
be more said? He is good and fair. Is Sir John Falstaff
here?

PAGE Sir, he is within; and I would I could do a good
office between you.

EVANS It is spoke as a Christians ought to speak.

SHALLOW He hath wronged me, Master Page.

PAGE Sir, he doth in some sort confess it.

SHALLOW If it be confessed, it is not redressed. Is not that
so, Master Page? He hath wronged me, indeed he hath,
100 at a word, he hath. Believe me — Robert Shallow,
Esquire, saith he is wronged.

PAGE Here comes Sir John.

Enter Sir John Falstaff, Bardolph, Nym, and Pistol

FALSTAFF Now, Master Shallow, you'll complain of me
to the King?

SHALLOW Knight, you have beaten my men, killed my
deer, and broke open my lodge.

FALSTAFF But not kissed your keeper's daughter?

SHALLOW Tut, a pin! This shall be answered.

FALSTAFF I will answer it straight. I have done all this.
110 That is now answered.

SHALLOW The Council shall know this.

FALSTAFF 'Twere better for you if it were known in
counsel. You'll be laughed at.

EVANS *Pauca verba*, Sir John, good worts.

FALSTAFF Good worts? Good cabbage! — Slender, I
broke your head. What matter have you against me?

SLENDER Marry, sir, I have matter in my head against
you, and against your cony-catching rascals, Bardolph,
Nym, and Pistol. They carried me to the tavern, and
120 made me drunk, and afterward picked my pocket.

BARDOLPH You Banbury cheese!

SLENDER Ay, it is no matter.

PISTOL How now, Mephostophilus?

SLENDER Ay, it is no matter.

NYM Slice, I say. *Pauca, pauca*. Slice! That's my humour.

SLENDER Where's Simple, my man? Can you tell, cousin?

EVANS Peace, I pray you. Now let us understand. There is three umpires in this matter, as I understand – that is, Master Page, *fidelicet* Master Page; and there is myself, *fidelicet* myself; and the three party is, lastly and finally, mine host of the Garter.   130

PAGE We three to hear it, and end it between them.

EVANS Fery goot. I will make a prief of it in my notebook, and we will afterwards 'ork upon the cause with as great discreetly as we can.

FALSTAFF Pistol!

PISTOL He hears with ears.

EVANS The tevil and his tam! What phrase is this, 'He hears with ear'? Why, it is affectations.   140

FALSTAFF Pistol, did you pick Master Slender's purse?

SLENDER Ay, by these gloves, did he – or I would I might never come in mine own great chamber again else – of seven groats in mill-sixpences, and two Edward shovel-boards, that cost me two shillings and twopence apiece of Yed Miller, by these gloves.

FALSTAFF Is this true, Pistol?

EVANS No, it is false, if it is a pickpurse.

PISTOL

Ha, thou mountain-foreigner! – Sir John and master mine,

I combat challenge of this latten bilbo.   150

Word of denial in thy *labras* here!

Word of denial! Froth and scum, thou liest!

SLENDER (*pointing to Nym*) By these gloves, then 'twas he.

NYM Be advised, sir, and pass good humours. I will say
'Marry trap with you', if you run the nuthook's humour
on me. That is the very note of it.

SLENDER By this hat, then he in the red face had it. For
though I cannot remember what I did when you made
me drunk, yet I am not altogether an ass.

160 FALSTAFF What say you, Scarlet and John?

BARDOLPH Why, sir, for my part, I say the gentleman
had drunk himself out of his five sentences.

EVANS It is his 'five senses'. Fie, what the ignorance is!

BARDOLPH And being fap, sir, was, as they say, cashiered.
And so conclusions passed the careers.

SLENDER Ay, you spake in Latin then too. But 'tis no
matter. I'll ne'er be drunk whilst I live again, but in
honest, civil, godly company, for this trick. If I be
drunk, I'll be drunk with those that have the fear of
170 God, and not with drunken knaves.

EVANS So Got 'udge me, that is a virtuous mind.

FALSTAFF You hear all these matters denied, gentlemen.
You hear it.

Enter Anne Page, with wine, Mistress Ford, and
Mistress Page

PAGE Nay, daughter, carry the wine in – we'll drink
within.

Exit Anne Page

SLENDER O heaven! This is Mistress Anne Page.

PAGE How now, Mistress Ford?

FALSTAFF Mistress Ford, by my troth, you are very well
met. By your leave, good mistress.

He kisses her

180 PAGE Wife, bid these gentlemen welcome. Come, we
have a hot venison pasty to dinner. Come, gentlemen, I
hope we shall drink down all unkindness.

Exeunt all except Slender

SLENDER I had rather than forty shillings I had my Book of Songs and Sonnets here.

Enter Simple

How now, Simple, where have you been? I must wait on myself, must I? You have not the Book of Riddles about you, have you?

SIMPLE Book of Riddles? Why, did you not lend it to Alice Shortcake upon Allhallowmas last, a fortnight afore Michaelmas?   190

Enter Shallow and Evans

SHALLOW Come, coz; come, coz; we stay for you. A word with you, coz. Marry, this, coz – there is as 'twere a tender, a kind of tender, made afar off by Sir Hugh here. Do you understand me?

SLENDER Ay, sir, you shall find me reasonable. If it be so, I shall do that that is reason.

SHALLOW Nay, but understand me.

SLENDER So I do, sir.

EVANS Give ear to his motions. Master Slender, I will description the matter to you, if you be capacity of it.   200

SLENDER Nay, I will do as my cousin Shallow says. I pray you pardon me. He's a justice of peace in his country, simple though I stand here.

EVANS But that is not the question. The question is concerning your marriage.

SHALLOW Ay, there's the point, sir.

EVANS Marry, is it, the very point of it – to Mistress Anne Page.

SLENDER Why, if it be so, I will marry her upon any reasonable demands.   210

EVANS But can you affection the 'oman? Let us command to know that of your mouth, or of your lips – for divers philosophers hold that the lips is parcel of the mouth.

Therefore, precisely, can you carry your good will to the maid?

SHALLOW Cousin Abraham Slender, can you love her?

SLENDER I hope, sir, I will do as it shall become one that would do reason.

EVANS Nay, Got's lords and his ladies! You must speak
220   possitable, if you can carry her your desires towards her.

SHALLOW That you must. Will you, upon good dowry, marry her?

SLENDER I will do a greater thing than that, upon your request, cousin, in any reason.

SHALLOW Nay, conceive me, conceive me, sweet coz — what I do is to pleasure you, coz. Can you love the maid?

SLENDER I will marry her, sir, at your request. But if there be no great love in the beginning, yet heaven may
230   decrease it upon better acquaintance when we are married and have more occasion to know one another. I hope upon familiarity will grow more content. But if you say 'Marry her', I will marry her — that I am freely dissolved, and dissolutely.

EVANS It is a fery discretion answer, save the fall is in the 'ord 'dissolutely'. The 'ort is, according to our meaning, 'resolutely'. His meaning is good.

SHALLOW Ay, I think my cousin meant well.

SLENDER Ay, or else I would I might be hanged, la!

Enter Anne Page

240   SHALLOW Here comes fair Mistress Anne. Would I were young for your sake, Mistress Anne!

ANNE The dinner is on the table. My father desires your worships' company.

SHALLOW I will wait on him, fair Mistress Anne.

EVANS 'Od's plessed will! I will not be absence at the grace.   *Exeunt Shallow and Evans*

ANNE Will't please your worship to come in, sir?

SLENDER No, I thank you, forsooth, heartily. I am very
well.

ANNE The dinner attends you, sir.   250

SLENDER I am not a-hungry, I thank you, forsooth.
(*To Simple*) Go, sirrah, for all you are my man, go wait
upon my cousin Shallow.   *Exit Simple*
A justice of peace sometime may be beholding to his
friend for a man. I keep but three men and a boy yet,
till my mother be dead. But what though? Yet I live
like a poor gentleman born.

ANNE I may not go in without your worship – they will
not sit till you come.

SLENDER I'faith, I'll eat nothing. I thank you as much as   260
though I did.

ANNE I pray you, sir, walk in.

SLENDER I had rather walk here, I thank you. I bruised my
shin th'other day with playing at sword and dagger with
a master of fence – three veneys for a dish of stewed
prunes – and, by my troth, I cannot abide the smell of
hot meat since. Why do your dogs bark so? Be there
bears i'th'town?

ANNE I think there are, sir. I heard them talked of.

SLENDER I love the sport well, but I shall as soon quarrel   270
at it as any man in England. You are afraid if you see the
bear loose, are you not?

ANNE Ay, indeed, sir.

SLENDER That's meat and drink to me, now. I have seen
Sackerson loose twenty times, and have taken him by
the chain. But, I warrant you, the women have so cried
and shrieked at it, that it passed. But women, indeed,
cannot abide 'em – they are very ill-favoured rough
things.
    Enter Page

280   PAGE Come, gentle Master Slender, come. We stay for
        you.
       SLENDER I'll eat nothing, I thank you, sir.
       PAGE By cock and pie, you shall not choose, sir! Come,
        come.
       SLENDER Nay, pray you lead the way.
       PAGE Come on, sir.
       SLENDER Mistress Anne, yourself shall go first.
       ANNE Not I, sir. Pray you keep on.
       SLENDER Truly, I will not go first, truly, la! I will not do
290   you that wrong.
       ANNE I pray you, sir.
       SLENDER I'll rather be unmannerly than troublesome.
        You do yourself wrong, indeed, la!   *Exeunt*

I.2   *Enter Evans and Simple*
       EVANS Go your ways, and ask of Doctor Caius's house
        which is the way. And there dwells one Mistress Quickly,
        which is in the manner of his nurse, or his dry nurse,
        or his cook, or his laundry, his washer, and his wringer.
       SIMPLE Well, sir.
       EVANS Nay, it is petter yet. Give her this letter, for it is a
        'oman that altogether's acquaintance with Mistress Anne
        Page. And the letter is to desire and require her to
        solicit your master's desires to Mistress Anne Page.
10   I pray you be gone. I will make an end of my dinner –
        there's pippins and cheese to come.   *Exeunt*

I.3   *Enter Falstaff, Host, Bardolph, Nym, Pistol, and
        Robin*
       FALSTAFF Mine host of the Garter –

HOST What says my bully rook? Speak scholarly and
    wisely.

FALSTAFF Truly, mine host, I must turn away some of
    my followers.

HOST Discard, bully Hercules, cashier. Let them wag;
    trot, trot.

FALSTAFF I sit at ten pounds a week.

HOST Thou'rt an emperor – Caesar, Keisar, and Pheazar.
    I will entertain Bardolph; he shall draw, he shall tap.   10
    Said I well, bully Hector?

FALSTAFF Do so, good mine host.

HOST I have spoke. Let him follow. (*To Bardolph*) Let me
    see thee froth and lime. I am at a word. Follow.   *Exit*

FALSTAFF Bardolph, follow him. A tapster is a good trade.
    An old cloak makes a new jerkin; a withered servingman
    a fresh tapster. Go, adieu.

BARDOLPH It is a life that I have desired. I will thrive.

PISTOL
    O base Hungarian wight! Wilt thou the spigot wield?
                                        Exit Bardolph

NYM He was gotten in drink. Is not the humour con-   20
    ceited?

FALSTAFF I am glad I am so acquit of this tinderbox.
    His thefts were too open. His filching was like an
    unskilful singer – he kept not time.

NYM The good humour is to steal at a minute's rest.

PISTOL
    'Convey', the wise it call. 'Steal'? Foh,
    A fico for the phrase!

FALSTAFF Well, sirs, I am almost out at heels.

PISTOL
    Why then, let kibes ensue.

FALSTAFF There is no remedy – I must cony-catch, I must   30
    shift.

PISTOL
    Young ravens must have food.

FALSTAFF Which of you know Ford of this town?

PISTOL
    I ken the wight. He is of substance good.

FALSTAFF My honest lads, I will tell you what I am about.

PISTOL Two yards, and more.

FALSTAFF No quips now, Pistol. Indeed, I am in the
waist two yards about. But I am now about no waste –
I am about thrift. Briefly, I do mean to make love to
Ford's wife. I spy entertainment in her. She discourses,
she carves, she gives the leer of invitation. I can construe
the action of her familiar style; and the hardest voice
of her behaviour – to be Englished rightly – is 'I am
Sir John Falstaff's'.

PISTOL He hath studied her will, and translated her will –
out of honesty into English.

NYM The anchor is deep. Will that humour pass?

FALSTAFF Now, the report goes she has all the rule of
her husband's purse. He hath a legion of angels.

PISTOL
    As many devils entertain! And 'To her, boy', say I.

NYM The humour rises – it is good. Humour me the
angels.

FALSTAFF I have writ me here a letter to her; and here
another to Page's wife, who even now gave me good eyes
too, examined my parts with most judicious œillades.
Sometimes the beam of her view gilded my foot, sometimes my portly belly.

PISTOL (*aside*)
    Then did the sun on dunghill shine.

NYM (*aside*) I thank thee for that humour.

FALSTAFF O, she did so course o'er my exteriors with
such a greedy intention that the appetite of her eye did

seem to scorch me up like a burning-glass. Here's
another letter to her. She bears the purse too. She is a
region in Guiana, all gold and bounty. I will be cheaters
to them both, and they shall be exchequers to me. They
shall be my East and West Indies, and I will trade to
them both. (*To Pistol*) Go, bear thou this letter to
Mistress Page; (*to Nym*) and thou this to Mistress Ford.
We will thrive, lads, we will thrive.

PISTOL
    Shall I Sir Pandarus of Troy become –   70
    And by my side wear steel? Then Lucifer take all!
NYM I will run no base humour. Here, take the humour-
    letter. I will keep the haviour of reputation.
FALSTAFF (*to Robin*)
    Hold, sirrah, bear you these letters tightly;
    Sail like my pinnace to these golden shores.
    Rogues, hence, avaunt! Vanish like hailstones, go!
    Trudge, plod away o'th'hoof, seek shelter, pack!
    Falstaff will learn the humour of the age,
    French thrift, you rogues – myself and skirted page.
                              Exeunt Falstaff and Robin
PISTOL
    Let vultures gripe thy guts! For gourd and fullam holds, 80
    And high and low beguiles the rich and poor.
    Tester I'll have in pouch when thou shalt lack,
    Base Phrygian Turk!
NYM I have operations which be humours of revenge.
PISTOL
    Wilt thou revenge?
NYM   By welkin and her star!
PISTOL
    With wit or steel?
NYM   With both the humours, I.
    I will discuss the humour of this love to Page.

PISTOL
　　And I to Ford shall eke unfold
　　　　How Falstaff, varlet vile,
90　　His dove will prove, his gold will hold,
　　　　And his soft couch defile.

NYM My humour shall not cool. I will incense Page to
　　deal with poison. I will possess him with yellowness, for
　　the revolt of mine is dangerous. That is my true humour.

PISTOL
　　Thou art the Mars of malcontents. I second thee. Troop
　　on.   *Exeunt*

I.4　　*Enter Mistress Quickly and Simple*

MISTRESS QUICKLY (*calling*) What, John Rugby!
　　Enter Rugby
　　I pray thee, go to the casement and see if you can see
　　my master, Master Doctor Caius, coming. If he do,
　　i'faith, and find anybody in the house, here will be an
　　old abusing of God's patience and the King's English.

RUGBY I'll go watch.

MISTRESS QUICKLY Go; and we'll have a posset for't
　　soon at night, in faith, at the latter end of a sea-coal
　　fire.   *Exit Rugby*
10　　An honest, willing, kind fellow, as ever servant shall
　　come in house withal; and, I warrant you, no tell-tale,
　　nor no breed-bate. His worst fault is that he is given to
　　prayer. He is something peevish that way, but nobody
　　but has his fault. But let that pass. – Peter Simple you
　　say your name is?

SIMPLE Ay, for fault of a better.

MISTRESS QUICKLY And Master Slender's your master?

SIMPLE Ay, forsooth.

MISTRESS QUICKLY Does he not wear a great round

beard like a glover's paring-knife?   20

SIMPLE No, forsooth. He hath but a little wee face, with a little yellow beard – a Cain-coloured beard.

MISTRESS QUICKLY A softly-sprighted man, is he not?

SIMPLE Ay, forsooth. But he is as tall a man of his hands as any is between this and his head. He hath fought with a warrener.

MISTRESS QUICKLY How say you? – O, I should remember him. Does he not hold up his head, as it were, and strut in his gait?

SIMPLE Yes, indeed, does he.   30

MISTRESS QUICKLY Well, heaven send Anne Page no worse fortune. Tell Master Parson Evans I will do what I can for your master. Anne is a good girl, and I wish –

Enter Rugby

RUGBY Out, alas! Here comes my master.

MISTRESS QUICKLY We shall all be shent. Run in here, good young man; go into this closet. He will not stay long.

She shuts Simple in the closet

What, John Rugby! John, what, John, I say! Go, John, go inquire for my master. I doubt he be not well, that   40
he comes not home.   *Exit Rugby*

She sings

And down, down, adown-a, *etc.*

Enter Doctor Caius

CAIUS Vat is you sing? I do not like dese toys. Pray you go and vetch me in my closet *un boîtier vert* – a box, a green-a box. Do intend vat I speak? A green-a box.

MISTRESS QUICKLY Ay, forsooth, I'll fetch it you. (*Aside*) I am glad he went not in himself. If he had found the young man, he would have been horn-mad.

Exit to the closet

CAIUS Fe, fe, fe, fe! *Ma foi, il fait fort chaud. Je m'en*
50   *vais à la cour — la grande affaire.*
    Enter Mistress Quickly with the box
MISTRESS QUICKLY Is it this, sir?
CAIUS *Oui, mette-le au mon* pocket. *Dépêche*, quickly. Vere
    is dat knave Rugby?
MISTRESS QUICKLY What, John Rugby! John!
    Enter Rugby
RUGBY Here, sir.
CAIUS You are John Rugby, and you are Jack Rugby.
    Come, take-a your rapier, and come after my heel to the
    court.
RUGBY 'Tis ready, sir, here in the porch.
60   CAIUS By my trot, I tarry too long. 'Od's me! *Qu'ai-je*
    oublié? Dere is some simples in my closet, dat I vill not
    for the varld I shall leave behind.   *Exit to the closet*
MISTRESS QUICKLY Ay me, he'll find the young man
    there, and be mad.
CAIUS (*within*) O, *diable, diable!* Vat is in my closet?
    Villainy! *Larron!*
    Enter Caius, pulling Simple out of the closet
    Rugby, my rapier!
MISTRESS QUICKLY Good master, be content.
CAIUS Wherefore shall I be content-a?
70   MISTRESS QUICKLY The young man is an honest man.
CAIUS What shall de honest man do in my closet? Dere is
    no honest man dat shall come in my closet.
MISTRESS QUICKLY I beseech you, be not so phlegmatic.
    Hear the truth of it. He came of an errand to me from
    Parson Hugh.
CAIUS Vell?
SIMPLE Ay, forsooth, to desire her to —
MISTRESS QUICKLY Peace, I pray you.

CAIUS Peace-a your tongue. (*To Simple*) Speak-a your
tale.   80

SIMPLE To desire this honest gentlewoman, your maid,
to speak a good word to Mistress Anne Page for my
master in the way of marriage.

MISTRESS QUICKLY This is all, indeed, la! But I'll
ne'er put my finger in the fire, and need not.

CAIUS Sir Hugh send-a you? – Rugby, *baille* me some
paper. (*To Simple*) Tarry you a little-a while.

    He writes

MISTRESS QUICKLY (*aside to Simple*) I am glad he is so
quiet. If he had been throughly moved, you should have
heard him so loud and so melancholy. But notwith-   90
standing, man, I'll do you your master what good I can.
And the very yea and the no is, the French doctor, my
master – I may call him my master, look you, for I keep
his house; and I wash, wring, brew, bake, scour, dress
meat and drink, make the beds, and do all myself –

SIMPLE (*aside to Mistress Quickly*) 'Tis a great charge to
come under one body's hand.

MISTRESS QUICKLY (*aside to Simple*) Are you avised
o'that? You shall find it a great charge – and to be up
early and down late. But notwithstanding – to tell you   100
in your ear, I would have no words of it – my master
himself is in love with Mistress Anne Page. But notwithstanding that, I know Anne's mind. That's neither
here nor there.

CAIUS You, jack'nape, give-a this letter to Sir Hugh. By
gar, it is a shallenge. I will cut his troat in de park, and I will
teach a scurvy jackanape priest to meddle or make. You
may be gone. It is not good you tarry here.

                                 Exit Simple

By gar, I will cut all his two stones. By gar, he shall not
have a stone to throw at his dog.   110

MISTRESS QUICKLY Alas, he speaks but for his friend.

CAIUS It is no matter-a ver dat. Do not you tell-a me dat I shall have Anne Page for myself? By gar, I vill kill de Jack priest. And I have appointed mine host of de Jarteer to measure our weapon. By gar, I will myself have Anne Page.

MISTRESS QUICKLY Sir, the maid loves you, and all shall be well. We must give folks leave to prate. What the good-year!

120 CAIUS Rugby, come to the court with me. (*To Mistress Quickly*) By gar, if I have not Anne Page, I shall turn your head out of my door. Follow my heels, Rugby.

Exeunt Caius and Rugby

MISTRESS QUICKLY You shall have An — fool's-head of your own. No, I know Anne's mind for that. Never a woman in Windsor knows more of Anne's mind than I do, nor can do more than I do with her, I thank heaven.

FENTON (*offstage*) Who's within there, ho?

MISTRESS QUICKLY Who's there, I trow? Come near the house, I pray you.

Enter Fenton

130 FENTON How now, good woman, how dost thou?

MISTRESS QUICKLY The better that it pleases your good worship to ask.

FENTON What news? How does pretty Mistress Anne?

MISTRESS QUICKLY In truth, sir, and she is pretty, and honest, and gentle — and one that is your friend. I can tell you that by the way, I praise heaven for it.

FENTON Shall I do any good, thinkest thou? Shall I not lose my suit?

MISTRESS QUICKLY Troth, sir, all is in His hands above.
140 But notwithstanding, Master Fenton, I'll be sworn on a book she loves you. Have not your worship a wart above your eye?

FENTON Yes, marry, have I. What of that?

MISTRESS QUICKLY Well, thereby hangs a tale. Good faith, it is such another Nan — but, I detest, an honest maid as ever broke bread. We had an hour's talk of that wart. I shall never laugh but in that maid's company. But, indeed, she is given too much to allicholy and musing. But for you — well — go to —

FENTON Well, I shall see her today. Hold, there's money for thee; let me have thy voice in my behalf. If thou seest her before me, commend me — 150

MISTRESS QUICKLY Will I? I'faith, that we will. And I will tell your worship more of the wart the next time we have confidence, and of other wooers.

FENTON Well, farewell. I am in great haste now.

MISTRESS QUICKLY Farewell to your worship.

Exit Fenton

Truly, an honest gentleman. But Anne loves him not, for I know Anne's mind as well as another does. Out upon't! What have I forgot?   *Exit* 160

*

Enter Mistress Page, with a letter   II.I

MISTRESS PAGE What, have I 'scaped love-letters in the holiday time of my beauty, and am I now a subject for them? Let me see.

(*She reads*)

Ask me no reason why I love you, for though Love use Reason for his precisian, he admits him not for his counsellor. You are not young, no more am I. Go to, then, there's sympathy. You are merry, so am I. Ha, ha, then there's more sympathy. You love sack, and so do I. Would you desire better sympathy? Let it suffice thee, Mistress

10 *Page – at the least if the love of soldier can suffice – that I*
love thee. I will not say, pity me – 'tis not a soldier-like
phrase – but I say, love me. By me,
    Thine own true knight,
    By day or night,
    Or any kind of light,
    With all his might
    For thee to fight,

                                    John Falstaff.

What a Herod of Jewry is this! O, wicked, wicked world!
20 One that is well-nigh worn to pieces with age to show
himself a young gallant! What an unweighed behaviour
hath this Flemish drunkard picked – with the devil's
name! – out of my conversation, that he dares in this
manner assay me? Why, he hath not been thrice in my
company. What should I say to him? I was then frugal
of my mirth – heaven forgive me! Why, I'll exhibit a
bill in the parliament for the putting down of men. How
shall I be revenged on him? For revenged I will be, as
sure as his guts are made of puddings.
    Enter Mistress Ford
30 MISTRESS FORD Mistress Page! Trust me, I was going to
    your house.
    MISTRESS PAGE And, trust me, I was coming to you.
    You look very ill.
    MISTRESS FORD Nay, I'll ne'er believe that. I have to
    show to the contrary.
    MISTRESS PAGE Faith, but you do, in my mind.
    MISTRESS FORD Well, I do, then. Yet I say I could show
    you to the contrary. O Mistress Page, give me some
    counsel.
40 MISTRESS PAGE What's the matter, woman?

MISTRESS FORD O woman, if it were not for one trifling respect, I could come to such honour.

MISTRESS PAGE Hang the trifle, woman, take the honour. What is it? Dispense with trifles. What is it?

MISTRESS FORD If I would but go to hell for an eternal moment or so, I could be knighted.

MISTRESS PAGE What? Thou liest. Sir Alice Ford? These knights will hack, and so thou shouldst not alter the article of thy gentry.

MISTRESS FORD We burn daylight. Here, read, read.   50 Perceive how I might be knighted. I shall think the worse of fat men as long as I have an eye to make difference of men's liking. And yet he would not swear; praised women's modesty; and gave such orderly and well-behaved reproof to all uncomeliness that I would have sworn his disposition would have gone to the truth of his words. But they do no more adhere and keep place together than the Hundredth Psalm to the tune of 'Greensleeves'. What tempest, I trow, threw this whale, with so many tuns of oil in his belly, ashore at Windsor?   60 How shall I be revenged on him? I think the best way were to entertain him with hope till the wicked fire of lust have melted him in his own grease. Did you ever hear the like?

MISTRESS PAGE (comparing the two letters) Letter for letter, but that the name of Page and Ford differs. To thy great comfort in this mystery of ill opinions, here's the twin-brother of thy letter. But let thine inherit first, for I protest mine never shall. I warrant he hath a thousand of these letters, writ with blank space for different names – sure, more – and these are of the second edition. He   70 will print them, out of doubt; for he cares not what he puts into the press, when he would put us two. I had rather be a giantess and lie under Mount Pelion. Well,

I will find you twenty lascivious turtles ere one chaste man.

She gives her letter to Mistress Ford

MISTRESS FORD Why, this is the very same: the very hand, the very words. What doth he think of us?

MISTRESS PAGE Nay, I know not. It makes me almost
80 ready to wrangle with mine own honesty. I'll entertain myself like one that I am not acquainted withal; for, sure, unless he know some strain in me that I know not myself, he would never have boarded me in this fury.

MISTRESS FORD 'Boarding' call you it? I'll be sure to keep him above deck.

MISTRESS PAGE So will I. If he come under my hatches, I'll never to sea again. Let's be revenged on him. Let's appoint him a meeting, give him a show of comfort in his suit, and lead him on with a fine-baited delay till he
90 hath pawned his horses to mine host of the Garter.

MISTRESS FORD Nay, I will consent to act any villainy against him that may not sully the chariness of our honesty. O that my husband saw this letter! It would give eternal food to his jealousy.

MISTRESS PAGE Why, look where he comes, and my good man too. He's as far from jealousy as I am from giving him cause – and that, I hope, is an unmeasurable distance.

MISTRESS FORD You are the happier woman.
100 MISTRESS PAGE Let's consult together against this greasy knight. Come hither.

They retire

Enter Ford with Pistol, and Page with Nym

FORD Well, I hope it be not so.

PISTOL
   Hope is a curtal dog in some affairs.
   Sir John affects thy wife.

FORD Why, sir, my wife is not young.

PISTOL

He woos both high and low, both rich and poor,
Both young and old, one with another, Ford.
He loves the gallimaufry. Ford, perpend.

FORD Love my wife?

PISTOL

With liver burning hot. Prevent. Or go thou   110
Like Sir Actaeon he, with Ringwood at thy heels.
O, odious is the name!

FORD What name, sir?

PISTOL

The horn, I say. Farewell.
Take heed, have open eye, for thieves do foot by night.
Take heed, ere summer comes or cuckoo-birds do sing.
Away, Sir Corporal Nym!
Believe it, Page; he speaks sense.   *Exit*

FORD (*aside*)

I will be patient. I will find out this.

NYM (*to Page*) And this is true. I like not the humour of   120
lying. He hath wronged me in some humours. I should
have borne the humoured letter to her, but I have a
sword and it shall bite upon my necessity. He loves your
wife. There's the short and the long. My name is
Corporal Nym. I speak, and I avouch 'tis true. My name
is Nym, and Falstaff loves your wife. Adieu. I love not
the humour of bread and cheese — and there's the
humour of it. Adieu.   *Exit*

PAGE 'The humour of it', quoth 'a! Here's a fellow frights
English out of his wits.   130

FORD (*aside*) I will seek out Falstaff.

PAGE (*aside*) I never heard such a drawling, affecting
rogue.

FORD (*aside*) If I do find it — well.

PAGE (*aside*) I will not believe such a Cataian, though the priest o'th'town commended him for a true man.

FORD (*aside*) 'Twas a good sensible fellow – well.

Mistress Page and Mistress Ford come forward

PAGE How now, Meg?

MISTRESS PAGE Whither go you, George? Hark you.

They speak aside

140 MISTRESS FORD How now, sweet Frank, why art thou melancholy?

FORD I melancholy? I am not melancholy. Get you home, go.

MISTRESS FORD Faith, thou hast some crotchets in thy head now. Will you go, Mistress Page?

MISTRESS PAGE Have with you. – You'll come to dinner, George?

Enter Mistress Quickly

(*Aside to Mistress Ford*) Look who comes yonder. She shall be our messenger to this paltry knight.

150 MISTRESS FORD (*aside to Mistress Page*) Trust me, I thought on her. She'll fit it.

MISTRESS PAGE You are come to see my daughter Anne?

MISTRESS QUICKLY Ay, forsooth; and, I pray, how does good Mistress Anne?

MISTRESS PAGE Go in with us and see. We have an hour's talk with you.

Exeunt Mistress Page, Mistress Ford,
and Mistress Quickly

PAGE How now, Master Ford?

FORD You heard what this knave told me, did you not?

PAGE Yes, and you heard what the other told me?

160 FORD Do you think there is truth in them?

PAGE Hang 'em, slaves! I do not think the knight would offer it. But these that accuse him in his intent towards

our wives are a yoke of his discarded men – very rogues,
now they be out of service.

FORD Were they his men?

PAGE Marry, were they.

FORD I like it never the better for that. Does he lie at the
Garter?

PAGE Ay, marry, does he. If he should intend this voyage
toward my wife, I would turn her loose to him; and   170
what he gets more of her than sharp words, let it lie on
my head.

FORD I do not misdoubt my wife, but I would be loath
to turn them together. A man may be too confident. I
would have nothing lie on my head. I cannot be thus
satisfied.

Enter Host

PAGE Look where my ranting host of the Garter comes.
There is either liquor in his pate or money in his purse
when he looks so merrily. – How now, mine host?

HOST How now, bully rook? Thou'rt a gentleman.   180

He turns and calls

Cavaliero justice, I say!

Enter Shallow

SHALLOW I follow, mine host, I follow. Good even and
twenty, good Master Page. Master Page, will you go with
us? We have sport in hand.

HOST Tell him, cavaliero justice; tell him, bully rook.

SHALLOW Sir, there is a fray to be fought between Sir
Hugh the Welsh priest and Caius the French doctor.

FORD Good mine host o'th'Garter, a word with you.

HOST What sayest thou, my bully rook?

They go aside

SHALLOW (*to Page*) Will you go with us to behold it?   190
My merry host hath had the measuring of their weapons,
and, I think, hath appointed them contrary places; for,

believe me, I hear the parson is no jester. Hark, I will
tell you what our sport shall be.

They go aside

HOST Hast thou no suit against my knight, my guest
cavaliero?

FORD None, I protest. But I'll give you a pottle of burnt
sack to give me recourse to him and tell him my name is
Brook – only for a jest.

200   HOST My hand, bully. Thou shalt have egress and
regress. – Said I well? – And thy name shall be Brook.
It is a merry knight. Will you go, Ameers?

SHALLOW Have with you, mine host.

PAGE I have heard the Frenchman hath good skill in his
rapier.

SHALLOW Tut, sir, I could have told you more. In these
times you stand on distance, your passes, stoccadoes,
and I know not what. 'Tis the heart, Master Page;
'tis here, 'tis here. I have seen the time, with my long

210   sword, I would have made you four tall fellows skip like
rats.

HOST Here, boys, here, here! Shall we wag?

PAGE Have with you. I had rather hear them scold than
fight.   *Exeunt Host, Shallow, and Page*

FORD Though Page be a secure fool and stands so firmly
on his wife's frailty, yet I cannot put off my opinion so
easily. She was in his company at Page's house, and what
they made there I know not. Well, I will look further
into't, and I have a disguise to sound Falstaff. If I find

220   her honest, I lose not my labour. If she be otherwise,
'tis labour well bestowed.   *Exit*

II.2   *Enter Falstaff and Pistol*

FALSTAFF I will not lend thee a penny.

PISTOL

Why then, the world's mine oyster,
Which I with sword will open. –
I will retort the sum in equipage.

FALSTAFF Not a penny. I have been content, sir, you
should lay my countenance to pawn. I have grated upon
my good friends for three reprieves for you and your
coach-fellow Nym, or else you had looked through the
grate, like a geminy of baboons. I am damned in hell
for swearing to gentlemen my friends you were good   10
soldiers and tall fellows. And when Mistress Bridget
lost the handle of her fan, I took't upon mine honour thou
hadst it not.

PISTOL

Didst thou not share? Hadst thou not fifteen pence?

FALSTAFF Reason, you rogue, reason. Thinkest thou
I'll endanger my soul gratis? At a word, hang no more
about me – I am no gibbet for you. Go – a short knife
and a throng – to your manor of Pickt-hatch, go. You'll
not bear a letter for me, you rogue? You stand upon
your honour! Why, thou unconfinable baseness, it is   20
as much as I can do to keep the terms of my honour
precise. I, I, I myself sometimes, leaving the fear of
God on the left hand and hiding mine honour in my
necessity, am fain to shuffle, to hedge, and to lurch; and
yet you, you rogue, will ensconce your rags, your cat-
a-mountain looks, your red-lattice phrases, and your
bold beating oaths, under the shelter of your honour!
You will not do it? You!

PISTOL

I do relent. What wouldst thou more of man?

Enter Robin

ROBIN Sir, here's a woman would speak with you.   30

FALSTAFF Let her approach.

Enter Mistress Quickly

MISTRESS QUICKLY Give your worship good morrow.

FALSTAFF Good morrow, good wife.

MISTRESS QUICKLY Not so, an't please your worship.

FALSTAFF Good maid, then.

MISTRESS QUICKLY

I'll be sworn,

As my mother was the first hour I was born.

FALSTAFF

I do believe the swearer. What with me?

MISTRESS QUICKLY Shall I vouchsafe your worship a
40   word or two?

FALSTAFF Two thousand, fair woman, and I'll vouchsafe thee the hearing.

MISTRESS QUICKLY There is one Mistress Ford – Sir,
I pray, come a little nearer this ways – I myself dwell
with Master Doctor Caius.

FALSTAFF Well, on. Mistress Ford, you say –

MISTRESS QUICKLY Your worship says very true – I
pray your worship, come a little nearer this ways.

FALSTAFF I warrant thee nobody hears – *(indicating*
50   *Pistol and Robin)* mine own people, mine own people.

MISTRESS QUICKLY Are they so? God bless them and
make them his servants!

FALSTAFF Well, Mistress Ford – what of her?

MISTRESS QUICKLY Why, sir, she's a good creature.
Lord, Lord, your worship's a wanton! Well, God forgive
you, and all of us, I pray –

FALSTAFF Mistress Ford – come, Mistress Ford.

MISTRESS QUICKLY Marry, this is the short and the long
of it: you have brought her into such a canaries as 'tis
60   wonderful. The best courtier of them all, when the
court lay at Windsor, could never have brought her to
such a canary; yet there has been knights, and lords,

and gentlemen, with their coaches, I warrant you, coach
after coach, letter after letter, gift after gift, smelling so
sweetly – all musk – and so rushling, I warrant you, in
silk and gold, and in such alligant terms, and in such
wine and sugar of the best and the fairest, that would
have won any woman's heart, and, I warrant you, they
could never get an eye-wink of her – I had myself twenty
angels given me this morning, but I defy all angels in   70
any such sort, as they say, but in the way of honesty –
and, I warrant you, they could never get her so much
as sip on a cup with the proudest of them all, and yet
there has been earls – nay, which is more, pensioners –
but, I warrant you, all is one with her.

FALSTAFF But what says she to me? Be brief, my good
she-Mercury.

MISTRESS QUICKLY Marry, she hath received your
letter, for the which she thanks you a thousand times,
and she gives you to notify that her husband will be   80
absence from his house between ten and eleven.

FALSTAFF Ten and eleven.

MISTRESS QUICKLY Ay, forsooth; and then you may
come and see the picture, she says, that you wot of.
Master Ford, her husband, will be from home. Alas,
the sweet woman leads an ill life with him – he's a very
jealousy man – she leads a very frampold life with him,
good heart.

FALSTAFF Ten and eleven. Woman, commend me to her.
I will not fail her.   90

MISTRESS QUICKLY Why, you say well. But I have
another messenger to your worship. Mistress Page
hath her hearty commendations to you too; and, let me
tell you in your ear, she's as fartuous a civil modest
wife, and one, I tell you, that will not miss you morning
nor evening prayer, as any is in Windsor, whoe'er be

the other. And she bade me tell your worship that her husband is seldom from home, but she hopes there will come a time. I never knew a woman so dote upon a man. Surely, I think you have charms, la! Yes, in truth.

FALSTAFF Not I, I assure thee. Setting the attraction of my good parts aside, I have no other charms.

MISTRESS QUICKLY Blessing on your heart for't!

FALSTAFF But I pray thee tell me this: has Ford's wife and Page's wife acquainted each other how they love me?

MISTRESS QUICKLY That were a jest indeed! They have not so little grace, I hope – that were a trick indeed! But Mistress Page would desire you to send her your little page, of all loves. Her husband has a marvellous infection to the little page; and, truly, Master Page is an honest man. Never a wife in Windsor leads a better life than she does. Do what she will, say what she will, take all, pay all, go to bed when she list, rise when she list, all is as she will. And, truly, she deserves it; for if there be a kind woman in Windsor, she is one. You must send her your page – no remedy.

FALSTAFF Why, I will.

MISTRESS QUICKLY Nay, but do so, then – and, look you, he may come and go between you both. And in any case have a nay-word, that you may know one another's mind, and the boy never need to understand anything; for 'tis not good that children should know any wickedness. Old folks, you know, have discretion, as they say, and know the world.

FALSTAFF Fare thee well; commend me to them both. There's my purse – I am yet thy debtor. Boy, go along with this woman.

Exeunt Mistress Quickly and Robin

This news distracts me.   130

PISTOL (*aside*)

This punk is one of Cupid's carriers.

Clap on more sails; pursue; up with your fights;

Give fire! She is my prize, or ocean whelm them all!

Exit

FALSTAFF Sayest thou so, old Jack? Go thy ways. I'll make more of thy old body than I have done. Will they yet look after thee? Wilt thou, after the expense of so much money, be now a gainer? Good body, I thank thee. Let them say 'tis grossly done – so it be fairly done, no matter.

Enter Bardolph

BARDOLPH Sir John, there's one Master Brook below   140 would fain speak with you, and be acquainted with you; and hath sent your worship a morning's draught of sack.

FALSTAFF Brook is his name?

BARDOLPH Ay, sir.

FALSTAFF Call him in.   *Exit Bardolph* Such Brooks are welcome to me, that o'erflows such liquor. Aha! Mistress Ford and Mistress Page, have I encompassed you? Go to; *via!*

Enter Bardolph, with Ford disguised as Brook

FORD Bless you, sir.   150

FALSTAFF And you, sir. Would you speak with me?

FORD I make bold to press with so little preparation upon you.

FALSTAFF You're welcome. What's your will? (*To Bardolph*) Give us leave, drawer.   *Exit Bardolph*

FORD Sir, I am a gentleman that have spent much. My name is Brook.

FALSTAFF Good Master Brook, I desire more acquaintance of you.

160 FORD Good Sir John, I sue for yours – not to charge
you – for I must let you understand I think myself in
better plight for a lender than you are, the which hath
something emboldened me to this unseasoned intrusion;
for they say if money go before, all ways do lie open.

FALSTAFF Money is a good soldier, sir, and will on.

FORD Troth, and I have a bag of money here troubles me.
If you will help to bear it, Sir John, take all, or half, for
easing me of the carriage.

FALSTAFF Sir, I know not how I may deserve to be your
170 porter.

FORD I will tell you, sir, if you will give me the hearing.

FALSTAFF Speak, good Master Brook. I shall be glad to
be your servant.

FORD Sir, I hear you are a scholar – I will be brief with
you – and you have been a man long known to me,
though I had never so good means as desire to make
myself acquainted with you. I shall discover a thing to
you wherein I must very much lay open mine own
imperfection. But, good Sir John, as you have one
180 eye upon my follies, as you hear them unfolded, turn
another into the register of your own, that I may pass
with a reproof the easier, sith you yourself know how
easy it is to be such an offender.

FALSTAFF Very well, sir. Proceed.

FORD There is a gentlewoman in this town – her husband's
name is Ford.

FALSTAFF Well, sir.

FORD I have long loved her, and, I protest to you, bestowed much on her, followed her with a doting ob-
190 servance, engrossed opportunities to meet her, fee'd
every slight occasion that could but niggardly give me

sight of her, not only bought many presents to give her but have given largely to many to know what she would have given. Briefly, I have pursued her as love hath pursued me, which hath been on the wing of all occasions. But whatsoever I have merited – either in my mind or in my means – meed, I am sure, I have received none, unless experience be a jewel. That I have purchased at an infinite rate, and that hath taught me to say this: 200
'Love like a shadow flies when substance love pursues,
Pursuing that that flies, and flying what pursues.'

FALSTAFF Have you received no promise of satisfaction at her hands?

FORD Never.

FALSTAFF Have you importuned her to such a purpose?

FORD Never.

FALSTAFF Of what quality was your love, then?

FORD Like a fair house built on another man's ground, so that I have lost my edifice by mistaking the place where   210
I erected it.

FALSTAFF To what purpose have you unfolded this to me?

FORD When I have told you that, I have told you all. Some say that though she appear honest to me, yet in other places she enlargeth her mirth so far that there is shrewd construction made of her. Now, Sir John, here is the heart of my purpose: you are a gentleman of excellent breeding, admirable discourse, of great admittance, authentic in your place and person, generally allowed for your many warlike, courtlike, and learned   220
preparations.

FALSTAFF O, sir!

FORD Believe it, for you know it. There is money. Spend it, spend it; spend more; spend all I have. Only give me so much of your time in exchange of it as to lay an amiable siege to the honesty of this Ford's wife. Use your art of wooing, win her to consent to you. If any man may, you may as soon as any.

FALSTAFF Would it apply well to the vehemency of your
230   affection that I should win what you would enjoy? Methinks you prescribe to yourself very preposterously.

FORD O, understand my drift. She dwells so securely on the excellency of her honour that the folly of my soul dares not present itself. She is too bright to be looked against. Now, could I come to her with any detection in my hand, my desires had instance and argument to commend themselves. I could drive her then from the ward of her purity, her reputation, her marriage-vow, and a thousand other her defences, which now are too
240   too strongly embattled against me. What say you to't, Sir John?

FALSTAFF Master Brook, I will first make bold with your money; next, give me your hand; and last, as I am a gentleman, you shall, if you will, enjoy Ford's wife.

FORD O good sir!

FALSTAFF I say you shall.

FORD Want no money, Sir John; you shall want none.

FALSTAFF Want no Mistress Ford, Master Brook; you shall want none. I shall be with her, I may tell you, by
250   her own appointment. Even as you came in to me, her assistant, or go-between, parted from me. I say I shall be with her between ten and eleven, for at that time the jealous rascally knave her husband will be forth. Come you to me at night, you shall know how I speed.

FORD I am blest in your acquaintance. Do you know Ford, sir?

FALSTAFF Hang him, poor cuckoldy knave! I know him not. Yet I wrong him to call him poor. They say the jealous wittolly knave hath masses of money, for the

which his wife seems to me well-favoured. I will use 260
her as the key of the cuckoldy rogue's coffer – and
there's my harvest-home.

FORD I would you knew Ford, sir, that you might avoid
him if you saw him.

FALSTAFF Hang him, mechanical salt-butter rogue! I will
stare him out of his wits. I will awe him with my cudgel;
it shall hang like a meteor o'er the cuckold's horns.
Master Brook, thou shalt know I will predominate over
the peasant, and thou shalt lie with his wife. Come to
me soon at night. Ford's a knave, and I will aggravate 270
his style. Thou, Master Brook, shalt know him for
knave and cuckold. Come to me soon at night.   *Exit*

FORD What a damned Epicurean rascal is this! My heart
is ready to crack with impatience. Who says this is
improvident jealousy? My wife hath sent to him, the
hour is fixed, the match is made. Would any man have
thought this? See the hell of having a false woman! My
bed shall be abused, my coffers ransacked, my reputation gnawn at; and I shall not only receive this villainous wrong, but stand under the adoption of abomin- 280
able terms, and by him that does me this wrong.
Terms! Names! Amaimon sounds well; Lucifer, well;
Barbason, well. Yet they are devils' additions, the names
of fiends. But Cuckold! Wittol! – Cuckold! The devil
himself hath not such a name. Page is an ass, a secure
ass. He will trust his wife, he will not be jealous. I will
rather trust a Fleming with my butter, Parson Hugh the
Welshman with my cheese, an Irishman with my
aqua-vitae bottle, or a thief to walk my ambling gelding,
than my wife with herself. Then she plots, then she 290
ruminates, then she devises. And what they think in
their hearts they may effect, they will break their
hearts but they will effect. God be praised for my

jealousy! Eleven o'clock the hour. I will prevent this, detect my wife, be revenged on Falstaff, and laugh at Page. I will about it. Better three hours too soon than a minute too late. Fie, fie, fie! Cuckold, cuckold, cuckold!

Exit

II.3   *Enter Doctor Caius and Rugby*

CAIUS Jack Rugby!

RUGBY Sir.

CAIUS Vat is the clock, Jack?

RUGBY 'Tis past the hour, sir, that Sir Hugh promised to meet.

CAIUS By gar, he has save his soul dat he is no come. He has pray his Pible well dat he is no come. By gar, Jack Rugby, he is dead already if he be come.

RUGBY He is wise, sir. He knew your worship would kill
10   him if he came.

CAIUS By gar, de herring is no dead so as I vill kill him. Take your rapier, Jack. I vill tell you how I vill kill him.

RUGBY Alas, sir, I cannot fence.

CAIUS Villainy, take your rapier.

RUGBY Forbear. Here's company.

Enter Host, Shallow, Slender, and Page

HOST Bless thee, bully doctor!

SHALLOW Save you, Master Doctor Caius!

PAGE Now, good Master Doctor!

SLENDER Give you good morrow, sir.

20 CAIUS Vat be you all, one, two, tree, four, come for?

HOST To see thee fight, to see thee foin, to see thee traverse, to see thee here, to see thee there, to see thee pass thy punto, thy stock, thy reverse, thy distance, thy montant. Is he dead, my Ethiopian? Is he dead, my Francisco? Ha, bully? What says my Aesculapius?

My Galen? My heart of elder? Ha? Is he dead, bully
stale? Is he dead?

CAIUS By gar, he is de coward Jack priest of de vorld. He
is not show his face.

HOST Thou art a Castalion-King-Urinal. Hector of   30
Greece, my boy!

CAIUS I pray you bear witness that me have stay six or
seven, two, tree hours for him, and he is no come.

SHALLOW He is the wiser man, Master Doctor. He is a
curer of souls, and you a curer of bodies. If you should
fight, you go against the hair of your professions. Is it
not true, Master Page?

PAGE Master Shallow, you have yourself been a great
fighter, though now a man of peace.

SHALLOW Bodykins, Master Page, though I now be old   40
and of the peace, if I see a sword out, my finger itches
to make one. Though we are justices and doctors and
churchmen, Master Page, we have some salt of our
youth in us. We are the sons of women, Master Page.

PAGE 'Tis true, Master Shallow.

SHALLOW It will be found so, Master Page. Master
Doctor Caius, I am come to fetch you home. I am
sworn of the peace. You have showed yourself a wise
physician, and Sir Hugh hath shown himself a wise and
patient churchman. You must go with me, Master   50
Doctor.

HOST Pardon, guest justice. — A word, Mounseur Mockwater.

CAIUS Mockvater? Vat is dat?

HOST Mockwater, in our English tongue, is valour, bully.

CAIUS By gar, then I have as much mockvater as de
Englishman. Scurvy jack-dog priest! By gar, me vill cut
his ears.

HOST He will clapper-claw thee tightly, bully.

60 CAIUS Clapper-de-claw? Vat is dat?

HOST That is, he will make thee amends.

CAIUS By gar, me do look he shall clapper-de-claw me, for, by gar, me vill have it.

HOST And I will provoke him to't, or let him wag.

CAIUS Me tank you for dat.

HOST And moreover, bully – (*Aside to the others*) But first, Master guest, and Master Page, and eke Cavaliero Slender, go you through the town to Frogmore.

PAGE Sir Hugh is there, is he?

70 HOST He is there. See what humour he is in; and I will bring the doctor about by the fields. Will it do well?

SHALLOW We will do it.

PAGE, SHALLOW, *and* SLENDER Adieu, good master Doctor.   *Exeunt*

CAIUS By gar, me vill kill de priest, for he speak for a jackanape to Anne Page.

HOST Let him die. Sheathe thy impatience; throw cold water on thy choler. Go about the fields with me through Frogmore. I will bring thee where Mistress

80 Anne Page is, at a farmhouse a-feasting; and thou shalt woo her. Cried game? Said I well?

CAIUS By gar, me dank you vor dat. By gar, I love you, and I shall procure-a you de good guest – de earl, de knight, de lords, de gentlemen, my patients.

HOST For the which I will be thy adversary toward Anne Page. Said I well?

CAIUS By gar, 'tis good. Vell said.

HOST Let us wag, then.

CAIUS Come at my heels, Jack Rugby.   *Exeunt*

*

Enter Evans and Simple   III.I

EVANS I pray you now, good Master Slender's serving-
man, and friend Simple by your name, which way have
you looked for Master Caius, that calls himself Doctor
of Physic?

SIMPLE Marry, sir, the pittie-ward, the park-ward,
every way; Old Windsor way, and every way but the
town way.

EVANS I most fehemently desire you you will also look
that way.

SIMPLE I will, sir.   *Exit* 10

EVANS Pless my soul, how full of chollors I am, and
trempling of mind! I shall be glad if he have deceived
me. How melancholies I am! I will knog his urinals
about his knave's costard when I have good opportunities
for the 'ork. Pless my soul!

He sings
> To shallow rivers, to whose falls
> Melodious birds sings madrigals.
> There will we make our peds of roses,
> And a thousand fragrant posies.
> To shallow —   20

Mercy on me! I have a great dispositions to cry.

He sings
> Melodious birds sing madrigals —
> Whenas I sat in Pabylon —
> And a thousand vagram posies.
> To shallow, *etc.*

Enter Simple

SIMPLE Yonder he is, coming this way, Sir Hugh.

EVANS He's welcome.

He sings
> To shallow rivers, to whose falls —

Heaven prosper the right! What weapons is he?

30 SIMPLE No weapons, sir. There comes my master, Master
    Shallow, and another gentleman, from Frogmore, over
    the stile, this way.

    EVANS Pray you, give me my gown – or else keep it in
    your arms.

        He takes a book and reads it
        Enter Page, Shallow, and Slender

    SHALLOW How now, Master Parson? Good morrow, good
    Sir Hugh. Keep a gamester from the dice, and a good
    student from his book, and it is wonderful.

    SLENDER (*aside*) Ah, sweet Anne Page!

    PAGE Save you, good Sir Hugh!

40 EVANS Pless you from his mercy sake, all of you!

    SHALLOW What, the sword and the word? Do you study
    them both, Master Parson?

    PAGE And youthful still – in your doublet and hose this
    raw rheumatic day?

    EVANS There is reasons and causes for it.

    PAGE We are come to you to do a good office, Master
    Parson.

    EVANS Fery well. What is it?

    PAGE Yonder is a most reverend gentleman, who, belike,
50 having received wrong by some person, is at most odds
    with his own gravity and patience that ever you saw.

    SHALLOW I have lived fourscore years and upward. I
    never heard a man of his place, gravity, and learning so
    wide of his own respect.

    EVANS What is he?

    PAGE I think you know him: Master Doctor Caius, the
    renowned French physician.

    EVANS Got's will and his passion of my heart! I had as
    lief you would tell me of a mess of porridge.

60 PAGE Why?

    EVANS He has no more knowledge in Hibocrates and

Galen – and he is a knave besides, a cowardly knave as
you would desires to be acquainted withal.

PAGE I warrant you, he's the man should fight with him.

SLENDER (*aside*) O sweet Anne Page!

SHALLOW It appears so by his weapons.

Enter Host, Caius, and Rugby

Keep them asunder; here comes Doctor Caius.

Evans and Caius offer to fight

PAGE Nay, good master Parson, keep in your weapon.

SHALLOW So do you, good Master Doctor.

HOST Disarm them, and let them question. Let them keep   70
their limbs whole and hack our English.

CAIUS I pray you let-a me speak a word with your ear.
Verefore vill you not meet-a me?

EVANS (*aside to Caius*) Pray you, use your patience.
(*Aloud*) In good time.

CAIUS By gar, you are de coward, de Jack dog, John ape.

EVANS (*aside to Caius*) Pray you, let us not be laughing-
stocks to other men's humours. I desire you in friendship, and I will one way or other make you amends.
(*Aloud*) I will knog your urinals about your knave's   80
cogscombs for missing your meetings and appointments.

CAIUS *Diable!* Jack Rugby, mine host de Jarteer, have I
not stay for him to kill him? Have I not, at de place I
did appoint?

EVANS As I am a Christians soul, now, look you, this is the
place appointed. I'll be judgement by mine host of the
Garter.

HOST Peace, I say, Gallia and Gaul, French and Welsh,
soul-curer and body-curer.   90

CAIUS Ay, dat is very good, excellent.

HOST Peace, I say. Hear mine host of the Garter. Am I
politic? Am I subtle? Am I a Machiavel? Shall I lose

my doctor? No; he gives me the potions and the motions. Shall I lose my parson? My priest? My Sir Hugh? No; he gives me the proverbs and the no-verbs. Give me thy hand, terrestrial; so. Give me thy hand, celestial; so. Boys of art, I have deceived you both. I have directed you to wrong places. Your hearts are mighty, your skins are whole, and let burnt sack be the issue. Come, lay their swords to pawn. Follow me, lads of peace; follow, follow, follow.   *Exit*

SHALLOW Trust me, a mad host. Follow, gentlemen, follow.

SLENDER (*aside*) O sweet Anne Page!
                    Exeunt Shallow, Slender, and Page

CAIUS Ha, do I perceive dat? Have you make-a de sot of us, ha, ha?

EVANS This is well. He has made us his vlouting-stog. I desire you that we may be friends, and let us knog our prains together to be revenge on this same scald, scurvy, cogging companion, the host of the Garter.

CAIUS By gar, with all my heart. He promise to bring me where is Anne Page. By gar, he deceive me too.

EVANS Well, I will smite his noddles. Pray you follow.
                    Exeunt

III.2   *Enter Mistress Page and Robin*

MISTRESS PAGE Nay, keep your way, little gallant. You were wont to be a follower, but now you are a leader. Whether had you rather, lead mine eyes, or eye your master's heels?

ROBIN I had rather, forsooth, go before you like a man than follow him like a dwarf.

MISTRESS PAGE O, you are a flattering boy. Now I see you'll be a courtier.

Enter Ford

FORD Well met, Mistress Page. Whither go you?

MISTRESS PAGE Truly, sir, to see your wife. Is she at   10
home?

FORD Ay; and as idle as she may hang together, for want
of company. I think, if your husbands were dead, you
two would marry.

MISTRESS PAGE Be sure of that — two other husbands.

FORD Where had you this pretty weathercock?

MISTRESS PAGE I cannot tell what the dickens his name
is that my husband had him of. What do you call your
knight's name, sirrah?

ROBIN Sir John Falstaff.   20

FORD Sir John Falstaff?

MISTRESS PAGE He, he. I can never hit on's name. There
is such a league between my good man and he. Is your
wife at home indeed?

FORD Indeed she is.

MISTRESS PAGE By your leave, sir. I am sick till I see her.
Exeunt Mistress Page and Robin

FORD Has Page any brains? Hath he any eyes? Hath he
any thinking? Sure, they sleep; he hath no use of them.
Why, this boy will carry a letter twenty mile as easy as a
cannon will shoot point-blank twelve score. He pieces   30
out his wife's inclination. He gives her folly motion and
advantage. And now she's going to my wife, and Falstaff's boy with her. A man may hear this shower sing
in the wind. And Falstaff's boy with her! Good plots!
They are laid; and our revolted wives share damnation
together. Well, I will take him, then torture my wife,
pluck the borrowed veil of modesty from the so-
seeming Mistress Page, divulge Page himself for a
secure and wilful Actaeon; and to these violent pro-
ceedings all my neighbours shall cry aim.   40

The town clock strikes
The clock gives me my cue, and my assurance bids me
search. There I shall find Falstaff. I shall be rather
praised for this than mocked, for it is as positive as the
earth is firm that Falstaff is there. I will go.

Enter Page, Shallow, Slender, Host, Evans, Caius,
and Rugby

ALL Well met, Master Ford.

FORD Trust me, a good knot. I have good cheer at home,
and I pray you all go with me.

SHALLOW I must excuse myself, Master Ford.

SLENDER And so must I, sir. We have appointed to dine
50   with Mistress Anne, and I would not break with her for
more money than I'll speak of.

SHALLOW We have lingered about a match between Anne
Page and my cousin Slender, and this day we shall have
our answer.

SLENDER I hope I have your good will, father Page.

PAGE You have, Master Slender – I stand wholly for you.
But my wife, Master Doctor, is for you altogether.

CAIUS Ay, be-gar, and de maid is love-a me – my nursh-a
Quickly tell me so mush.

60 HOST What say you to young Master Fenton? He capers,
he dances, he has eyes of youth, he writes verses, he
speaks holiday, he smells April and May. He will
carry't, he will carry't. 'Tis in his buttons he will
carry't.

PAGE Not by my consent, I promise you. The gentleman
is of no having. He kept company with the wild Prince
and Poins. He is of too high a region, he knows too
much. No, he shall not knit a knot in his fortunes with
the finger of my substance. If he take her, let him take
70   her simply. The wealth I have waits on my consent, and
my consent goes not that way.

FORD I beseech you heartily, some of you go home with
me to dinner. Besides your cheer, you shall have sport –
I will show you a monster. Master Doctor, you shall go.
So shall you, Master Page, and you, Sir Hugh.
SHALLOW Well, fare you well. We shall have the freer
wooing at Master Page's. *Exeunt Shallow and Slender*
CAIUS Go home, John Rugby. I come anon. *Exit Rugby*
HOST Farewell, my hearts. I will to my honest knight
Falstaff, and drink canary with him.   *Exit*   80
FORD (*aside*) I think I shall drink in pipe-wine first with
him; I'll make him dance. – Will you go, gentles?
ALL Have with you to see this monster.   *Exeunt*

Enter Mistress Ford and Mistress Page   III.3
MISTRESS FORD What, John! What, Robert!
MISTRESS PAGE Quickly, quickly! Is the buck-basket –
MISTRESS FORD I warrant. What, Robert, I say!
Enter John and Robert with a great buck-basket
MISTRESS PAGE Come, come, come.
MISTRESS FORD Here, set it down.
MISTRESS PAGE Give your men the charge. We must be
brief.
MISTRESS FORD Marry, as I told you before, John and
Robert, be ready here hard by in the brew-house. And
when I suddenly call you, come forth, and, without any   10
pause or staggering, take this basket on your shoulders.
That done, trudge with it in all haste, and carry it
among the whitsters in Datchet Mead, and there empty
it in the muddy ditch close by the Thames side.
MISTRESS PAGE You will do it?
MISTRESS FORD I ha' told them over and over – they
lack no direction. – Be gone, and come when you are
called.   *Exeunt John and Robert*

Enter Robin

MISTRESS PAGE Here comes little Robin.

20 MISTRESS FORD How now, my eyas-musket, what news
with you?

ROBIN My master, Sir John, is come in at your back-
door, Mistress Ford, and requests your company.

MISTRESS PAGE You little Jack-a-Lent, have you been
true to us?

ROBIN Ay, I'll be sworn. My master knows not of your
being here, and hath threatened to put me into ever-
lasting liberty if I tell you of it; for he swears he'll turn
me away.

30 MISTRESS PAGE Thou'rt a good boy. This secrecy of
thine shall be a tailor to thee and shall make thee a new
doublet and hose. I'll go hide me.

MISTRESS FORD Do so. (*To Robin*) Go tell thy master I
am alone.   *Exit Robin*
Mistress Page, remember you your cue.

MISTRESS PAGE I warrant thee. If I do not act it, hiss me.

MISTRESS FORD Go to, then. We'll use this unwholesome
humidity, this gross watery pumpion. We'll teach him
to know turtles from jays.   *Exit Mistress Page*

Enter Falstaff

40 FALSTAFF Have I caught thee, my heavenly jewel? Why,
now let me die, for I have lived long enough. This is
the period of my ambition. O this blessed hour!

MISTRESS FORD O sweet Sir John!

FALSTAFF Mistress Ford, I cannot cog, I cannot prate,
Mistress Ford. Now shall I sin in my wish: I would thy
husband were dead. I'll speak it before the best lord,
I would make thee my lady.

MISTRESS FORD I your lady, Sir John? Alas, I should be
a pitiful lady.

50 FALSTAFF Let the court of France show me such another.

I see how thine eye would emulate the diamond. Thou
hast the right arched beauty of the brow that becomes
the ship-tire, the tire-valiant, or any tire of Venetian
admittance.

MISTRESS FORD A plain kerchief, Sir John. My brows
become nothing else, nor that well neither.

FALSTAFF Thou art a tyrant to say so. Thou wouldst
make an absolute courtier, and the firm fixture of thy
foot would give an excellent motion to thy gait in a
semi-circled farthingale. I see what thou wert if For-   60
tune, thy foe, were – not Nature – thy friend. Come,
thou canst not hide it.

MISTRESS FORD Believe me, there's no such thing in me.

FALSTAFF What made me love thee? Let that persuade
thee there's something extraordinary in thee. Come, I
cannot cog and say thou art this and that, like a many of
these lisping hawthorn-buds that come like women in
men's apparel and smell like Bucklersbury in simple-
time. I cannot. But I love thee, none but thee; and thou
deservest it.   70

MISTRESS FORD Do not betray me, sir. I fear you love
Mistress Page.

FALSTAFF Thou mightst as well say I love to walk by the
Counter-gate, which is as hateful to me as the reek of a
lime-kiln.

MISTRESS FORD Well, heaven knows how I love you, and
you shall one day find it.

FALSTAFF Keep in that mind – I'll deserve it.

MISTRESS FORD Nay, I must tell you, so you do, or else
I could not be in that mind.   80

　　Enter Robin

ROBIN Mistress Ford, Mistress Ford! Here's Mistress
Page at the door, sweating and blowing and looking
wildly, and would needs speak with you presently.

FALSTAFF She shall not see me. I will ensconce me behind the arras.

MISTRESS FORD Pray you, do so. She's a very tattling woman.

Falstaff hides himself
Enter Mistress Page

What's the matter? How now?

MISTRESS PAGE O Mistress Ford, what have you done?
90   You're shamed, you're overthrown, you're undone for ever.

MISTRESS FORD What's the matter, good Mistress Page?

MISTRESS PAGE O well-a-day, Mistress Ford, having an honest man to your husband, to give him such cause of suspicion!

MISTRESS FORD What cause of suspicion?

MISTRESS PAGE What cause of suspicion? Out upon you! How am I mistook in you!

MISTRESS FORD Why, alas, what's the matter?

100   MISTRESS PAGE Your husband's coming hither, woman, with all the officers in Windsor, to search for a gentleman that he says is here now in the house, by your consent, to take an ill advantage of his absence. You are undone.

MISTRESS FORD 'Tis not so, I hope.

MISTRESS PAGE Pray heaven it be not so that you have such a man here! But 'tis most certain your husband's coming, with half Windsor at his heels, to search for such a one. I come before to tell you. If you know yourself clear, why, I am glad of it. But if you have a friend here,
110   convey, convey him out. Be not amazed, call all your senses to you, defend your reputation, or bid farewell to your good life for ever.

MISTRESS FORD What shall I do? There is a gentleman, my dear friend; and I fear not mine own shame so much

as his peril. I had rather than a thousand pound he were
out of the house.

MISTRESS PAGE For shame, never stand 'you had rather'
and 'you had rather'! Your husband's here at hand.
Bethink you of some conveyance. In the house you
cannot hide him. – O, how have you deceived me! – Look,   120
here is a basket. If he be of any reasonable stature, he
may creep in here; and throw foul linen upon him, as if
it were going to bucking. Or – it is whiting-time – send
him by your two men to Datchet Mead.

MISTRESS FORD He's too big to go in there. What shall I
do?

Falstaff rushes out of hiding

FALSTAFF Let me see't, let me see't. O, let me see't! I'll
in, I'll in. Follow your friend's counsel. I'll in.

MISTRESS PAGE What, Sir John Falstaff? (*Aside to him*)
Are these your letters, knight?   130

FALSTAFF (*aside to Mistress Page*) I love thee, and none
but thee. Help me away. Let me creep in here. I'll
never –

*He gets into the basket; they cover him with foul
linen*

MISTRESS PAGE (*to Robin*) Help to cover your master,
boy. Call your men, Mistress Ford. (*Aside to Falstaff*)
You dissembling knight!   *Exit Robin*

MISTRESS FORD What, John! Robert! John!

Enter John and Robert

Go, take up these clothes here. Quickly! Where's the
cowl-staff? Look how you drumble! Carry them to the
laundress in Datchet Mead. Quickly! Come.   140

Enter Ford, Page, Caius, and Evans

FORD (*to his companions*) Pray you, come near. If I suspect
without cause, why then make sport at me; then let me

be your jest; I deserve it. (*To John and Robert*) How now?
Whither bear you this?

JOHN *and* ROBERT To the laundress, forsooth.

MISTRESS FORD Why, what have you to do whither they
bear it? You were best meddle with buck-washing.

FORD Buck? I would I could wash myself of the buck!
Buck, buck, buck! Ay, buck! I warrant you, buck – and
150   of the season too, it shall appear.

>   *Exeunt John and Robert with the basket*
Gentlemen, I have dreamed tonight. I'll tell you my
dream. Here, here, here be my keys. Ascend my chambers. Search, seek, find out. I'll warrant we'll unkennel
the fox. Let me stop this way first.

>   *He locks the door*

So; now escape.

PAGE Good master Ford, be contented. You wrong yourself too much.

FORD True, Master Page. Up, gentlemen, you shall see
sport anon. Follow me, gentlemen.   *Exit*

160   EVANS This is fery fantastical humours and jealousies.

CAIUS By gar, 'tis no the fashion of France. It is not
jealous in France.

PAGE Nay, follow him, gentlemen. See the issue of his
search.   *Exeunt Page, Caius, and Evans*

MISTRESS PAGE Is there not a double excellency in this?

MISTRESS FORD I know not which pleases me better –
that my husband is deceived, or Sir John.

MISTRESS PAGE What a taking was he in when your
husband asked who was in the basket!

170   MISTRESS FORD I am half afraid he will have need of
washing; so throwing him into the water will do him a
benefit.

MISTRESS PAGE Hang him, dishonest rascal! I would all
of the same strain were in the same distress.

MISTRESS FORD I think my husband hath some special suspicion of Falstaff's being here, for I never saw him so gross in his jealousy till now.

MISTRESS PAGE I will lay a plot to try that, and we will yet have more tricks with Falstaff. His dissolute disease will scarce obey this medicine.   180

MISTRESS FORD Shall we send that foolish carrion Mistress Quickly to him, and excuse his throwing into the water, and give him another hope to betray him to another punishment?

MISTRESS PAGE We will do it. Let him be sent for tomorrow eight o'clock, to have amends.

    Enter Ford, Page, Caius, and Evans

FORD I cannot find him. Maybe the knave bragged of that he could not compass.

MISTRESS PAGE (*aside to Mistress Ford*) Heard you that?

MISTRESS FORD You use me well, Master Ford! Do you?   190

FORD Ay, I do so.

MISTRESS FORD Heaven make you better than your thoughts.

FORD Amen.

MISTRESS PAGE You do yourself mighty wrong, Master Ford.

FORD Ay, ay, I must bear it.

EVANS If there be anypody in the house, and in the chambers, and in the coffers, and in the presses, heaven forgive my sins at the day of judgement.   200

CAIUS By gar, nor I too. There is nobodies.

PAGE Fie, fie, Master Ford, are you not ashamed? What spirit, what devil suggests this imagination? I would not ha' your distemper in this kind for the wealth of Windsor Castle.

FORD 'Tis my fault, Master Page. I suffer for it.

EVANS You suffer for a pad conscience. Your wife is as

honest a 'omans as I will desires among five thousand,
and five hundred too.

210 CAIUS By gar, I see 'tis an honest woman.

FORD Well, I promised you a dinner. Come, come, walk
in the Park. I pray you pardon me. I will hereafter make
known to you why I have done this. Come, wife, come,
Mistress Page, I pray you pardon me. Pray heartily
pardon me.

PAGE Let's go in, gentlemen; but, trust me, we'll mock
him. I do invite you tomorrow morning to my house to
breakfast. After, we'll a-birding together. I have a fine
hawk for the bush. Shall it be so?

220 FORD Anything.

EVANS If there is one, I shall make two in the company.

CAIUS If there be one or two, I shall make-a the turd.

FORD Pray you go, Master Page.

Exeunt all but Evans and Caius

EVANS I pray you now, remembrance tomorrow on the
lousy knave, mine host.

CAIUS Dat is good. By gar, with all my heart.

EVANS A lousy knave, to have his gibes and his mockeries.

Exeunt

III.4   *Enter Fenton and Anne Page*

FENTON
    I see I cannot get thy father's love;
    Therefore no more turn me to him, sweet Nan.
ANNE
    Alas, how then?
FENTON   Why, thou must be thyself.
    He doth object I am too great of birth,
    And that, my state being galled with my expense,
    I seek to heal it only by his wealth.

Besides these, other bars he lays before me –
My riots past, my wild societies;
And tells me 'tis a thing impossible
I should love thee but as a property.   10

ANNE
Maybe he tells you true.

FENTON
No, heaven so speed me in my time to come!
Albeit, I will confess, thy father's wealth
Was the first motive that I wooed thee, Anne;
Yet, wooing thee, I found thee of more value
Than stamps in gold or sums in sealèd bags.
And 'tis the very riches of thyself
That now I aim at.

ANNE   Gentle Master Fenton,
Yet seek my father's love, still seek it, sir.
If opportunity and humblest suit   20
Cannot attain it, why then – hark you hither.
      They talk aside
      Enter Shallow, Slender, and Mistress Quickly

SHALLOW Break their talk, Mistress Quickly. My kinsman shall speak for himself.

SLENDER I'll make a shaft or a bolt on't. 'Slid, 'tis but
venturing.

SHALLOW Be not dismayed.

SLENDER No, she shall not dismay me. I care not for
that, but that I am afeard.

MISTRESS QUICKLY (*to Anne*) Hark ye, Master Slender
would speak a word with you.

ANNE   30
I come to him. (*Aside*) This is my father's choice.
O, what a world of vile ill-favoured faults
Looks handsome in three hundred pounds a year!

MISTRESS QUICKLY And how does good Master Fenton?
Pray you, a word with you.
They talk aside

SHALLOW She's coming. To her, coz. O boy, thou hadst
a father!

SLENDER I had a father, Mistress Anne. My uncle can
tell you good jests of him. Pray you, uncle, tell Mistress
40   Anne the jest how my father stole two geese out of a pen,
good uncle.

SHALLOW Mistress Anne, my cousin loves you.

SLENDER Ay, that I do, as well as I love any woman in
Gloucestershire.

SHALLOW He will maintain you like a gentlewoman.

SLENDER Ay, that I will, come cut and long-tail, under
the degree of a squire.

SHALLOW He will make you a hundred and fifty pounds
jointure.

50   ANNE Good Master Shallow, let him woo for himself.

SHALLOW Marry, I thank you for it; I thank you for that
good comfort. She calls you, coz. I'll leave you.

ANNE Now, Master Slender –

SLENDER Now, good Mistress Anne –

ANNE What is your will?

SLENDER My will? 'Od's heartlings, that's a pretty jest
indeed! I ne'er made my will yet, I thank heaven. I am
not such a sickly creature, I give heaven praise.

ANNE I mean, Master Slender, what would you with me?

60   SLENDER Truly, for mine own part, I would little or
nothing with you. Your father and my uncle hath made
motions. If it be my luck, so; if not, happy man be his
dole. They can tell you how things go better than I can.
You may ask your father; here he comes.
Enter Page and Mistress Page

PAGE

Now, Master Slender. Love him, daughter Anne –
Why, how now? What does Master Fenton here?
You wrong me, sir, thus still to haunt my house.
I told you, sir, my daughter is disposed of.

FENTON

Nay, Master Page, be not impatient.

MISTRESS PAGE

Good Master Fenton, come not to my child.   70

PAGE

She is no match for you.

FENTON

Sir, will you hear me?

PAGE   No, good Master Fenton.
Come, Master Shallow, come, son Slender, in.
Knowing my mind, you wrong me, Master Fenton.
                    Exeunt Page, Shallow, and Slender

MISTRESS QUICKLY

Speak to Mistress Page.

FENTON

Good Mistress Page, for that I love your daughter
In such a righteous fashion as I do,
Perforce, against all checks, rebukes, and manners,
I must advance the colours of my love
And not retire. Let me have your good will.   80

ANNE

Good mother, do not marry me to yond fool.

MISTRESS PAGE

I mean it not – I seek you a better husband.

MISTRESS QUICKLY That's my master, Master Doctor.

ANNE

Alas, I had rather be set quick i'th'earth,
And bowled to death with turnips.

MISTRESS PAGE

    Come, trouble not yourself. Good Master Fenton,
    I will not be your friend, nor enemy.
    My daughter will I question how she loves you,
    And as I find her, so am I affected.
90   Till then, farewell, sir. She must needs go in;
    Her father will be angry.

FENTON

    Farewell, gentle mistress. Farewell, Nan.

Exeunt Mistress Page and Anne

MISTRESS QUICKLY This is my doing now. 'Nay,' said
I, 'will you cast away your child on a fool, and a
physician? Look on Master Fenton.' This is my doing.

FENTON

    I thank thee, and I pray thee once tonight
    Give my sweet Nan this ring. There's for thy pains.

MISTRESS QUICKLY Now heaven send thee good fortune! *Exit Fenton*
100   A kind heart he hath. A woman would run through fire
and water for such a kind heart. But yet I would my
master had Mistress Anne; or I would Master Slender
had her; or, in sooth, I would Master Fenton had her.
I will do what I can for them all three, for so I have
promised, and I'll be as good as my word – but speciously
for Master Fenton. Well, I must of another errand to Sir
John Falstaff from my two mistresses. What a beast am
I to slack it! *Exit*

III.5   *Enter Falstaff and Bardolph*

FALSTAFF Bardolph, I say!

BARDOLPH Here, sir.

FALSTAFF Go fetch me a quart of sack – put a toast in't.

Exit Bardolph

Have I lived to be carried in a basket like a barrow of
butcher's offal? And to be thrown in the Thames? Well,
if I be served such another trick, I'll have my brains
ta'en out and buttered, and give them to a dog for a new-
year's gift. The rogues slighted me into the river with as
little remorse as they would have drowned a blind
bitch's puppies, fifteen i'th'litter. And you may know   10
by my size that I have a kind of alacrity in sinking. If the
bottom were as deep as hell, I should down. I had been
drowned but that the shore was shelvy and shallow – a
death that I abhor, for the water swells a man, and what
a thing should I have been when I had been swelled!
I should have been a mountain of mummy.

Enter Bardolph with sack

BARDOLPH Here's Mistress Quickly, sir, to speak with
you.

FALSTAFF Come, let me pour in some sack to the Thames
water, for my belly's as cold as if I had swallowed   20
snowballs for pills to cool the reins. Call her in.

BARDOLPH Come in, woman.

Enter Mistress Quickly

MISTRESS QUICKLY By your leave; I cry you mercy.
Give your worship good morrow.

FALSTAFF Take away these chalices. Go, brew me a
pottle of sack finely.

BARDOLPH With eggs, sir?

FALSTAFF Simple of itself. I'll no pullet-sperm in my
brewage.   *Exit Bardolph*
How now?   30

MISTRESS QUICKLY Marry, sir, I come to your worship
from Mistress Ford.

FALSTAFF Mistress Ford? I have had ford enough. I
was thrown into the ford. I have my belly full of ford.

MISTRESS QUICKLY Alas the day, good heart, that was

not her fault. She does so take on with her men; they
mistook their erection.

FALSTAFF So did I mine, to build upon a foolish woman's
promise.

40 MISTRESS QUICKLY Well, she laments, sir, for it, that
it would yearn your heart to see it. Her husband goes
this morning a-birding. She desires you once more to
come to her between eight and nine. I must carry her
word quickly. She'll make you amends, I warrant you.

FALSTAFF Well, I will visit her. Tell her so, and bid her
think what a man is. Let her consider his frailty, and
then judge of my merit.

MISTRESS QUICKLY I will tell her.

FALSTAFF Do so. Between nine and ten, sayest thou?

50 MISTRESS QUICKLY Eight and nine, sir.

FALSTAFF Well, begone. I will not miss her.

MISTRESS QUICKLY Peace be with you, sir.   *Exit*

FALSTAFF I marvel I hear not of Master Brook. He sent
me word to stay within. I like his money well. O, here
he comes.

    Enter Ford disguised as Brook

FORD Bless you, sir.

FALSTAFF Now, Master Brook, you come to know what
hath passed between me and Ford's wife?

FORD That, indeed, Sir John, is my business.

60 FALSTAFF Master Brook, I will not lie to you. I was at her
house the hour she appointed me.

FORD And sped you, sir?

FALSTAFF Very ill-favouredly, Master Brook.

FORD How so, sir? Did she change her determination?

FALSTAFF No, Master Brook, but the peaking cornuto
her husband, Master Brook, dwelling in a continual
'larum of jealousy, comes me in the instant of our
encounter, after we had embraced, kissed, protested,

and, as it were, spoke the prologue of our comedy; and
at his heels a rabble of his companions, thither provoked   70
and instigated by his distemper, and, forsooth, to
search his house for his wife's love.

FORD What? While you were there?

FALSTAFF While I was there.

FORD And did he search for you, and could not find you?

FALSTAFF You shall hear. As good luck would have it,
comes in one Mistress Page, gives intelligence of Ford's
approach, and, in her invention and Ford's wife's dis-
traction, they conveyed me into a buck-basket.

FORD A buck-basket?   80

FALSTAFF By the Lord, a buck-basket! Rammed me in
with foul shirts and smocks, socks, foul stockings,
greasy napkins, that, Master Brook, there was the
rankest compound of villainous smell that ever offended
nostril.

FORD And how long lay you there?

FALSTAFF Nay, you shall hear, Master Brook, what I
have suffered to bring this woman to evil for your good.
Being thus crammed in the basket, a couple of Ford's
knaves, his hinds, were called forth by their mistress to   90
carry me in the name of foul clothes to Datchet Lane.
They took me on their shoulders, met the jealous knave
their master in the door, who asked them once or twice
what they had in their basket. I quaked for fear lest the
lunatic knave would have searched it; but Fate, or-
daining he should be a cuckold, held his hand. Well, on
went he for a search, and away went I for foul clothes.
But mark the sequel, Master Brook. I suffered the
pangs of three several deaths: first, an intolerable fright
to be detected with a jealous rotten bell-wether;   100
next, to be compassed like a good bilbo in the circum-
ference of a peck, hilt to point, heel to head; and then, to

be stopped in, like a strong distillation, with stinking clothes that fretted in their own grease. Think of that, a man of my kidney – think of that – that am as subject to heat as butter; a man of continual dissolution and thaw. It was a miracle to 'scape suffocation. And in the height of this bath, when I was more than half stewed in grease, like a Dutch dish, to be thrown into the Thames, and cooled, glowing hot, in that surge, like a horse-shoe. Think of that – hissing hot – think of that, Master Brook!

FORD In good sadness, sir, I am sorry that for my sake you have suffered all this. My suit, then, is desperate? You'll undertake her no more?

FALSTAFF Master Brook, I will be thrown into Etna, as I have been into Thames, ere I will leave her thus. Her husband is this morning gone a-birding. I have received from her another embassy of meeting. 'Twixt eight and nine is the hour, Master Brook.

FORD 'Tis past eight already, sir.

FALSTAFF Is it? I will then address me to my appoint-ment. Come to me at your convenient leisure, and you shall know how I speed; and the conclusion shall be crowned with your enjoying her. Adieu. You shall have her, Master Brook; Master Brook, you shall cuckold Ford.   *Exit*

FORD Hum! Ha! Is this a vision? Is this a dream? Do I sleep? Master Ford, awake; awake, Master Ford! There's a hole made in your best coat, Master Ford. This 'tis to be married; this 'tis to have linen and buck-baskets! Well, I will proclaim myself what I am. I will now take the lecher. He is at my house. He cannot 'scape me. 'Tis impossible he should. He cannot creep into a halfpenny purse, nor into a pepperbox. But, lest the devil that guides him should aid him, I will search impossible places. Though what I am I cannot avoid, yet to be what I would not shall not make me tame. If I have horns to make one mad, let the proverb go with me – I'll be horn-mad.   *Exit*   140

*

Enter Mistress Page, Mistress Quickly, and William   IV.1

MISTRESS PAGE Is he at Master Ford's already, thinkest thou?

MISTRESS QUICKLY Sure he is by this, or will be presently. But truly he is very courageous mad about his throwing into the water. Mistress Ford desires you to come suddenly.

MISTRESS PAGE I'll be with her by and by – I'll but bring my young man here to school. Look where his master comes.

Enter Sir Hugh Evans

'Tis a playing day, I see. How now, Sir Hugh, no school   10
today?

EVANS No. Master Slender is let the boys leave to play.

MISTRESS QUICKLY Blessing of his heart!

MISTRESS PAGE Sir Hugh, my husband says my son profits nothing in the world at his book. I pray you, ask him some questions in his accidence.

EVANS Come hither, William. Hold up your head. Come.

MISTRESS PAGE Come on, sirrah. Hold up your head. Answer your master, be not afraid.

EVANS William, how many numbers is in nouns?   20

WILLIAM Two.

MISTRESS QUICKLY Truly, I thought there had been one number more, because they say "Od's nouns'.

EVANS Peace your tattlings. What is 'fair', William?

WILLIAM *Pulcher*.

MISTRESS QUICKLY Polecats! There are fairer things than polecats, sure.

EVANS You are a very simplicity 'oman. I pray you peace. What is *lapis*, William?

30 WILLIAM A stone.

EVANS And what is 'a stone', William?

WILLIAM A pebble.

EVANS No, it is *lapis*. I pray you remember in your prain.

WILLIAM *Lapis*.

EVANS That is a good William. What is he, William, that does lend articles?

WILLIAM Articles are borrowed of the pronoun, and be thus declined: *Singulariter, nominativo, hic, haec, hoc*.

EVANS *Nominativo, hig, hag, hog*. Pray you mark:
40 *genitivo, hujus*. Well, what is your accusative case?

WILLIAM *Accusativo, hinc*.

EVANS I pray you have your remembrance, child. *Accusativo, hung, hang, hog*.

MISTRESS QUICKLY 'Hang-hog' is Latin for bacon, I warrant you.

EVANS Leave your prabbles, 'oman. What is the focative case, William?

WILLIAM O – *vocativo, O*.

EVANS Remember, William. Focative is *caret*.

50 MISTRESS QUICKLY And that's a good root.

EVANS 'Oman, forbear.

MISTRESS PAGE Peace!

EVANS What is your genitive case plural, William?

WILLIAM Genitive case?

EVANS Ay.

WILLIAM Genitive – *horum, harum, horum*.

MISTRESS QUICKLY Vengeance of Jenny's case! Fie on her! Never name her, child, if she be a whore.

EVANS For shame, 'oman.

MISTRESS QUICKLY You do ill to teach the child such   60
words. He teaches him to hick and to hack, which they'll
do fast enough of themselves, and to call 'horum'. Fie
upon you!

EVANS 'Oman, art thou lunatics? Hast thou no under-
standings for thy cases and the numbers of the genders?
Thou art as foolish Christian creatures as I would
desires.

MISTRESS PAGE Prithee hold thy peace.

EVANS Show me now, William, some declensions of your
pronouns.   70

WILLIAM Forsooth, I have forgot.

EVANS It is *qui, quae, quod*. If you forget your *qui*s, your
*quae*s, and your *quod*s, you must be preeches. Go your
ways and play. Go.

MISTRESS PAGE He is a better scholar than I thought he
was.

EVANS He is a good sprag memory. Farewell, Mistress
Page.

MISTRESS PAGE Adieu, good Sir Hugh.   *Exit Evans*
Get you home, boy. Come, we stay too long.   *Exeunt*   80

Enter Falstaff and Mistress Ford   IV.2

FALSTAFF Mistress Ford, your sorrow hath eaten up my
sufferance. I see you are obsequious in your love, and I
profess requital to a hair's breadth, not only, Mistress
Ford, in the simple office of love, but in all the accoutrement, complement, and ceremony of it. But are you sure
of your husband now?

MISTRESS FORD He's a-birding, sweet Sir John.

MISTRESS PAGE (*within*) What ho, gossip Ford. What ho!

MISTRESS FORD Step into the chamber, Sir John.

Exit Falstaff

Enter Mistress Page

10 MISTRESS PAGE How now, sweetheart; who's at home besides yourself?

MISTRESS FORD Why, none but mine own people.

MISTRESS PAGE Indeed?

MISTRESS FORD No, certainly. (*Aside to her*) Speak louder.

MISTRESS PAGE Truly, I am so glad you have nobody here.

MISTRESS FORD Why?

MISTRESS PAGE Why, woman, your husband is in his
20   old lines again. He so takes on yonder with my husband, so rails against all married mankind, so curses all Eve's daughters, of what complexion soever, and so buffets himself on the forehead, crying 'Peer out, peer out!', that any madness I ever yet beheld seemed but tameness, civility, and patience to this his distemper he is in now. I am glad the fat knight is not here.

MISTRESS FORD Why, does he talk of him?

MISTRESS PAGE Of none but him, and swears he was carried out, the last time he searched for him, in a
30   basket; protests to my husband he is now here, and hath drawn him and the rest of their company from their sport, to make another experiment of his suspicion. But I am glad the knight is not here. Now he shall see his own foolery.

MISTRESS FORD How near is he, Mistress Page?

MISTRESS PAGE Hard by, at street end. He will be here anon.

MISTRESS FORD I am undone. The knight is here.

MISTRESS PAGE Why, then, you are utterly shamed, and
40   he's but a dead man. What a woman are you! Away with him, away with him! Better shame than murder.

MISTRESS FORD Which way should he go? How should
I bestow him? Shall I put him into the basket again?
Enter Falstaff

FALSTAFF No, I'll come no more i'th'basket. May I not
go out ere he come?

MISTRESS PAGE Alas, three of Master Ford's brothers
watch the door with pistols, that none shall issue out.
Otherwise you might slip away ere he came. But what
make you here?

FALSTAFF What shall I do? I'll creep up into the chim- 50
ney.

MISTRESS FORD There they always use to discharge their
birding pieces.

MISTRESS PAGE Creep into the kiln-hole.

FALSTAFF Where is it?

MISTRESS FORD He will seek there, on my word. Neither
press, coffer, chest, trunk, well, vault, but he hath an
abstract for the remembrance of such places, and goes
to them by his note. There is no hiding you in the
house. 60

FALSTAFF I'll go out, then.

MISTRESS PAGE If you go out in your own semblance,
you die, Sir John. Unless you go out disguised —

MISTRESS FORD How might we disguise him?

MISTRESS PAGE Alas the day, I know not. There is no
woman's gown big enough for him. Otherwise he might
put on a hat, a muffler, and a kerchief, and so escape.

FALSTAFF Good hearts, devise something. Any extremity
rather than a mischief.

MISTRESS FORD My maid's aunt, the fat woman of 70
Brainford, has a gown above.

MISTRESS PAGE On my word, it will serve him. She's as
big as he is; and there's her thrummed hat and her
muffler too. Run up, Sir John.

MISTRESS FORD Go, go, sweet Sir John. Mistress Page and I will look some linen for your head.

MISTRESS PAGE Quick, quick! We'll come dress you straight. Put on the gown the while.   *Exit Falstaff*

MISTRESS FORD I would my husband would meet him in this shape. He cannot abide the old woman of Brainford. He swears she's a witch, forbade her my house, and hath threatened to beat her.

MISTRESS PAGE Heaven guide him to thy husband's cudgel, and the devil guide his cudgel afterwards!

MISTRESS FORD But is my husband coming?

MISTRESS PAGE Ay, in good sadness, is he, and talks of the basket too, howsoever he hath had intelligence.

MISTRESS FORD We'll try that; for I'll appoint my men to carry the basket again, to meet him at the door with it, as they did last time.

MISTRESS PAGE Nay, but he'll be here presently. Let's go dress him like the witch of Brainford.

MISTRESS FORD I'll first direct my men what they shall do with the basket. Go up. I'll bring linen for him straight.

MISTRESS PAGE Hang him, dishonest varlet! We cannot misuse him enough.

We'll leave a proof, by that which we will do,
Wives may be merry, and yet honest too.
We do not act that often jest and laugh;
'Tis old but true: 'Still swine eats all the draff.'   *Exit*
Enter John and Robert

MISTRESS FORD Go, sirs, take the basket again on your shoulders. Your master is hard at door. If he bid you set it down, obey him. Quickly, dispatch.   *Exit*

JOHN Come, come, take it up.

ROBERT Pray heaven it be not full of knight again.

JOHN I hope not. I had as lief bear so much lead.

Enter Ford, Page, Shallow, Caius, and Evans

FORD Ay, but if it prove true, Master Page, have you any
way then to unfool me again? Set down the basket,
villains. Somebody call my wife. Youth in a basket! O   110
you panderly rascals! There's a knot, a ging, a pack, a
conspiracy against me. Now shall the devil be shamed.
What, wife, I say! Come, come forth! Behold what
honest clothes you send forth to bleaching!

PAGE Why, this passes, Master Ford. You are not to go
loose any longer. You must be pinioned.

EVANS Why, this is lunatics. This is mad as a mad dog.

SHALLOW Indeed, Master Ford, this is not well, indeed.

FORD So say I too, sir.

Enter Mistress Ford

Come hither, Mistress Ford. Mistress Ford, the honest   120
woman, the modest wife, the virtuous creature, that
hath the jealous fool to her husband! I suspect without
cause, mistress, do I?

MISTRESS FORD Heaven be my witness, you do, if you
suspect me in any dishonesty.

FORD Well said, brazen-face. Hold it out. – Come forth,
sirrah!

He pulls clothes out of the basket

PAGE This passes!

MISTRESS FORD Are you not ashamed? Let the clothes
alone.   130

FORD I shall find you anon.

EVANS 'Tis unreasonable. Will you take up your wife's
clothes? Come away.

FORD Empty the basket, I say.

MISTRESS FORD Why, man, why?

FORD Master Page, as I am a man, there was one conveyed out of my house yesterday in this basket. Why
may not he be there again? In my house I am sure he is.

My intelligence is true. My jealousy is reasonable.
140 Pluck me out all the linen.

MISTRESS FORD If you find a man there, he shall die a
flea's death.

PAGE Here's no man.

SHALLOW By my fidelity, this is not well, Master Ford.
This wrongs you.

EVANS Master Ford, you must pray, and not follow the
imaginations of your own heart. This is jealousies.

FORD Well, he's not here I seek for.

PAGE No, nor nowhere else but in your brain.

150 FORD Help to search my house this one time. If I find
not what I seek, show no colour for my extremity. Let
me for ever be your table sport. Let them say of me 'As
jealous as Ford, that searched a hollow walnut for his
wife's leman'. Satisfy me once more. Once more search
with me.   *Exeunt John and Robert with the basket*

MISTRESS FORD What ho, Mistress Page, come you and
the old woman down. My husband will come into the
chamber.

FORD Old woman? What old woman's that?

160 MISTRESS FORD Why, it is my maid's aunt of Brainford.

FORD A witch, a quean, an old cozening quean! Have I not
forbid her my house? She comes of errands, does she?
We are simple men; we do not know what's brought to
pass under the profession of fortune-telling. She works
by charms, by spells, by th'figure; and such daubery as
this is beyond our element – we know nothing. Come
down, you witch, you hag, you. Come down, I say!

MISTRESS FORD Nay, good sweet husband! – Good
gentlemen, let him not strike the old woman.

*Enter Falstaff in woman's clothes, and Mistress
Page*

MISTRESS PAGE Come, Mother Prat, come, give me your   170
hand.

FORD I'll prat her.

He beats Falstaff

Out of my door, you witch, you rag, you baggage, you
polecat, you ronyon! Out, out! I'll conjure you, I'll
fortune-tell you.   *Exit Falstaff*

MISTRESS PAGE Are you not ashamed? I think you have
killed the poor woman.

MISTRESS FORD Nay, he will do it. – 'Tis a goodly credit
for you.

FORD Hang her, witch!   180

EVANS By yea and no, I think the 'oman is a witch indeed.
I like not when a 'oman has a great peard. I spy a great
peard under his muffler.

FORD Will you follow, gentlemen? I beseech you, follow.
See but the issue of my jealousy. If I cry out thus upon
no trail, never trust me when I open again.

PAGE Let's obey his humour a little further. Come,
gentlemen.

Exeunt Ford, Page, Shallow, Caius, and Evans

MISTRESS PAGE Trust me, he beat him most pitifully.

MISTRESS FORD Nay, by th'mass, that he did not. He   190
beat him most unpitifully, methought.

MISTRESS PAGE I'll have the cudgel hallowed and hung
o'er the altar. It hath done meritorious service.

MISTRESS FORD What think you? May we, with the
warrant of womanhood and the witness of a good
conscience, pursue him with any further revenge?

MISTRESS PAGE The spirit of wantonness is sure scared
out of him. If the devil have him not in fee simple, with
fine and recovery, he will never, I think, in the way of
waste, attempt us again.   200

MISTRESS FORD Shall we tell our husbands how we have served him?

MISTRESS PAGE Yes, by all means, if it be but to scrape the figures out of your husband's brains. If they can find in their hearts the poor unvirtuous fat knight shall be any further afflicted, we two will still be the ministers.

MISTRESS FORD I'll warrant they'll have him publicly shamed, and methinks there would be no period to the jest, should he not be publicly shamed.

210 MISTRESS PAGE Come, to the forge with it, then. Shape it. I would not have things cool.   *Exeunt*

IV.3   *Enter Host and Bardolph*

BARDOLPH Sir, the Germans desire to have three of your horses. The Duke himself will be tomorrow at court, and they are going to meet him.

HOST What duke should that be comes so secretly? I hear not of him in the court. Let me speak with the gentlemen. They speak English?

BARDOLPH Ay, sir. I'll call them to you.

HOST They shall have my horses, but I'll make them pay. I'll sauce them. They have had my house a week at
10   command. I have turned away my other guests. They must come off. I'll sauce them. Come.   *Exeunt*

IV.4   *Enter Page, Ford, Mistress Page, Mistress Ford, and Evans*

EVANS 'Tis one of the best discretions of a 'oman as ever I did look upon.

PAGE And did he send you both these letters at an instant?

MISTRESS PAGE Within a quarter of an hour.

FORD

Pardon me, wife. Henceforth do what thou wilt.
I rather will suspect the sun with cold
Than thee with wantonness. Now doth thy honour
    stand,
In him that was of late an heretic,
As firm as faith.

PAGE   'Tis well, 'tis well. No more.
Be not as extreme in submission   10
As in offence.
But let our plot go forward. Let our wives
Yet once again, to make us public sport,
Appoint a meeting with this old fat fellow,
Where we may take him and disgrace him for it.

FORD

There is no better way than that they spoke of.

PAGE How? To send him word they'll meet him in the
Park at midnight? Fie, fie, he'll never come.

EVANS You say he has been thrown in the rivers, and has
been grievously peaten as an old 'oman. Methinks there   20
should be terrors in him, that he should not come.
Methinks his flesh is punished; he shall have no desires.

PAGE So think I too.

MISTRESS FORD

Devise but how you'll use him when he comes,
And let us two devise to bring him thither.

MISTRESS PAGE

There is an old tale goes that Herne the Hunter,
Sometime a keeper here in Windsor Forest,
Doth all the winter-time, at still midnight,
Walk round about an oak, with great ragg'd horns;
And there he blasts the tree, and takes the cattle,   30
And makes milch-kine yield blood, and shakes a chain
In a most hideous and dreadful manner.

You have heard of such a spirit, and well you know
The superstitious idle-headed eld
Received and did deliver to our age
This tale of Herne the Hunter for a truth.

PAGE

Why, yet there want not many that do fear
In deep of night to walk by this Herne's Oak.
But what of this?

MISTRESS FORD   Marry, this is our device:

40   That Falstaff at that oak shall meet with us,
Disguised like Herne, with huge horns on his head.

PAGE

Well, let it not be doubted but he'll come.
And in this shape, when you have brought him thither,
What shall be done with him? What is your plot?

MISTRESS PAGE

That likewise have we thought upon, and thus:
Nan Page my daughter, and my little son,
And three or four more of their growth, we'll dress
Like urchins, ouphes, and fairies, green and white,
With rounds of waxen tapers on their heads,

50   And rattles in their hands. Upon a sudden,
As Falstaff, she, and I are newly met,
Let them from forth a sawpit rush at once
With some diffusèd song. Upon their sight,
We two in great amazedness will fly.
Then let them all encircle him about,
And, fairy-like, to pinch the unclean knight,
And ask him why, that hour of fairy revel,
In their so sacred paths he dares to tread
In shape profane.

MISTRESS FORD   And till he tell the truth,

60   Let the supposèd fairies pinch him sound
And burn him with their tapers.

MISTRESS PAGE   The truth being known,
We'll all present ourselves, dis-horn the spirit,
And mock him home to Windsor.

FORD   The children must
Be practised well to this, or they'll ne'er do't.

EVANS I will teach the children their behaviours, and I
will be like a jackanapes also, to burn the knight with
my taber.

FORD
That will be excellent. I'll go buy them vizards.

MISTRESS PAGE
My Nan shall be the Queen of all the Fairies,
Finely attirèd in a robe of white.   70

PAGE
That silk will I go buy. (*Aside*) And in that time
Shall Master Slender steal my Nan away
And marry her at Eton. (*To them*) Go, send to Falstaff
    straight.

FORD
Nay, I'll to him again in name of Brook.
He'll tell me all his purpose. Sure, he'll come.

MISTRESS PAGE
Fear not you that. Go get us properties
And tricking for our fairies.

EVANS Let us about it. It is admirable pleasures and fery
honest knaveries.   *Exeunt Page, Ford, and Evans*

MISTRESS PAGE
Go, Mistress Ford,   80
Send Quickly to Sir John, to know his mind.
                                 Exit Mistress Ford
I'll to the doctor. He hath my good will,
And none but he, to marry with Nan Page.
That Slender, though well landed, is an idiot;
And he my husband best of all affects.

The doctor is well moneyed, and his friends
Potent at court. He, none but he, shall have her,
Though twenty thousand worthier come to crave her.

Exit

IV.5   *Enter Host and Simple*

HOST What wouldst thou have, boor? What, thick-skin?
Speak, breathe, discuss; brief, short, quick, snap.

SIMPLE Marry, sir, I come to speak with Sir John Falstaff
from Master Slender.

HOST There's his chamber, his house, his castle, his
standing-bed and truckle-bed. 'Tis painted about with
the story of the Prodigal, fresh and new. Go, knock and
call. He'll speak like an Anthropophaginian unto thee.
Knock, I say.

10 SIMPLE There's an old woman, a fat woman, gone up into
his chamber. I'll be so bold as stay, sir, till she come
down. I come to speak with her, indeed.

HOST Ha! A fat woman? The knight may be robbed. I'll
call. Bully knight! Bully Sir John! Speak from thy
lungs military. Art thou there? It is thine host, thine
Ephesian, calls.

FALSTAFF (*above*) How now, mine host?

HOST Here's a Bohemian-Tartar tarries the coming down
of thy fat woman. Let her descend, bully, let her des-
20   cend. My chambers are honourable. Fie, privacy, fie!

Enter Falstaff

FALSTAFF There was, mine host, an old fat woman even
now with me, but she's gone.

SIMPLE Pray you, sir, was't not the wise woman of
Brainford?

FALSTAFF Ay, marry, was it, mussel-shell. What would
you with her?

SIMPLE My master, sir, my Master Slender, sent to her, seeing her go thorough the streets, to know, sir, whether one Nym, sir, that beguiled him of a chain, had the chain or no.   30

FALSTAFF I spake with the old woman about it.

SIMPLE And what says she, I pray, sir?

FALSTAFF Marry, she says that the very same man that beguiled Master Slender of his chain cozened him of it.

SIMPLE I would I could have spoken with the woman herself. I had other things to have spoken with her too, from him.

FALSTAFF What are they? Let us know.

HOST Ay, come. Quick!

SIMPLE I may not conceal them, sir.   40

HOST Conceal them, or thou diest.

SIMPLE Why, sir, they were nothing but about Mistress Anne Page: to know if it were my master's fortune to have her or no.

FALSTAFF 'Tis, 'tis his fortune.

SIMPLE What, sir?

FALSTAFF To have her or no. Go, say the woman told me so.

SIMPLE May I be bold to say so, sir?

FALSTAFF Ay, sir; like who more bold.   50

SIMPLE I thank your worship. I shall make my master glad with these tidings.   *Exit*

HOST Thou art clerkly, thou art clerkly, Sir John. Was there a wise woman with thee?

FALSTAFF Ay, that there was, mine host, one that hath taught me more wit than ever I learned before in my life. And I paid nothing for it neither, but was paid for my learning.

    Enter Bardolph

BARDOLPH Out, alas, sir, cozenage, mere cozenage!

60 HOST Where be my horses? Speak well of them, varletto.

BARDOLPH Run away with the cozeners. For so soon as
    I came beyond Eton, they threw me off, from behind
    one of them, in a slough of mire; and set spurs and
    away, like three German devils, three Doctor Faustuses.

HOST They are gone but to meet the Duke, villain. Do
    not say they be fled. Germans are honest men.

    Enter Evans

EVANS Where is mine host?

HOST What is the matter, sir?

EVANS Have a care of your entertainments. There is a
70 friend of mine come to town tells me there is three
    cozen-germans that has cozened all the hosts of Readins,
    of Maidenhead, of Colebrook, of horses and money. I
    tell you for good will, look you. You are wise, and full of
    gibes and vlouting-stocks, and 'tis not convenient you
    should be cozened. Fare you well.   *Exit*

    Enter Caius

CAIUS Vere is mine host de Jarteer?

HOST Here, Master Doctor, in perplexity and doubtful
    dilemma.

CAIUS I cannot tell vat is dat. But it is tell-a me dat you
80 make grand preparation for a duke de Jamany. By my
    trot, dere is no duke that the court is know to come. I
    tell you for good will. Adieu.   *Exit*

HOST Hue and cry, villain, go! Assist me, knight. I am
    undone! Fly, run, hue and cry, villain! I am undone!

                        Exeunt Host and Bardolph

FALSTAFF I would all the world might be cozened, for I
    have been cozened and beaten too. If it should come to
    the ear of the court how I have been transformed, and
    how my transformation hath been washed and cudgelled,
    they would melt me out of my fat drop by drop, and
90 liquor fishermen's boots with me. I warrant they would

whip me with their fine wits till I were as crestfallen as a
dried pear. I never prospered since I forswore myself at
primero. Well, if my wind were but long enough to say
my prayers, I would repent.

Enter Mistress Quickly

Now, whence come you?

MISTRESS QUICKLY From the two parties, forsooth.

FALSTAFF The devil take one party, and his dam the
other! And so they shall be both bestowed. I have
suffered more for their sakes, more than the villainous
inconstancy of man's disposition is able to bear.   100

MISTRESS QUICKLY And have not they suffered? Yes, I
warrant; speciously one of them. Mistress Ford, good
heart, is beaten black and blue, that you cannot see a
white spot about her.

FALSTAFF What tellest thou me of black and blue? I
was beaten myself into all the colours of the rainbow;
and I was like to be apprehended for the witch of
Brainford. But that my admirable dexterity of wit, my
counterfeiting the action of an old woman, delivered me,
the knave constable had set me i'th'stocks, i'th'common   110
stocks, for a witch.

MISTRESS QUICKLY Sir, let me speak with you in your
chamber. You shall hear how things go, and, I warrant,
to your content. Here is a letter will say somewhat.
Good hearts, what ado here is to bring you together!
Sure, one of you does not serve heaven well, that you are
so crossed.

FALSTAFF Come up into my chamber.   *Exeunt*

Enter Fenton and Host   IV.6

HOST Master Fenton, talk not to me. My mind is heavy.
I will give over all.

FENTON
    Yet hear me speak. Assist me in my purpose,
    And, as I am a gentleman, I'll give thee
    A hundred pound in gold more than your loss.
HOST I will hear you, Master Fenton, and I will, at the
    least, keep your counsel.
FENTON
    From time to time I have acquainted you
    With the dear love I bear to fair Anne Page,
10   Who mutually hath answered my affection,
    So far forth as herself might be her chooser,
    Even to my wish. I have a letter from her
    Of such contents as you will wonder at,
    The mirth whereof so larded with my matter
    That neither singly can be manifested
    Without the show of both. Fat Falstaff
    Hath a great scene. The image of the jest
    I'll show you here at large. Hark, good mine host:
    Tonight at Herne's Oak, just 'twixt twelve and one,
20   Must my sweet Nan present the Fairy Queen –
    The purpose why is here – in which disguise,
    While other jests are something rank on foot,
    Her father hath commanded her to slip
    Away with Slender, and with him at Eton
    Immediately to marry. She hath consented.
    Now, sir,
    Her mother – ever strong against that match
    And firm for Doctor Caius – hath appointed
    That he shall likewise shuffle her away,
30   While other sports are tasking of their minds,
    And at the deanery, where a priest attends,
    Straight marry her. To this her mother's plot
    She, seemingly obedient, likewise hath
    Made promise to the doctor. Now thus it rests:

Her father means she shall be all in white,
And in that habit, when Slender sees his time
To take her by the hand and bid her go,
She shall go with him. Her mother hath intended,
The better to denote her to the doctor –
For they must all be masked and vizarded –   40
That quaint in green she shall be loose enrobed,
With ribands pendent, flaring 'bout her head;
And when the doctor spies his vantage ripe,
To pinch her by the hand, and, on that token,
The maid hath given consent to go with him.

HOST
Which means she to deceive, father or mother?

FENTON
Both, my good host, to go along with me.
And here it rests – that you'll procure the vicar
To stay for me at church 'twixt twelve and one,
And, in the lawful name of marrying,   50
To give our hearts united ceremony.

HOST
Well, husband your device. I'll to the vicar.
Bring you the maid, you shall not lack a priest.

FENTON
So shall I evermore be bound to thee;
Besides, I'll make a present recompense.   *Exeunt*

*

Enter Falstaff and Mistress Quickly   V.I
FALSTAFF Prithee no more prattling. Go. I'll hold. This
is the third time; I hope good luck lies in odd numbers.
Away; go. They say there is divinity in odd numbers,
either in nativity, chance, or death. Away.

MISTRESS QUICKLY I'll provide you a chain, and I'll do what I can to get you a pair of horns.

FALSTAFF Away, I say; time wears. Hold up your head, and mince.   *Exit Mistress Quickly*

Enter Ford disguised as Brook

How now, Master Brook! Master Brook, the matter will be known tonight or never. Be you in the Park about midnight, at Herne's Oak, and you shall see wonders.

FORD Went you not to her yesterday, sir, as you told me you had appointed?

FALSTAFF I went to her, Master Brook, as you see, like a poor old man. But I came from her, Master Brook, like a poor old woman. That same knave Ford, her husband, hath the finest mad devil of jealousy in him, Master Brook, that ever governed frenzy. I will tell you: he beat me grievously, in the shape of a woman; for in the shape of man, Master Brook, I fear not Goliath with a weaver's beam, because I know also life is a shuttle. I am in haste. Go along with me. I'll tell you all, Master Brook. Since I plucked geese, played truant and whipped top, I knew not what 'twas to be beaten till lately. Follow me. I'll tell you strange things of this knave Ford, on whom tonight I will be revenged. And I will deliver his wife into your hand. Follow. Strange things in hand, Master Brook! Follow.   *Exeunt*

V.2   *Enter Page, Shallow, and Slender*

PAGE Come, come. We'll couch i'th'Castle ditch till we see the light of our fairies. Remember, son Slender, my daughter.

SLENDER Ay, forsooth. I have spoke with her, and we have a nay-word how to know one another. I come to her in

white, and cry 'mum'; she cries 'budget'; and by that
we know one another.

SHALLOW That's good too. But what needs either your
'mum' or her 'budget'? The white will decipher her
well enough. It hath struck ten o'clock.   10

PAGE The night is dark. Light and spirits will become it
well. Heaven prosper our sport! No man means evil but
the devil, and we shall know him by his horns. Let's
away. Follow me.   *Exeunt*

Enter Mistress Page, Mistress Ford, and Doctor Caius   V.3

MISTRESS PAGE Master Doctor, my daughter is in green.
When you see your time, take her by the hand, away
with her to the deanery, and dispatch it quickly. Go
before into the Park. We two must go together.

CAIUS I know vat I have to do. Adieu.

MISTRESS PAGE Fare you well, sir.   *Exit Caius*
My husband will not rejoice so much at the abuse of
Falstaff as he will chafe at the doctor's marrying my
daughter. But 'tis no matter. Better a little chiding
than a great deal of heartbreak.   10

MISTRESS FORD Where is Nan now, and her troop of
fairies, and the Welsh devil Hugh?

MISTRESS PAGE They are all couched in a pit hard by
Herne's Oak, with obscured lights, which, at the very
instant of Falstaff's and our meeting, they will at once
display to the night.

MISTRESS FORD That cannot choose but amaze him.

MISTRESS PAGE If he be not amazed, he will be mocked.
If he be amazed, he will every way be mocked.

MISTRESS FORD We'll betray him finely.   20

MISTRESS PAGE
Against such lewdsters and their lechery,

Those that betray them do no treachery.

MISTRESS FORD The hour draws on. To the Oak, to the Oak!   *Exeunt*

V.4   *Enter Evans disguised as a Satyr, and others as Fairies*

EVANS Trib, trib, fairies. Come. And remember your parts. Be pold, I pray you. Follow me into the pit, and when I give the watch-'ords, do as I pid you. Come, come; trib, trib.   *Exeunt*

V.5   *Enter Falstaff disguised as Herne, with a buck's head upon him*

FALSTAFF The Windsor bell hath struck twelve; the minute draws on. Now, the hot-blooded gods assist me! Remember, Jove, thou wast a bull for thy Europa. Love set on thy horns. O powerful love, that in some respects makes a beast a man, in some other a man a beast. You were also, Jupiter, a swan for the love of Leda. O omnipotent love, how near the god drew to the complexion of a goose! A fault done first in the form of a beast – O Jove, a beastly fault – and then another fault
10   in the semblance of a fowl – think on't, Jove, a foul fault! When gods have hot backs, what shall poor men do? For me, I am here a Windsor stag, and the fattest, I think, i'th'forest. Send me a cool rut-time, Jove, or who can blame me to piss my tallow? Who comes here? My doe?

Enter Mistress Ford and Mistress Page

MISTRESS FORD Sir John! Art thou there, my deer, my male deer?

FALSTAFF My doe with the black scut! Let the sky rain

potatoes. Let it thunder to the tune of 'Greensleeves',
hail kissing-comfits, and snow eringoes. Let there come   20
a tempest of provocation, I will shelter me here.

He embraces her

MISTRESS FORD Mistress Page is come with me, sweetheart.

FALSTAFF Divide me like a bribed buck, each a haunch.
I will keep my sides to myself, my shoulders for the
fellow of this walk, and my horns I bequeath your
husbands. Am I a woodman, ha? Speak I like Herne
the Hunter? Why, now is Cupid a child of conscience;
he makes restitution. As I am a true spirit, welcome!

A noise of horns

MISTRESS PAGE Alas, what noise?   30

MISTRESS FORD Heaven forgive our sins!

FALSTAFF What should this be?

MISTRESS FORD *and* MISTRESS PAGE Away, away!

They run off

FALSTAFF I think the devil will not have me damned, lest
the oil that's in me should set hell on fire. He would
never else cross me thus.

*Enter Evans as a Satyr, Mistress Quickly as the
Queen of Fairies, Pistol as Hobgoblin, Anne Page
and boys as Fairies. They carry tapers*

MISTRESS QUICKLY *as Queen of Fairies*
Fairies black, grey, green, and white,
You moonshine revellers, and shades of night,
You orphan heirs of fixèd destiny,
Attend your office and your quality.   40
Crier Hobgoblin, make the fairy oyes.

PISTOL *as Hobgoblin*
Elves, list your names; silence, you airy toys.
Cricket, to Windsor chimneys shalt thou leap.
Where fires thou findest unraked and hearths unswept,
There pinch the maids as blue as bilberry.

Our radiant Queen hates sluts and sluttery.

FALSTAFF

They are fairies; he that speaks to them shall die.
I'll wink and couch; no man their works must eye.
He lies down upon his face

EVANS *as a Satyr*

Where's Bead? Go you, and where you find a maid
50   That, ere she sleep, has thrice her prayers said,
Raise up the organs of her fantasy,
Sleep she as sound as careless infancy.
But those as sleep and think not on their sins,
Pinch them, arms, legs, backs, shoulders, sides, and shins.

MISTRESS QUICKLY *as Queen of Fairies*

About, about!
Search Windsor Castle, elves, within and out.
Strew good luck, ouphes, on every sacred room,
That it may stand till the perpetual doom
In state as wholesome as in state 'tis fit,
60   Worthy the owner and the owner it.
The several chairs of order look you scour
With juice of balm and every precious flower.
Each fair instalment, coat, and several crest,
With loyal blazon, evermore be blest!
And nightly, meadow-fairies, look you sing,
Like to the Garter's compass, in a ring.
Th'expressure that it bears, green let it be,
More fertile-fresh than all the field to see;
And *Honi soit qui mal y pense* write
70   In emerald tufts, flowers purple, blue, and white,
Like sapphire, pearl, and rich embroidery,
Buckled below fair knighthood's bending knee.
Fairies use flowers for their charactery.
Away, disperse! But till 'tis one o'clock,
Our dance of custom round about the oak
Of Herne the Hunter let us not forget.

EVANS *as a Satyr*

Pray you, lock hand in hand; yourselves in order set;

And twenty glow-worms shall our lanterns be,
To guide our measure round about the tree.
But stay — I smell a man of middle earth.   80

FALSTAFF Heavens defend me from that Welsh fairy,
lest he transform me to a piece of cheese.

PISTOL *as Hobgoblin*
Vile worm, thou wast o'erlooked even in thy birth.

MISTRESS QUICKLY *as Queen of Fairies*
With trial-fire touch me his finger-end.
If he be chaste, the flame will back descend
And turn him to no pain; but if he start,
It is the flesh of a corrupted heart.

PISTOL *as Hobgoblin*
A trial, come.

EVANS *as a Satyr*
   Come, will this wood take fire?
 They burn him with their tapers

FALSTAFF O, O, O!

MISTRESS QUICKLY *as Queen of Fairies*
Corrupt, corrupt, and tainted in desire!   90
About him, fairies, sing a scornful rhyme,
And, as you trip, still pinch him to your time.

    The Song
 Fie on sinful fantasy!
 Fie on lust and luxury!
 Lust is but a bloody fire,
 Kindled with unchaste desire,
 Fed in heart, whose flames aspire,
 As thoughts do blow them, higher and higher.
 Pinch him, fairies, mutually,
 Pinch him for his villainy.   100
Pinch him, and burn him, and turn him about,
Till candles and starlight and moonshine be out.
During this song they pinch Falstaff; and Doctor

Caius comes one way, and steals away a boy in green;
Slender another way, and takes off a boy in white;
and Fenton comes, and steals away Anne Page. A noise
of hunting is made within; and all the Fairies run
away. Falstaff pulls off his buck's head, and rises up.
Enter Page, Ford, Mistress Page, and Mistress Ford

PAGE
Nay, do not fly; I think we have watched you now.
Will none but Herne the Hunter serve your turn?

MISTRESS PAGE
I pray you, come, hold up the jest no higher.
Now, good Sir John, how like you Windsor wives?
She points to the horns
See you these, husband? Do not these fair yokes
Become the forest better than the town?

FORD Now, sir, who's a cuckold now? Master Brook,
110   Falstaff's a knave, a cuckoldy knave. Here are his
horns, Master Brook. And, Master Brook, he hath
enjoyed nothing of Ford's but his buck-basket, his
cudgel, and twenty pounds of money, which must be
paid to Master Brook. His horses are arrested for it,
Master Brook.

MISTRESS FORD Sir John, we have had ill luck; we could
never meet. I will never take you for my love again, but
I will always count you my deer.

FALSTAFF I do begin to perceive that I am made an ass.
120   FORD Ay, and an ox too. Both the proofs are extant.

FALSTAFF And these are not fairies? I was three or four
times in the thought they were not fairies; and yet the
guiltiness of my mind, the sudden surprise of my
powers, drove the grossness of the foppery into a
received belief, in despite of the teeth of all rhyme and
reason, that they were fairies. See now how wit may be
made a Jack-a-Lent when 'tis upon ill employment.

EVANS Sir John Falstaff, serve Got and leave your desires, and fairies will not pinse you.

FORD Well said, fairy Hugh.   130

EVANS And leave your jealousies too, I pray you.

FORD I will never mistrust my wife again till thou art able to woo her in good English.

FALSTAFF Have I laid my brain in the sun and dried it, that it wants matter to prevent so gross o'erreaching as this? Am I ridden with a Welsh goat too? Shall I have a coxcomb of frieze? 'Tis time I were choked with a piece of toasted cheese.

EVANS Seese is not good to give putter. Your belly is all putter.   140

FALSTAFF 'Seese' and 'putter'? Have I lived to stand at the taunt of one that makes fritters of English? This is enough to be the decay of lust and late-walking through the realm.

MISTRESS PAGE Why, Sir John, do you think, though we would have thrust virtue out of our hearts by the head and shoulders, and have given ourselves without scruple to hell, that ever the devil could have made you our delight?

FORD What, a hodge-pudding? A bag of flax?   150

MISTRESS PAGE A puffed man?

PAGE Old, cold, withered, and of intolerable entrails?

FORD And one that is as slanderous as Satan?

PAGE And as poor as Job?

FORD And as wicked as his wife?

EVANS And given to fornications, and to taverns, and sack, and wine, and metheglins, and to drinkings, and swearings and starings, pribbles and prabbles?

FALSTAFF Well, I am your theme. You have the start of me. I am dejected. I am not able to answer the Welsh   160

flannel. Ignorance itself is a plummet o'er me. Use me as
you will.

FORD Marry, sir, we'll bring you to Windsor, to one
Master Brook, that you have cozened of money, to whom
you should have been a pander. Over and above that
you have suffered, I think to repay that money will be a
biting affliction.

PAGE Yet be cheerful, knight. Thou shalt eat a posset
tonight at my house, where I will desire thee to laugh at
170 my wife that now laughs at thee. Tell her Master Slender
hath married her daughter.

MISTRESS PAGE (*aside*) Doctors doubt that. If Anne Page
be my daughter, she is, by this, Doctor Caius's wife.
     Enter Slender

SLENDER Whoa, ho, ho, father Page!

PAGE Son, how now? How now, son? Have you dispatched?

SLENDER Dispatched? I'll make the best in Gloucestershire know on't. Would I were hanged, la, else!

PAGE Of what, son?

180 SLENDER I came yonder at Eton to marry Mistress Anne
Page, and she's a great lubberly boy. If it had not been
i'th'church, I would have swinged him, or he should
have swinged me. If I did not think it had been Anne
Page, would I might never stir! And 'tis a postmaster's
boy.

PAGE Upon my life, then, you took the wrong.

SLENDER What need you tell me that? I think so, when I
took a boy for a girl. If I had been married to him, for all
he was in woman's apparel, I would not have had him.

190 PAGE Why, this is your own folly. Did not I tell you how
you should know my daughter by her garments?

SLENDER I went to her in white, and cried 'mum', and
she cried 'budget', as Anne and I had appointed. And

yet it was not Anne, but a postmaster's boy.

MISTRESS PAGE Good George, be not angry. I knew of
your purpose, turned my daughter into green; and
indeed she is now with the Doctor at the deanery, and
there married.

Enter Doctor Caius

CAIUS Vere is Mistress Page? By gar, I am cozened. I ha'
married *un garçon*, a boy; *un paysan*, by gar, a boy. It is   200
not Anne Page. By gar, I am cozened.

MISTRESS PAGE Why? Did you take her in green?

CAIUS Ay, by gar, and 'tis a boy. By gar, I'll raise all
Windsor.   *Exit*

FORD This is strange. Who hath got the right Anne?

PAGE
My heart misgives me. Here comes Master Fenton.

Enter Fenton and Anne Page

How now, Master Fenton?

ANNE
Pardon, good father. Good my mother, pardon.

PAGE Now, mistress, how chance you went not with
Master Slender?   210

MISTRESS PAGE
Why went you not with Master Doctor, maid?

FENTON
You do amaze her. Hear the truth of it.
You would have married her most shamefully
Where there was no proportion held in love.
The truth is, she and I, long since contracted,
Are now so sure that nothing can dissolve us.
Th'offence is holy that she hath committed,
And this deceit loses the name of craft,
Of disobedience, or unduteous title,
Since therein she doth evitate and shun   220
A thousand irreligious cursèd hours

Which forcèd marriage would have brought upon her.

FORD

Stand not amazed. Here is no remedy.

In love the heavens themselves do guide the state.

Money buys lands, and wives are sold by fate.

FALSTAFF I am glad, though you have ta'en a special
stand to strike at me, that your arrow hath glanced.

PAGE

Well, what remedy? Fenton, heaven give thee joy!

What cannot be eschewed must be embraced.

FALSTAFF

230 When night-dogs run, all sorts of deer are chased.

MISTRESS PAGE

Well, I will muse no further. Master Fenton,

Heaven give you many, many merry days.

Good husband, let us every one go home,

And laugh this sport o'er by a country fire;

Sir John and all.

FORD   Let it be so. Sir John,

To Master Brook you yet shall hold your word,

For he tonight shall lie with Mistress Ford.   *Exeunt*

An Account of the Text

The Merry Wives of Windsor first saw print in 1602, when it was published as a quarto. The title-page, which is not without its interest, runs, when modernized, thus: 'A most pleasant and excellent conceited comedy of Sir John Falstaff and the Merry Wives of Windsor, intermixed with sundry variable and pleasing humours of Sir Hugh the Welsh knight, Justice Shallow, and his wise cousin Master Slender, with the swaggering vein of Ancient Pistol, and Corporal Nym. By William Shakespeare. As it hath been divers times acted by the Right Honourable my Lord Chamberlain's Servants, both before her majesty and elsewhere.' This is evidently a publisher's blurb, singling out the characters that could be expected to have an immediate appeal to anyone who knew the two parts of *Henry IV* and *Henry V*. It is also curiously erratic. The description of Slender, a new character, could hardly be bettered, yet that of Evans, the other new character named, suggests that whoever was responsible for it had neither seen nor read the play. The text itself has something of the same hit-and-miss quality. Nevertheless, it was reprinted, with a few minor alterations, in 1619. Then, in 1623, came the Folio edition of the plays, in which *The Merry Wives of Windsor* appears as the third of the Comedies, between *The Two Gentlemen of Verona* and *Measure for Measure*. The text of the Folio is very different from that of the Quarto. It is almost twice the length, running to over 2,700 lines as compared with a mere 1,600. It contains five scenes – IV.1 and V.1–4 – which are not to be found at all in the Quarto. It introduces one character, Page's son little William, who does not appear in the Quarto, and allots a speaking part to another, Falstaff's page Robin, who is mute in the text of 1602. Moreover, it is carefully divided into acts and scenes, whereas the Quarto has no such divisions. Most important of all, however, the Folio presents a much fuller, better written and far more coherent play than does the Quarto.

The superiority of the Folio text was soon recognized at a very practical level. The Quarto of 1602 had been printed for a bookseller called Arthur Johnson. In January 1630 Johnson made over his rights in *The Merry Wives of Windsor* to another bookseller, R. Meighen. But, when Meighen had the play reprinted as a quarto, later in the same year, it was not the 1602 text, or the 1619, which he used, but that of the Folio. The judgement about the relative values of the two texts, implicit in this choice, is one that all editors of the comedy have concurred with; they are unanimous in basing their texts on that of the Folio.

This does not mean, however, that the editor can afford to ignore the Quarto completely. Rowe did so in his edition of 1709, the first edited Shakespeare that we have, but only for the simple reason that he did not know of its existence. Pope, Shakespeare's second editor, though unaware of the 1602 version, knew that of 1619, and recognized that at one point it offered a demonstrably better reading than the Folio. When Ford asks the Host for his connivance in Ford's plan to present himself to Falstaff under an assumed name, he says in the Folio: 'tell him my name is *Broome*: onely for a iest' (II.1.198–9). Thereafter in the Folio the name under which he talks to Falstaff is consistently 'Broome'. In the Quarto Ford's request is: 'tell him my name | Is *Rrooke*, onlie for a Iest'. The Host's reply, 'thy | Name shall be *Brooke*', makes it clear that the improbable 'Rrooke' is merely a misprint; and from this point onwards the name is always 'Brooke' in the Quarto. At this stage in the action there is nothing to indicate which of the two names is the one that Shakespeare originally wrote, though 'Brooke' has obvious associations with 'Ford' while 'Broome' has none. The issue is settled in the next scene. At II.2.140–48, the following exchanges between Bardolph and Falstaff occur in the Folio:

Bar. Sir *Iohn*, there's one Master *Broome* below would faine speake
with you, and be acquainted with you; and hath sent your worship
a mornings draught of Sacke.
Fal. *Broome* is his name?
Bar. I Sir.
Fal. Call him in: such *Broomes* are welcome to mee, that ore'flowes
such liquor . . .

Falstaff's final speech here makes no sense. It is evident that
something has gone wrong. The corresponding passage in the
Quarto runs thus:

Bar. Sir heer's a Gentleman,
    One M. *Brooke*, would speak with you,
    He hath sent you a cup of sacke.
Fal. M. *Brooke*, hees welcome: Bid him come vp,
    Such *Brookes* are alwaies welcome to me . . .

The Quarto clearly has the name right: the substitution of 'Brooke'
for 'Broome' turns the Folio nonsense into a characteristically
Falstaffian jest. In every other respect, however, the Quarto text
is plainly inferior to that of the Folio here. Quite apart from
the fact that it prints prose as though it were verse, it almost
ruins the joke by missing out Falstaff's explanation of why 'Such
Brookes' are welcome to him. Moreover, its repetition of the
word 'welcome' is feeble. The lively, natural quality of the Folio's
dialogue, with its use of question and answer, has been flattened
out and made pedestrian. The Quarto version here – and it is
representative of the general level of the Quarto as a whole –
has all the appearance of something inadequately remembered.
   Pope, while realizing that 'Brooke' is the correct reading,
missed the other instance in which the Quarto text preserves
what Shakespeare wrote. It was spotted by the dramatist's
third editor, Lewis Theobald (1733). At III.1.92, the Host,
seeking to reconcile Caius and Evans, whom he has already
addressed as '*Gallia* and *Gaule*, *French & Welch*, Soule-Curer,
and Body-Curer' (89–90), puts his plea to them in the following
form in the Folio:

> Peace, I say: heare mine Host of the Garter,
> Am I politicke? Am I subtle? Am I a Machiuell?
> Shall I loose my Doctor? No, hee giues me the Potions and the Motions.
> Shall I loose my Parson? my Priest? my Sir *Hugh*? No, he giues me
> the Prouerbes, and the No-verbes. Giue me thy hand (Celestiall) so:
> Boyes of Art, I haue deceiu'd you both ...

The Quarto version of this same speech is:

> Peace *I* say, heare mine host of the garter,
> Am *I* wise? am I polliticke? am *I* Matchauil?
> Shall *I* lose my doctor? No, he giues me the motions
> And the potions. Shall *I* lose my parson, my sir *Hu*?
> No, he giues me the prouerbes, and the nouerbes:
> Giue me thy hand terestiall,
> So giue me thy hand celestiall:
> So boyes of art I haue deceiued you both ...

The words 'Give me thy hand, terrestrial' — the form 'teres-
tiall' is merely a misspelling — are demanded by the action,
since the Host wishes to end the quarrel, and by the whole
structure of the speech, which is built on carefully contrived
antitheses. Moreover, it is easy to see how the compositor, or
the scribe who prepared the text of the play for the printer,
came to miss these five words. He set the first four of them,
and then his eye jumped from the Host's appeal to Caius to
his appeal to Evans, which starts with the same four words.
    There are other instances in which the Quarto offers a
reading that is tempting, but none of them has the patent
rightness of the two just cited. For example, in the opening
scene Slender answers Falstaff's brazen query, 'What matter have
you against me?' (I.i.116), by saying in the Folio text: 'Marry
sir, I haue matter in my head against you, and against your
cony-catching Rascalls, *Bardolf*, *Nym*, and *Pistoll*.' The Quarto
at this point is far more explicit. It reads: 'I haue matter in
my head against you and your cogging companions, *Pistoll*
and *Nym*. They carried mee to the Tauerne and made mee
drunke, and afterward picked my pocket.' To the present editor

it appears that the second sentence, not to be found in the Folio, is required to lead on to Falstaff's question, 'Pistol, did you pick Master Slender's purse?' (141). It has, however, been argued that a much subtler effect is achieved here if Slender, as in the Folio, has not yet made any specific complaint, since Falstaff's question then reveals that he knows perfectly well that Slender's purse was picked. This is undoubtedly true; so how does one decide whether to include the sentence from the Quarto or not? The answer will depend on whether one sees *The Merry Wives of Windsor* as a play of broad humour, written for an audience that needed to have things spelled out, or whether one regards it as a sophisticated comedy, designed for a learned queen and her court.

The whole problem would have been easier had the Folio text been set up from Shakespeare's own manuscript of the play, or even from the playhouse prompt copy. It was not. Two features of it are bound to strike anyone who looks at it with a little care. In the first place, there is only one stage direction within the scene in the entire play. This occurs at V.5.36, in the form '*Enter Fairies*'. Secondly, the only other entrances marked come at the beginning of each scene, and they name all the characters who take part in that scene, irrespective of whether they are onstage from the outset or do not appear until later. The Folio text, as it stands, cannot be used as a prompt book. It is not the work of a man of the theatre. The 'massed entries', as they are called, together with certain other peculiarities, such as the prodigal use of parentheses, have led modern scholars to the conclusion that the copy which the printers of the Folio had at their disposal was a transcript made by a professional scribe, Ralph Crane. Crane has done the work of tidying-up so thoroughly that it is impossible to say what sort of manuscript he was working from. What is practically certain is that he must have introduced some errors of his own in the process of copying.

The Folio text also represents a version of the play that has been submitted to some form of censorship. One mark of this is the substitution in it of 'Broome' for the 'Brooke' of the Quarto. The most likely reasons for it are either that the use of 'Brooke' somehow gave offence to the powerful family of that name, or that it was thought unwise to remind James I, who had *The Merry Wives of Windsor* performed before him at court on 4 November 1604, of this same family, which had been implicated in the Bye Plot and the Main Plot. The change of the name could well be the work of Shakespeare himself. The other evidence of censorship is the weakness of the oaths in the Folio as compared with those in the Quarto. For example, when Falstaff is describing his adventure in the buck-basket to the disguised Ford, he says in the Folio, replying to Ford's incredulous question 'A Buck-basket?', 'Yes: a Buck-basket' (III.5.80–81). In the Quarto, however, his answer to the same question is 'By the Lord a buck-basket', which sounds much more convincing. The purging of oaths of this kind from the text, which again may well be the work of Shakespeare himself, probably took place after the passing of an act, in 1606, to prohibit the profane use of God's name on the stage.

Pope thought of the Quarto as an early draft of the comedy, which Shakespeare later revised and expanded. This remained, with some modifications, the general view of scholars until 1910, when W. W. Greg, in a brilliant piece of textual analysis, showed that the peculiarities of the 1602 text could be explained far more satisfactorily by the hypothesis that it represents a version of the Folio put together from memory by an actor, or actors, who had taken part in performances of it. The prime culprit he identified as an actor who had played the Host, because his speeches, as the one quoted on p. 98 amply demonstrates, are remarkably close to their counterparts in the Folio. The part of Falstaff, though not quite so well preserved as that of the Host, is also fairly full and accurate, as are the entire scenes in which one or the other of these two characters is involved. When neither of them is onstage, things fall apart. Passages from one scene find their way into another; the point of jokes is lost; and there is much feeble repetition. There are some differences between the two texts, however, which cannot be explained by this theory alone. The complete omission of the examination in Latin grammar (IV.1) and of the first four scenes of Act V shows that there was also deliberate abridgement. Greg's view, with which the present editor fully agrees, is that the Quarto was vamped up by two actors, who had played the parts of the Host and Falstaff, in order to put together a shortened version of the play suitable for production in the provinces. Greg thinks further that the report was compiled by someone other than the two actors, who drew on the recollections of each of them. Some such assumption is made necessary by the extraordinary reading the Quarto provides of the Host's speech at IV.5.83. In the Folio it runs:

> Huy and cry, (villaine) goe: assist me Knight, I am vndone: fly, run: huy, and cry (villaine) I am vndone.

In the Quarto it takes the following form:

> *I* am cosened H*ugh*, and coy *Bardolfe*,
> Sweet knight assist me, *I* am cosened.

The nonsensical 'H*ugh*, and coy *Bardolfe*' seems to be the work of an amanuensis mishearing and misunderstanding the Host's 'Hue and cry, Bardolph'.

The Quarto is, in fact, a 'bad Quarto', and, as such, wholly unreliable and of no authority. Yet it is not without its uses and its delights.

COLLATIONS

The following lists are selective. They do not include corrections of obvious misprints or changes of punctuation. Q refers to the Quarto text of 1602 and F to the first Folio of 1623. Quotations from these texts are not modernized except for the printing of 'long s' (∫) as 's'.

1

The readings listed below derive from the Q, not from the F. Stage directions are not included in this list; they are given separately in list 3. The reading to the left of the bracket is that of the present edition; the reading to the right of it that of F.

I.I
119–20 They carried me to the tavern, and made me
       drunk, and afterward picked my pocket] *not in* F
   150 latten] Latine

I.3
    14 lime] liue
    49 a legion] (Q: legians); a legend
    78 humour] honor
    87 Page] *Ford*
    88 Ford] *Page*

II.1
127–8 and there's the humour of it] *not in* F
   197 FORD] *Shal.*
   199 (*and for the rest of the play*) Brook] *Broome*

II.2
     4 I will retort the sum in equipage] (*line* 2 *in* Q);
       not in F
    23 God] heauen
    29 wouldst] would
 51, 55 God] heauen
   293 God] Heauen

II.3
    52 word] *not in* F

III.1
    80 urinals] Vrinal
    81 cogscombs] (Q: cockcomes); Cogs-combe
  81–2 for missing your meetings and appointments] *not*
       in F
    97 Give me thy hand, terrestrial; so] *not in* F
   101 lads] Lad

III.3
131–2 and none but thee] *not in* F

III.5
    81 By the Lord] Yes

IV.3
     7 them] him
     9 house] houses

V.4

41 Disguised like Herne, with huge horns on his
head] *not in* F

V.5

93–4 to say my prayers] *not in* F

2

The following list contains the substantial departures from the
text of F, other than those given above, that are to be found
in the present edition. The F reading is to the right of the
bracket. Stage directions are not included. Readings thought
to be peculiar to the present edition are marked '*this edition*'.

The Characters in the Play] *not in* F *or* Q

I.1

26 py'r lady] per-lady
31 compromises] compremises
39 swort] sword
42 George] *Thomas*
54, 57 SHALLOW] *Slen.*
70 Got's] go't's
111, 113 Council . . . counsel] Councell . . . councell
165 careers] Car-eires

I.3

55 œillades] illiads
77 o'th'] ith'
92 Page] *Ford*

I.4

44 *un boîtier vert*] vnboyteene verd
49–50 *Ma foi, il fait fort chaud. Je m'en vais à la cour – la
grande affaire*] mai foy, il fait for ehando, Ie man voi
a le Court la grand affaires
52 *Dépêche*] de-peech
86 *baille*] ballow
119 good-year] good-ier

II.1

1 have I 'scaped] haue scap'd
54 praised] praise
58 Hundredth Psalm] hundred Psalms

195–6 guest cavaliero] guest-Caualeire
202 Ameers] An-heires

II.2

25 you, you rogue] (*this edition*); you Rogue
225 exchange] enchange

II.3

26 Galen] *Galien*
73 PAGE, SHALLOW, *and* SLENDER] *All.*

III.1

110 scald] scall

III.2

45 ALL] *Shal. Page, &c.*

III.3

3 Robert] *Robin*
145 JOHN *and* ROBERT] *Ser.*
155 escape] (*this edition*); vncape
181 foolish] foolishion

III.4

12 FENTON] *not in* F
66 Fenton] *Fenter*

II.5

28 pullet-sperm] Pullet-Spersme

IV.1

32 pebble] Peeble
43 *hung*] *hing*
57 Jenny's] Ginyes
64 lunatics] Lunaties
72–3 *quae . . . quaes*] *que . . . Ques*

IV.2

54 MISTRESS PAGE] *not in* F
62 MISTRESS PAGE] *Mist. Ford.*
93 direct] direct direct
97 misuse him enough] misuse enough
110 villains] villaine
111 ging] gin
118 this] thi
169 him not strike] him strike

IV.3

1 Germans desire] Germane desires

IV.4
   6 cold] gold
  31 makes] make
  59 MISTRESS FORD] *Ford.*
  64 ne'er] neu'r
  81 Quickly] quickly
IV.5
  40 SIMPLE] *Fal.*
IV.6
  27 ever] euen
  39 denote] deuote
V.2
  2–3 my daughter] my
V.3
  12 Welsh devil Hugh] Welch-deuill Herne
V.5
  68 More] Mote
  70 emerald tufts] Emrold-tuffes
  192 white] greene
  196 into green] into white
  200 *un garçon*] oon Garsoon
     un paysan] oon pesant
  202 green] white

3

The stage directions of F are of such a kind (see p. 99) as to make them almost useless to the editor or director. The stage directions in the present edition are therefore mainly editorial. A considerable number of them, however, derive from Q, which is far more helpful in this respect. Indeed, some of the Q directions are of great interest, since they indicate what the reporters could remember of the actual stage business that had occurred in productions they had taken part in. The following list contains the stage directions of the present text which have some basis in the Q and/or F. The reading of this text is to the left of the bracket; that of the Q and/or F to the right of it. When no direction is given, none exists.

I.1

    0 *Enter Justice Shallow, Slender, and Sir Hugh Evans*]
       Enter Iustice Shallow, *Syr* Hugh, *Maister* Page, *and*
       Slender Q; *Enter Iustice* Shallow, Slender, *Sir* Hugh
       Euans, *Master* Page, Falstoffe, Bardolph, Nym,
       Pistoll, Anne Page, *Mistresse* Ford, *Mistresse* Page,
       Simple F

  102 *Enter Sir John Falstaff, Bardolph, Nym, and Pistol*]
       Enter Syr Iohn Falstaffe, Pistoll, Bardolfe, *and* Nim
       Q

  173 *Enter Anne Page, with wine, Mistress Ford, and Mistress
       Page*] *Enter Mistresse* Foord, *Mistresse* Page, *and her
       daughter* Anne Q

  179 *He kisses her*] *Syr* Iohn kisses her Q

  182 *Exeunt all except Slender*] *Exit all, but* Slender *and
       mistresse* Anne Q

I.1

  279 *Enter Page*] *Enter Maister* Page Q

  293 *Exeunt*] *Exit omnes* Q; *Exeunt* F

I.2

    0 *Enter Evans and Simple*] *Enter sir* Hugh *and* Simple,
       from dinner Q; *Enter Euans, and Simple* F

   11 *Exeunt*] *Exit omnes* Q; *Exeunt* F

I.3

    0 *Enter Falstaff, Host, Bardolph, Nym, Pistol, and
       Robin*] *Enter sir* Iohn Falstaffes *Host of the Garter*,
       Nym, Bardolfe, Pistoll, *and the boy* Q; *Enter Falstaffe,
       Host, Bardolfe, Nym, Pistoll, Page* F

   14 *Exit*] *Exit Host* Q

   19 *Exit Bardolph*] *Exit Bardolfe* Q (*after line* 18)

   79 *Exeunt Falstaff and Robin*] *Exit Falstaffe, and the
       Boy* Q

   95 *Exeunt*] *Exit omnes* Q; *Exeunt* F

I.4

    0 *Enter Mistress Quickly and Simple*] *Enter Mistresse
       Quickly, and* Simple Q; *Enter Mistris Quickly, Simple,
       Iohn Rugby, Doctor, Caius, Fenton* F

   38 *She shuts Simple in the closet*] *He steps into the
       Counting-house* Q

42 *Enter Doctor Caius*] *And she opens the doore* Q
54 *Enter Rugby*] *Enter Iohn* Q
87 *He writes*] *The Doctor writes* Q
122 *Exeunt Caius and Rugby*] *Exit Doctor* Q
160 *Exit*] *Exit omnes* Q; *Exit* F

II.1

0 *Enter Mistress Page, with a letter*] *Enter Mistresse*
   Page, *reading of a Letter* Q; *Enter Mistris* Page,
   Mistris Ford, *Master* Page, *Master* Ford, Pistoll, Nim,
   Quickly, Host, Shallow F
29 *Enter Mistress Ford*] *Enter Mistresse* Foord Q
101 *Enter Ford with Pistol, and Page with Nym*] *Enter*
    Ford, *Page, Pistoll and Nym* Q
118 *Exit*] *Exit Pistoll* Q
128 *Exit*] *Exit Nym* Q
147 *Enter Mistress Quickly*] *Enter Mistresse Quickly* Q
    (after line 139)
156 *Exeunt Mistress Page, Mistress Ford, and Mistress*
    Quickly] *Exit Mistresse* Ford, *Mis.* Page, *and* Quickly
    Q
176 *Enter Host*] *Enter Host and Shallow* Q
189 *They go aside*] Ford *and the* Host *talkes* Q
214 *Exeunt Host, Shallow, and Page*] *Exit Host and*
    Shallow Q
221 *Exit*] *Exit omnes* Q; *Exeunt* F

II.2

0 *Enter Falstaff and Pistol*] *Enter Syr Iohn, and* Pistoll
   Q; *Enter* Falstaffe, Pistoll, Robin, Quickly, Bardolffe,
   Ford F
31 *Enter Mistress Quickly*] *Enter Mistresse Quickly* Q
129 *Exeunt Mistress Quickly and Robin*] *Exit Mistresse*
    Quickly Q
139 *Enter Bardolph*] *Enter Bardolfe* Q
149 *Enter Bardolph, with Ford disguised as Brook*]
    Enter Foord *disguised like* Brooke Q
272 *Exit*] *Exit Falstaffe* Q
297 *Exit*] *Exit Ford* Q; *Exti* F

II.3

0 *Enter Doctor Caius and Rugby*] *Enter the Doctor and*

his man Q; *Enter Caius, Rugby, Page, Shallow, Slender, Host* F

15   *Enter Host, Shallow, Slender, and Page*] *Enter Shallow, Page, my Host, and Slender* Q

74   *Exeunt*] *Exit all but the Host and Doctor* Q

89   *Exeunt*] *Exit omnes* Q; *Exeunt* F

III.1

0   *Enter Evans and Simple*] *Enter Syr Hugh and Simple* Q; *Enter Euans, Simple, Page, Shallow, Slender, Host, Caius, Rugby* F

34   *Enter Page, Shallow, and Slender*] *Enter Page, shallow, and Slender* Q

66, 67   *Enter Host, Caius, and Rugby . . . Evans and Caius offer to fight*] *Enter Doctor and the Host, they offer to fight* Q (*after line 64*)

102   *Exit*] *Exit Host* Q

114   *Exeunt*] *Exit omnes* Q

III.2

0   *Enter Mistress Page and Robin*] *Mist. Page, Robin, Ford, Page, Shallow, Slender, Host, Euans, Caius* F

8   *Enter Ford*] *Enter M. Foord* Q

44   *Enter Page, Shallow, Slender, Host, Evans, Caius, and Rugby*] *Enter Shallow, Page, host, Slender, Doctor, and sir Hugh* Q

77   *Exeunt Shallow and Slender*] *Exit Shallow and Slender* Q

80   *Exit*] *Exit host* Q

83   *Exeunt*] *Exit omnes* Q; *Exeunt* F

III.3

0   *Enter Mistress Ford and Mistress Page*] *Enter Mistresse Ford, with two of her men, and a great buck busket* Q; *Enter M. Ford, M. Page, Seruants, Robin, Falstaffe, Ford, Page, Caius, Euans* F

18   *Exeunt John and Robert*] *Exit seruant* Q

39   *Enter Falstaff*] *Enter Sir Iohn* Q

87   *Falstaff hides himself*] *Falstaffe stands behind the aras* Q
Enter Mistress Page] *Enter Mistresse Page* Q (*after line 75*)

129 *Aside to him*] *A side* Q
133 *He gets into the basket; they cover him with foul linen*]
     Sir Iohn goes into the basket, they put cloathes ouer
     him, the two men carries it away: Foord meetes it, and
     all the rest, Page, Doctor, Priest, Slender, Shallow Q
164 *Exeunt Page, Caius, and Evans*] *Exit omnes* Q
186 *Enter Ford, Page, Caius, and Evans*] *Enter all* Q
227 *Exeunt*] *Exit omnes* Q; *Exeunt* F

III.4

  0 *Enter Fenton and Anne Page*] *Enter M. Fenton, Page,*
     and mistresse Quickly Q; *Enter Fenton, Anne, Page,*
     Shallow, Slender, Quickly, Page, Mist. Page F
 64 *Enter Page and Mistress Page*] *Enter M. Page his wife,*
     M. Shallow, and Slender Q
 99 *Exit Fenton*] *Exit Fen.* Q
108 *Exit*] *Exit* Q; *Exeunt* F

III.5

  0 *Enter Falstaff and Bardolph*] *Enter Sir Iohn Falstaffe*
     Q; *Enter Falstaffe, Bardolfe, Quickly, Ford* F
 22 *Enter Mistress Quickly*] *Enter Mistresse Quickly* Q
 52 *Exit*] *Exit mistresse Quickly* Q
 55 *Enter Ford disguised as Brook*] *Enter Brooke* Q
127 *Exit*] *Exit Falstaffe* Q
140 *Exit*] *Exit omnes* Q; *Exeunt* F

IV.1

  0 *Enter Mistress Page, Mistress Quickly, and William*]
     Enter Mistris Page, Quickly, William, Euans F
 80 *Exeunt*] *Exeunt* F

IV.2

  0 *Enter Falstaff and Mistress Ford*] *Enter misteris Ford*
     and her two men Q; *Enter Falstoffe, Mist. Ford, Mist.*
     Page, Seruants, Ford, Page, Caius, Euans, Shallow F
  9 *Exit Falstaff*] *He steps behind the arras* Q
     Enter Mistress Page] *Enter mistresse Page* Q (*after*
     line 7)
 78 *Exit Falstaff*] *Exit Mis. Page, & Sir Iohn* Q
107 *Enter Ford, Page, Shallow, Caius, and Evans*] *Enter*
     M. Ford, Page, Priest, Shallow, the two men carries
     the basket, and Ford meets it Q

169, 172, 175   *Enter Falstaff in woman's clothes, and Mistress
                Page . . . He beats Falstaff . . . Exit Falstaff*] *Enter
                Falstaffe disguised like an old woman, and misteris
                Page with him, Ford beates him, and hee runnes away*
                Q *(after line* 167)

        188   *Exeunt Ford, Page, Shallow, Caius, and Evans*] *Exit
              omnes* Q

        211   *Exeunt*] *Exit both* Q; *Exeunt* F

IV.3

          0   *Enter Host and Bardolph*] *Enter Host and Bardolfe* Q;
              Enter Host and Bardolfe F

         11   *Exeunt*] *Exit omnes* Q; *Exeunt* F

IV.4

          0   *Enter Page, Ford, Mistress Page, Mistress Ford, and
              Evans*] *Enter Ford, Page, their wiues, Shallow, and
              Slender. Syr Hu.* Q; *Enter Page, Ford, Mistris Page,
              Mistris Ford, and Euans* F

IV.4

         88   *Exit*] *Exit omnes* Q

IV.5

          0   *Enter Host and Simple*] *Enter Host and Simple* Q;
              *Enter Host, Simple, Falstaffe, Bardolfe, Euans, Caius,
              Quickly* F

         20   *Enter Falstaff*] *Enter Sir Iohn* Q

         58   *Enter Bardolph*] *Enter Bardolfe* Q

         66   *Enter Evans*] *Enter Sir Hugh* Q *(after Caius's exit)*

         75   *Exit*] *Exit* Q *(before line* 83)
              Enter Caius] *Enter Doctor* Q *(after line* 64)

         82   *Exit*] *Exit.* Q *(before Evans's entry)*

         84   *Exeunt Host and Bardolph*] *Exit* Q

         94   *Enter Mistress Quickly*] *Enter Mistresse Quickly* Q

        118   *Exeunt*] *Exit omnes.* Q; *Exeunt* F

IV.6

          0   *Enter Fenton and Host*] *Enter Host and Fenton* Q;
              Enter Fenton, Host F

         55   *Exeunt*] *Exit omnes* Q; *Exeunt* F

V.1

          0   *Enter Falstaff and Mistress Quickly*] *Enter Falstaffe,
              Quickly, and Ford* F

28 *Exeunt*] *Exeunt* F

V.2

0 *Enter Page, Shallow, and Slender*] *Enter Page, Shallow, Slender* F

14 *Exeunt*] *Exeunt* F

V.3

0 *Enter Mistress Page, Mistress Ford, and Doctor Caius*] *Enter Mist. Page, Mist. Ford, Caius* F

24 *Exeunt*] *Exeunt* F

V.4

0 *Enter Evans disguised as a Satyr, and others as Fairies*] *Enter Euans and Fairies* F

4 *Exeunt*] *Exeunt* F

V.5

0 *Enter Falstaff disguised as Herne, with a buck's head upon him*] *Enter sir Iohn with a Bucks head vpon him* Q; *Enter Falstaffe, Mistris Page, Mistris Ford, Euans, Anne Page, Fairies, Page, Ford, Quickly, Slender, Fenton, Caius, Pistoll* F

15 *Enter Mistress Ford and Mistress Page*] *Enter mistris Page, and mistris Ford* Q

29 *A noise of horns*] *There is a noise of hornes, the two women run away* Q

36 *Enter Evans as a Satyr, Mistress Quickly as the Queen of Fairies, Pistol as Hobgoblin, Anne Page and boys as Fairies. They carry tapers*] *Enter sir Hugh like a Satyre, and boyes drest like Fayries, mistresse Quickly, like the Queene of Fayries: they sing a song about him, and afterward speake* Q; *Enter Fairies* F

88 *They burn him with their tapers*] *They put the Tapers to his fingers, and he starts* Q

102 *During this song they pinch Falstaff; and Doctor Caius comes one way, and steals away a boy in green; Slender another way, and takes off a boy in white; and Fenton comes, and steals away Anne Page. A noise of hunting is made within; and all the Fairies run away. Falstaff pulls off his buck's head, and rises up. Enter Page, Ford, Mistress Page, and Mistress Ford*] *Here they pinch him, and sing about him, & the Doctor comes*

> *one way & steales away a boy in red. And Slender*
> *another way he takes a boy in greene: And Fenton*
> *steales misteris Anne, being in white. And a noyse of*
> *hunting is made within: and all the* Fairies *runne away.*
> Falstaffe *pulles of his bucks head, and rises vp. And*
> *enters* M. Page, M. Ford, *and their wiues,* M. Shallow,
> Sir Hugh Q

173 *Enter Slender*] *Enter Slender* Q (*but after the entry of*
    Caius)

198 *Enter Doctor Caius*] *Enter the Doctor* Q (*but preceding*
    the entry of Slender)

206 *Enter Fenton and Anne Page*] *Enter Fenton and Anne*
    Q

237 *Exeunt*] *Exit omnes* Q; *Exeunt* F

4

The following list contains some of the more interesting and
plausible emendations, not adopted in the present edition, which
have been made by editors from the time of Nicholas Rowe
(1709) onwards. Those which originate in modern scholarly
editions are acknowledged. The reading to the left of the bracket
is that of the present edition; the reading to the right of the
bracket is the rejected emendation.

I.1

21 coat] cod (*Sir A. T. Quiller-Couch and J. Dover*
   Wilson, 1921)

232 content] contempt

235 fall] fault

I.2

11 cheese] seese

I.3

25 minute's] minim's; minim- (*Sir A. T. Quiller-Couch*
   and J. Dover Wilson, 1921)

I.4

21 wee] whey-

22 Cain-coloured] cane-colour'd

II.1

  5 *precisian*] physician

  129 'The humour of it'] The 'humour' of it (*H. J. Oliver,*
    1971)

  202 Ameers] (An-heires F); myn-heers

II.2

  22 I, I, I] I, ay, I; Ay, ay, I (*Sir A. T. Quiller-Couch
    and J. Dover Wilson, 1921*)

  27 bold beating] bull-baiting

II.3

  52–3 Mockwater] Make-water (*C. J. Sisson, 1954*)

III.2

  63 buttons] fortunes (*C. J. Sisson, 1954*)

II.3

  155 escape] (vncape F); uncouple; uncope (*Sir A. T.
    Quiller-Couch and J. Dover Wilson, 1921*); uncase
    (*C. J. Sisson, 1954*)

IV.2

  20 lines] lunes

V.5

  117 meet] mate (*Sir A. T. Quiller-Couch and J. Dover
    Wilson, 1921*)

Commentary

The act and scene divisions are those of the Folio. Biblical quotations are from the Bishops' Bible (1568, etc.), the official translation of Elizabeth's reign. Q refers to the Quarto text of *The Merry Wives of Windsor* (1602) and F to the text in the first Folio of 1623.

I.I

This opening scene is, for part of its course, something of a false start. It gives the impression that Shallow's complaint against Falstaff is going to be one of the play's main concerns. In fact, however, once the scene is over, nothing more is made of the matter. It is Falstaff's meeting with Mistress Ford and Mistress Page that launches the principal intrigue, and Evans's plan for a match between Slender and Anne Page that introduces the secondary action of the comedy. Nevertheless, Shakespeare knew what he was doing in beginning as he did. For an audience familiar with *Henry IV, Part I* the mere mention of Falstaff in the first speech would have been full of promise, catching their attention at once – a matter of prime importance on the open stage of the Elizabethan theatre, where there were no lights to go down. And, skilled man of the theatre that he was, Shakespeare would know that winning the interest of his audience at the outset was far more necessary than fulfilling all the expectations roused in doing it. He could rely on his failure to make

anything further of the Falstaff–Shallow relationship
going unnoticed in performance, provided that there
was other matter to take its place. Moreover, the
deer-stealing motif looks forward to the subsequent
action, where Falstaff seeks to steal those who are
dear to Page and Ford.

1 *Sir Hugh*: Parsons were normally addressed as 'Sir',
a title of respect in Shakespeare's England.
persuade me not: Don't try to dissuade me.

2 *Star-Chamber*: The Court of Star Chamber, so called
because the ceiling of the room in which it sat was
decorated with stars, tried cases which did not come
under the jurisdiction of the ordinary courts of law.
Offences such as riot and charges involving noblemen
came within its purview.

3 *abuse*: Wrong; ill-use.

4 *Esquire*: In Shakespeare's day this title meant that
the owner of it held a definite place in the social
hierarchy. He was immediately below a knight in
rank.

6 *Coram*: This word is a corrupt form of the Latin
'*Quorum*' ('of whom'). It was used to designate
certain justices whose presence was necessary to
constitute a bench of magistrates.

7 *cousin*: Kinsman. According to what Slender says at
III.4.38, Shallow is his uncle.
Custalorum: The *Custos Rotulorum*, of which
Custalorum is a corruption, was the keeper of the rolls,
the chief of the justices in a county, having in his
care the records of the sessions.

8 *Ratolorum*: Slender's version of *Rotulorum*.

9 *writes*: Designates; signs.
Armigero: Esquire; one entitled to bear heraldic arms.

10 *bill*: Bill of exchange; money order.
quittance: Receipt; acknowledgement of discharge
from debt.
obligation: Bond; contract.

11–12 *Ay, that I do . . . three hundred years*: Shallow means
that his family has borne arms for three centuries.

13 *hath*: Shakespeare on occasions uses this form of the third-person plural.

15 *give*: Display.
   luces: Pikes (the fresh-water fish).
   coat: Coat of arms.

17 *louses*: It is not clear whether this is a genuine mistake on the part of Evans, whose pronunciation of English is not his strong point, or whether he is punning.

18 *passant*: Walking (a heraldic term).
   familiar beast to man: Creature that is on a family footing with man. 'A louse is a man's companion' was a common proverb.

20–21 *The salt fish is an old coat*: Shallow seems to be alluding to Evans's pronunciation of 'coat' as 'cod', but the joke, if there is one, is by no means clear.

22 *quarter*: Add another family's coat of arms to my own.
   coʒ: Kinsman.

25 *Not a whit*: Not at all; not in the least.

26 *py'r lady*: By our lady (as Evans pronounces it). F reads *per-lady*.

27 *skirts*: Lower part of a coat or gown taking the form of four panels.

31 *atonements*: Reconciliations.

32 *Council*: Privy Council (sitting as the Court of Star Chamber).

33 *meet*: Fitting; proper.

35–6 *Take your viʒaments in*: Take account of; consider.

37 *O'my*: On my (colloquial).

39 *swort*: F reads *Sword*, but *swort* seems to be needed because Evans is quibbling on 'sword' and 'sort', meaning 'issue' or 'outcome'.

42 *George*: F reads *Thomas*, but as Page is called *George* whenever his name occurs elsewhere in the play the change seems necessary. It is quite possible that Shakespeare began by thinking of him as 'Thomas' and then changed his mind.

45 *small*: In a soprano voice.

46 *'orld*: Evans's pronunciation of 'world'; he habitually omits the initial 'w'.

just: Exactly.

48 *is*: Did. Evans has trouble with auxiliary verbs.

51 *pribbles and prabbles*: Empty chatter and petty quarrels. *prabbles* is Evans's version of 'brabbles', and *pribbles* a word of his own making.

54–5 *Did her grandsire leave her seven hundred pound*: F
allots this speech to Slender, but it is Shallow who
is more interested in Anne Page's fortune.

56 *is make her a petter penny*: Will provide her with
much more in addition.

57–8 *I know the young gentlewoman. She has good gifts*:
Like lines 54–5, these words are given to Slender in
F; but it is plain from what he says at 44 that he
has no real knowledge of Anne. The speech is therefore allotted to Shallow in this edition.

58 *gifts*: Qualities of mind and body.

59 *possibilities*: Prospects of inheriting wealth.

66 *your well-willers*: Those who wish you well.

72 *peradventures*: Perhaps.

72 *tell you another tale*: Have something further to say
to you.

78 *ill killed*: Not killed in the proper manner. There
seems to be a suggestion here that the deer from which
the venison came was one of those killed by Falstaff,
but nothing is made of it.

79 *la*: Indeed! (exclamation used to emphasize a conven-
tional phrase).

81 *By yea and no*: A mild oath.

83 *fallow*: Fawn-coloured.

84 *Cotsall*: The Cotswold Hills in Gloucestershire, a
great centre for coursing matches.

85 *judged*: Determined; fairly decided.

87 *'Tis your fault*: The meaning of this phrase is
disputed. Some think *fault* means 'misfortune', as it
does at III.3.206; others are of the opinion that it
means 'the check caused by a dog's losing the scent
of his quarry'. The latter explanation would seem
to be ruled out because greyhounds hunt by sight
not scent. To the present editor the most probable

meaning appears to be: 'You are mistaken; you are
in the wrong.' 'Fault' in the sense of 'mistake' is
common in Elizabethan English.

93–4 *I would I could do a good office between you*: Literally,
'I wish I could perform a good service between you',
meaning negotiate between you.

95 *a Christians*: Shakespeare's rendering of Evans's
Welsh accent.

97 *in some sort*: To some extent.

100 *at a word*: In short.

103 *of*: About.

106 *lodge*: House in a park or forest occupied by the
keeper.

108 *pin*: Trifle.
shall be answered: Must be atoned for.

109 *straight*: (1) Immediately; (2) straightforwardly.

112–13 *in counsel*: In private; in secret.

114 *Pauca verba*: Few words (Latin). Evans refers to two
Elizabethan proverbs: 'Few words show men wise'
and 'Few words are best'.
worts: (1) Words (as pronounced by Evans); (2)
cabbages (the sense in which Falstaff takes it).

116 *broke your head*: Drew blood by breaking the skin
of your head.
matter: Subject of complaint.

117 *matter*: (1) Matter of consequence; (2) pus.

118 *cony-catching*: Cheating; swindling (rogues' cant –
the dupe of a confidence trick being described as a
cony or rabbit).

119–20 *They carried me . . . my pocket*: This sentence is
taken from Q. That the copy for F, from which it
is omitted, must once have contained it, or something very like it, is made almost certain by Falstaff's
question to Pistol at 141: *did you pick Master Slender's
purse?* See An Account of the Text.

119 *carried*: Led; conducted.

121 *Banbury cheese*: A scornful allusion to Slender's figure
– Banbury cheeses being proverbially thin.

123 *Mephostophilus*: The name of the devil in Marlowe's

play *Doctor Faustus*; used here as a term of abuse.

125 *Slice*: (1) Slice of cheese; (2) cut to pieces.

humour: Temperament; mood. The word 'humour' seems to have been badly overworked in the last decade of the sixteenth century. Through Nym, who uses it ad nauseam with no sense of its original meaning, Shakespeare appears to be satirizing the excessive use of it.

Pauca, pauca: Cf. note to 114. Sword strokes rather than words are implied here.

130 *fidelicet*: videlicet (Latin for 'namely').

134 *prief*: Brief; summary; abstract.

139 *The tevil and his tam*: Evans means 'The devil and his dam [mother]', as an explosion of frustration at Pistol's phrase.

143 *great chamber*: Most impressive room of an elite house. Slender is boasting by calling it his own.

144 *seven groats in mill-sixpences*: A groat was worth fourpence; and a mill-sixpence was a sixpence made by a mechanical process in a stamping mill, instead of being hammered into shape as coins had been in the past. Slender seems rather confused about it all, because *seven groats* amount to two shillings and fourpence, a sum that is not divisible by six.

144–5 *Edward shovel-boards*: Old broad shillings, dating from the reign of Edward VI (1547–53), used in the game of shovelboard, in which coins were sent sliding along a polished board into holes at the end of it. Worn smooth with age, shillings issued under Edward VI would have been well adapted for use in this game, and, judging by the price that Slender has paid for his, would seem to have been much prized on this account.

146 *Yed*: Shortened form of the name Edward, like 'Ned'.

148 *it is false, if it is*: Evans means to say 'he is false, if he is'.

149 *mountain-foreigner*: Pistol's elaborately abusive term for 'Welshman'.

150 *combat challenge of*: Challenge to trial by combat.

latten bilbo: Man whose sword (*bilbo*) is made of brass (*latten*).

151 *labras*: Lips. Pistol's Latin is not very good – the word should be '*labra*'.

154 *Be advised*: Take my advice; think carefully.
pass good humours: Make the best of it, behave properly.

155 *Marry trap with you*: The precise meaning of this cant phrase, which occurs only here, is not known. Dr Johnson takes it to be 'an exclamation of insult, when a man is caught in his own trap'; others have suggested that it means 'be off with you'. It is clear from the context that it expresses contempt.

155–6 *run the nuthook's humour on me*: Threaten me with the constable. *nuthook* was a cant term for the catchpole or constable.

156 *very note of it*: Truth of the matter. The reference is to a musical note; and the literal meaning is 'the right tune of it'.

157 *he in the red face*: Meaning Bardolph.

160 *Scarlet and John*: Will Scarlet and Little John were two of Robin Hood's 'merry men'. The main allusion here is to Bardolph's scarlet complexion, but Falstaff also seems to be suggesting that Bardolph combines the thieving propensities of both the outlaws.

162 *five sentences*: Bardolph's blundering version of 'five senses'.

164 *fap*: Drunk (West Midland dialect).
cashiered: Relieved of his cash; robbed. Normally in Shakespeare's work 'cashier' has its usual meaning of 'discard from service' (cf. its use at I.3.6); but here Bardolph appears to be punning on a compound word of his own devising, 'cash-sheared', a rather neat equivalent for 'fleeced'. Bardolph relies, of course, on Slender's not understanding what he says.

165 *conclusions passed the careers*: The things that finally happened to him went far beyond what he had planned; matters got out of hand. The word 'career'

is employed here, it would seem, in the sense of a fixed course laid out for a gallop.

166 *in Latin*: Slender means that Bardolph's use of thieves' cant was 'Greek to him' then, just as it is now.

167 *but*: Except.

171 *'udge*: Judge (as pronounced by Evans).
  mind: Sentiment; intention.

179 *He kisses her*: This direction is adapted from Q, which reads: *Syr Iohn kisses her*; but it is implicit in F's *By your leaue good Mistris*, for kissing, as Erasmus noticed with pleasure on his first visit to England in 1499, was the usual form of greeting between a man and a woman.

181 *to*: For.

183 *had rather*: Would rather.

183–4 *Book of Songs and Sonnets*: Slender is referring to one of the many anthologies of love poetry that were available in Shakespeare's day. The most famous of them was the *Songes and Sonettes* published by Richard Tottel in 1557 and frequently reprinted. Slender needs it, of course, in order to cull from it some choice expressions of devotion that he can use on Anne Page. Courtly compliments do not come readily to his simple mind.

189 *Allhallowmas*: All Saints' Day, 1 November.

190 *Michaelmas*: St Michael's Day, 29 September. Simple, it is worth noticing, characteristically gets the two feasts the wrong way round and halves the interval between them in the process.

191 *stay*: Wait.

192 *Marry*: A mild oath of interjection, coming originally from the name of the Virgin Mary.

193 *tender*: Proposal of marriage.
  afar off: Indirectly; in a roundabout manner.

195 *reasonable*: Fair-minded. Slender is under the impression that Evans's *tender* is for some kind of accommodation between him and his enemies.

199 *motions*: Proposals.

203 *country*: District; part of the country.

          simple though: As sure as.

210 *demands*: Requests.

212 *divers*: Some; several.

213 *parcel*: Part.

214 *carry your good will to*: Feel affection for; love.

219 *Got's lords and his ladies*: This strange oath appears to be one of Evans's inventions.

220 *possitable*: Evans's version of 'positively'.

220–21 *carry her your desires towards her*: Direct your affection towards her. The curious expression *carry her* may be yet another instance of Evans's imperfect command of English, or it may be his pronunciation of 'career', meaning 'gallop'.

222 *upon good dowry*: On the strength of a good dowry being forthcoming. The bride's dowry, a normal part of the marriage settlement in Shakespeare's England, was the money and estate that she brought with her to her husband. It was, of course, provided by her father.

226 *conceive me*: Understand me; realize my meaning.

230 *decrease*: Slender means 'increase' and is alluding to the proverb 'Marry first and love will come after'.

234 *dissolved*: Slender's mistake for 'resolved'.
          dissolutely: For 'resolutely', as Evans notices, missing the previous error over 'resolved'.

235 *fall*: Fault; mistake.

240 *Would I*: I wish I.

244 *wait on him*: Join him.

245 *'Od's*: God's.

250 *attends*: Awaits.

252 *sirrah*: Sir (used only in addressing social inferiors or boys).
          for all: Although.

252–3 *wait upon*: Serve; attend.

254 *beholding*: Beholden; under obligation.

256 *till my mother be dead*: Slender's mother evidently curbs his desire to cut a figure.
          what though: What of it; no matter.

264–5 *playing at sword and dagger with a master of fence*:

Fencing with a rapier in one hand and a dagger in the other was introduced into England in the last decade of the sixteenth century and became very fashionable. Italian fencing masters set up schools in London. Mercutio, in *Romeo and Juliet* (II.4.19–35), pours scorn on the craze and on the technical terms belonging to it.

265 *master of fence*: Fencing master.

veneys: Bouts.

265–6 *a dish of stewed prunes*: The prize for the winner. Slender, without being aware of it, is speaking bawdily, since *stewed prunes* was a common term for prostitutes.

266 *by my troth*: By my faith (a mild oath).

268 *i'th'*: In the (colloquial).

270 *the sport*: Bear-baiting, in which a chained bear was attacked by dogs.

270–71 *quarrel at*: Object to; take exception to. Slender is evidently a puritan of sorts, for it was the Puritans who, to their credit, disapproved of the barbarous sport of bear-baiting.

275 *Sackerson*: Name of a famous bear belonging to the Paris Garden, a well-known bear-baiting ring not far from the Globe Theatre.

277 *passed*: Surpassed all belief; beggared description.

278 *ill-favoured*: Ugly-looking.

283 *By cock and pie*: An oath of asseveration. *Cock* is a perversion of 'God', and *pie* a late medieval word meaning 'directory for divine service'.

shall not choose: Must.

288 *keep on*: Go ahead.

289–90 *do you that wrong*: Insult you in that way; be so impolite to you.

292 *I'll rather be unmannerly than troublesome*: Slender is resorting to proverbs again; 'Better be unmannerly than troublesome' was a common saying of the time.

I.2

1 *Caius*: Pronounced to rhyme with 'try us'.

3 *dry nurse*: Housekeeper.

4 *laundry*: Laundress.

7 *altogether's acquaintance*: Is thoroughly acquainted.

11 *pippins*: Apples.

   cheese: This is the reading of both F and Q at this
   point. Most editors emend to 'seese' in order to
   bring the pronunciation into line with that indicated
   by F's *Seese* at V.5.139.

I.3

2 *bully rook*: Brave fellow.

4 *turn away*: Discard; dismiss.

6 *wag*: Go off; go their ways.

8 *sit at*: Live at the rate of; am spending.

9 *Thou'rt*: Thou art (colloquial).

   Keisar: Emperor (old form of 'Kaiser').

   Pheazar: Person of overwhelming presence. This
   word is either the Host's version of 'vizier' or a
   word of his own making derived from the verb
   'pheeze' meaning 'frighten away'.

10 *entertain*: Employ.

   draw: Draw liquor.

   tap: Serve as a tapster.

11 *Hector*: The Trojan hero, often cited in Shakespeare's
   works as the model of valour.

14 *froth*: Create a large head of foam on a mug of beer
   in order to cheat the customer with short measure.

   lime: Adulterate wine with lime in order to make it
   sparkle. Cf. *Henry IV, Part I*, II.4.120, where Falstaff
   says to the drawer Francis: 'You rogue, here's lime
   in this sack too.' This reading is taken from Q. The
   F version is *liue*, which makes good sense but does
   not carry the overtone of 'cheating' which seems
   necessary in this context.

14 *I am at a word*: I mean what I say; with me it's a
   case of no sooner said than done.

16 *An old cloak makes a new jerkin*: An adaptation of
   the proverb 'His old cloak will buy you a new kirtle'.

   jerkin: Close-fitting jacket, worn by men in
   Shakespeare's day.

19 *Hungarian wight*: Beggarly fellow. 'Hungarian' was

an Elizabethan cant term for 'beggarly' through its
punning association with 'hungry'.

spigot: Peg (in the tap of a barrel).

20 *gotten in drink*: Begotten when his parents were drunk.

20–21 *Is not the humour conceited*: Isn't that a clever turn
of phrase? Isn't that an ingenious witticism?

22 *acquit*: Rid; freed.

tinderbox: Alluding to Bardolph's red nose and flaming
complexion.

23 *open*: Obvious; easily detected.

25 *good humour*: Right trick of the trade.

at a minute's rest: In the space of a minute. The
emendation of *minute's* to 'minim's' is an attractive
one; but both F and Q read *minutes*.

26 *Convey*: Steal (thieves' cant).

it call: Call it. Pistol is much given to inversion.
His syntax, like his verse, owes much to the ranting
plays of the period 1570–90.

27 *fico*: (1) Fig; (2) female genitals. This Italian word
was used as an insult and was commonly accompanied by an obscene gesture.

28 *out at heels*: (1) Penniless, destitute (the sense in
which Falstaff uses the phrase); (2) in a state where
the heels of the shoes or stockings are worn through
(the sense in which Pistol takes it).

29 *kibes*: Chilblains.

30 *cony-catch*: Take to cheating.

31 *shift*: Resort to stratagems; live by my wits.

32 *Young ravens must have food*: Pistol is alluding to
the proverb 'Small birds must have meat'. The *Young
ravens* he has in mind are, of course, himself and
Nym.

34 *ken*: Know.

wight: Person.

of substance good: Well off; a man of means.

35 *about*: (1) Engaged in, planning (the sense in which
Falstaff means it); (2) about the waist, in circum-
ference (the sense in which Pistol takes it).

40 *entertainment*: (1) Kindness, readiness to meet

advances; (2) a source of provision.

discourses: Is affable; talks with familiarity.

41 *carves*: Minces her words; speaks affectedly.

leer of invitation: Inviting glance; come-hither look.

41–2 *construe the action of her familiar style*: Interpret the
meaning of her familiarities of speech and behaviour.

42 *hardest voice*: Harshest judgement; most severe interpretation. There is an elaborate grammatical pun in
this sentence turning on the use of *construe* and *voice*.

45 *will*: (1) Intention; (2) sexual desires; (3) legal will.

46 *honesty*: Chastity.

into English: There may well be a pun here on the
verb 'ingle', meaning 'to cuddle'. Pistol would then
be saying that Falstaff has transformed Mistress Ford
from an honest woman into one who is now 'ingle-
ish' – ready for and responsive to his advances.

47 *The anchor is deep*: The precise meaning of this
remark is not known, though Nym clearly thinks it
very clever. The likeliest interpretation is 'This is a
deep plot'.

Will that humour pass: What do you think of that
for a neat phrase?

49 *legion*: F reads *legend*; but most editors prefer *legion*,
which is supported by the reading *legians* in Q.

angels: This is one of the commonest of Elizabethan
puns. An 'angel' was a gold coin, bearing the figure
of Michael the archangel and worth about ten
shillings.

50 *As many devils entertain*: Let as many devils do battle
with them. Pistol implies that Falstaff is a legion of
devils in himself.

To her, boy: Cry of encouragement to a dog engaged
in hunting.

51 *The humour rises . . . the angels*: The joke and the
plot are becoming more intense.

51–2 *Humour me the angels*: Both 'Make more of the joke
about angels' and 'Bring me the angels' – Nym wants
money, if he can get it, as well as the joke, and is

also asking for the assistance (the 'humour' of the angels).

53 *writ me*: Written, I'd have you notice. The *me* (ethic dative) is really superfluous, but it is added by the speaker – Nym does it in the previous line – as a means of calling attention to himself and adding colour and liveliness to what he is saying.

54 *even now*: Just now.

good eyes: Approving glances.

55 *parts*: Appearance.

œillades: Looks of love. F reads *illiads*, a form that represents the Elizabethan pronunciation of this word, newly borrowed from the French.

60 *course o'er*: Examine; run her eye over.

62 *burning-glass*: Lens used to concentrate the sun's rays so as to set fire to something.

64 *Guiana*: Sir Walter Raleigh had made an expedition to Guiana in 1595 and had published an account of his discoveries in the following year, emphasizing the wealth and fertility of the land.

cheaters: (1) Escheators (officers of the Crown, whose task was to notify the Exchequer when lands fell due to the King); (2) sharpers.

70 *Sir Pandarus*: By Shakespeare's day Pandarus, the uncle of Cressida in Chaucer's *Troilus and Criseyde* who brings the lovers together, had become the type of the pander, a word that derives from his name. It is in this role that he is portrayed in Shakespeare's own *Troilus and Cressida*.

71 *And by my side wear steel*: And still keep my reputation as a soldier.

73 *haviour of reputation*: Appearance of respectability.

74 *tightly*: Safely (like a 'tight' ship).

75 *pinnace*: Small fast-sailing ship, often in attendance on a larger ship.

76 *avaunt*: Be off with you; be gone.

77 *o'th'hoof*: On foot (colloquial contraction of 'on the hoof').

pack: Be off; take yourselves off.

78 *humour*: Fashion. This is the Q reading. F has '*honor*', which does not give a satisfactory apposition to *French thrift*.

79 *French thrift*: Perhaps an allusion to the fashion of discarding several servingmen and replacing them by a single French page.

skirted: Wearing a coat with full skirts

80 *gripe*: Seize on.

gourd and fullam: Kinds of false dice used by cheaters.

holds: Hold good; can still be relied on. Shakespeare often uses the form of the third-person singular when two or more singular nouns precede the verb.

81 *high and low*: False dice weighted in such a way as to throw high or low numbers as required.

82 *Tester*: Sixpenny piece.

83 *Phrygian Turk*: A term of abuse – the Turks being the inveterate enemies of Christendom.

84 *operations*: Plans (probably Nym's version of 'inspirations').

85 *welkin*: Sky.

86 *With wit or steel*: By ingenuity or by force.

humours: Methods.

87 *discuss*: Disclose; make known.

87, 88 *Page . . . Ford*: These are both Q readings. F reads '*Ford . . . Page*', which does not correspond to what happens in II.1. Nym's speech at 92 would, however, be much more appropriate if it were about Ford. It could well be that at this stage Shakespeare meant Nym to address Ford, and Pistol Page, but then changed his mind.

88 *eke*: Also.

90 *prove*: Test the fidelity of.

92 *Page*: F reads *Ford*.

93 *deal with*: Make use of; resort to.

93 *possess*: Fill.

yellowness: Jealousy.

94 *the revolt of mine*: My revolt.

95 *Mars*: Roman god of war.

I.4

5 *old*: Plentiful.

7 *posset*: A drink made of hot milk curdled with wine or ale.

8 *soon at night*: As soon as night comes.

8–9 *sea-coal fire*: Fire made with mined coal brought by sea from Newcastle.

11 *withal*: With.

12 *breed-bate*: Troublemaker.

13 *something*: Somewhat.
   peevish: Silly; foolish.

16 *for fault of*: For lack of; in default of.

22 *Cain-coloured*: Reddish-yellow (the traditional colour of Cain's beard in tapestries). *Caine colourd* is the reading of F; Q has *kane colored*, which some editors prefer, taking it to mean 'yellowish' (the colour of a cane).

23 *softly-sprighted*: Gentle-spirited.

24 *as tall a man of his hands*: As brave a man in action (a proverbial phrase).

25 *between this and his head*: In these parts (another proverbial phrase).

26 *warrener*: Keeper of a warren (piece of land used for breeding and preserving game, especially rabbits).

35 *Out, alas*: An expression of dismay.

36 *shent*: Scolded; rebuked.

37 *closet*: Private room; study.

40 *doubt he be*: Fear he is.

42 *And down, down, adown-a, etc.*: A popular refrain sung to many songs of the time – cf. Ophelia's use of it in *Hamlet*, IV.5.172–3. The implication of *etc.* would seem to be that Mistress Quickly goes on repeating the refrain until Caius interrupts her.

43 *toys*: Frivolous trifling songs.

45 *Do intend*: Do you hear (French '*entendre*').

48 *horn-mad*: Furious with rage (like a mad bull prepared to horn anyone).

49–50 *Ma foi . . . la grande affaire*: By my faith, it is very hot (French). I'm going to the court – important business.

52 *Oui, mette-le au mon pocket. Dépêche*: Yes, put it in my pocket. Hurry.

56 *Jack*: A term of abuse.

60 *trot*: Troth (as pronounced by Caius).
   'Od's me: God save me.

60–61 *Qu'ai-je oublié*: What have I forgotten?

61 *simples*: Medicines made from herbs. Though Caius does not yet know it, there is indeed a Simple in his closet.

64 *mad*: Angry; mad with rage.

65 *diable*: Devil.

66 *Larron*: Thief.

68 *content*: Calm; quiet.

73 *phlegmatic*: Mistress Quickly's mistake for 'choleric'.

74 *of an*: On an.

85 *put my finger in the fire, and need not*: Meddle where there is no need to (a proverbial expression).

86 *buille*: Fetch.

89 *throughly*: Thoroughly; really.
   moved: Angered.

90 *melancholy*: Mistress Quickly means 'choleric' (cf. 73), but she invariably hits on any 'humour' but the right one.

91 *you*: For you; since you ask me.

94–5 *dress meat*: Prepare food.

96 *charge*: Burden; load of work.

98 *avised*: Aware.

105 *jack'nape*: Caius's version of 'jackanapes', meaning 'tame monkey'.

106 *gar*: Caius's pronunciation of 'God'.
    troat: Throat (as pronounced by Caius).

107 *make*: Interfere.

109 *cut all his two stones*: Castrate him.
    stones: Testicles.

112 *no matter-a ver dat*: Never mind that.

114 *Jack*: Knavish; contemptible.

115 *measure our weapon*: Act as umpire in our duel.

118–19 *What the good-year*: The meaning of this expression has not been satisfactorily explained, though here

something like 'What the deuce' seems to be
intended.

123 *An*: (1) Anne; (2) an.

128 *trow*: Wonder.

    Come near: Enter.

135 *honest*: Chaste.

    gentle: Full of good qualities.

    your friend: Favourably disposed towards you.

141 *Have not your worship*: Mistress Quickly is mixing
two constructions: 'Have not you' and 'Has not your
worship'.

145 *it is such another Nan*: Nan (diminutive form of
'Anne') is such a merry girl.

    detest: Mistress Quickly's version of 'protest'.

147 *but*: Except.

148 *allicholy*: A corruption of 'melancholy'.

149 *go to*: Come.

151 *voice*: Good word; support.

155 *confidence*: For 'conference'.

159–60 *Out upon't*: An exclamation of dismay.

II.I

1 *'scaped*: Escaped; been free from.

2 *holiday time*: Festive time; prime.

5 *precisian*: Austere spiritual adviser; puritan minister.
Falstaff is thinking of *Love* as a king who asks the
opinion of *Reason* but does not make him a member
of his privy council.

7 *sympathy*: Agreement; common ground between us.

8 *sack*: The general name for a class of white wines
imported from Spain and the Canaries.

19 *Herod of Jewry*: Audacious villain. In the miracle
plays, which were still being acted occasionally in
the late sixteenth century, Herod was portrayed as
an out-and-out villain, delighting in his own wickedness.

21 *What an unweighed behaviour*: What unguarded
action; what ill-judged piece of behaviour.

22 *Flemish drunkard*: The Flemings were often cited (in

the England of Shakespeare's day) as the most
drunken race in Europe.

22–3 *with the devils' name*: Exclamation which has the
effect of linking Falstaff to the devil.

23 *conversation*: Behaviour in his company.

24 *assay me*: Assail my virtue with words; address me
with proposals of love.

25 *should I say*: Can I have said.

26 *exhibit*: Propose.

27 *putting down*: Suppression (possibly with bawdy
implications).

29 *puddings*: Sausages; stuffing.

30 *Trust me*: Believe me.

33 *ill*: (1) Annoyed, savage (the sense in which Mistress
Page means it); (2) unattractive (the sense in which
Mistress Ford takes it).

34–5 *have to show*: Have something (the letter) to show.

42 *respect*: Consideration.
come to: Attain; achieve.
honour: Rank; position of dignity.

44 *Dispense with*: Disregard; have done with.

45 *go to hell*: For committing adultery.

48 *hack*: The precise sense of this word is doubtful,
but, when its use here is related to its use at IV.1.61,
it seems likely that some meaning such as 'make a
hackney (prostitute) of a woman' is intended. There
could also be a quibble on 'hack', meaning 'strike
with a weapon', employed with sexual connotations.

49 *article of thy gentry*: Character of your rank.

50 *burn daylight*: Waste time; engage in futilities (proverbial).

52–3 *make difference of*: Discriminate between.

53 *liking*: Physical appearance; looks.

55 *uncomeliness*: Improper behaviour.

56 *disposition*: Character.
gone to: Been in keeping with; accorded with.

57 *adhere*: Agree; accord.

59 *Greensleeves*: A popular love song, sometimes associated with harlotry in Shakespeare's day, to the tune

of which numerous lyrics were set.

trow: Wonder.

62 *entertain him*: Engage his thoughts; fill his mind.

67 *ill opinions*: Falstaff's belief that the wives are light women.

68 *inherit*: Take possession (of Falstaff's offer).

69–73 *I warrant . . . us two*: Referring to the way authors dedicated their work to different individuals in the hope of securing patronage from the greatest number of people.

72 *out of doubt*: Indubitably.

73 *press*: (1) Printing-press; (2) pressure of sexual intercourse.

74 *Mount Pelion*: Mountain in Thessaly. In classical mythology the Titans, when they rebelled against the gods, sought to reach the top of Olympus by piling Mount Ossa on Pelion. In revenge the gods buried them under the mountains they had sought to move.

75 *turtles*: Turtle-doves (proverbially true to their mates).

80 *wrangle*: Quarrel.

honesty: Chastity.

entertain: Treat.

81 *withal*: With.

82 *strain*: Tendency; quality.

83 *boarded*: Accosted; made advances to (the figurative use of 'to board' in the nautical sense).

fury: Impetuous fashion.

85 *under my hatches*: Below deck, extending the bawdy puns about sailing.

88 *comfort*: Encouragement.

89 *a fine-baited delay*: Delaying tactics full of tempting allurements.

91 *villainy*: Sharp practice.

92–3 *chariness of our honesty*: Scrupulous integrity of our good names.

95–6 *good man*: Husband.

103 *curtal dog*: Dog that has had its tail docked (with

the result that it is no longer a 'true' dog but an unreliable one).

104 *affects*: Loves; feels an inclination for.

107 *one with another*: Indiscriminately; promiscuously.

108 *gallimaufry*: Whole lot.

   perpend: Consider; take note.

110 *liver*: Supposed to be the seat of love in Shakespeare's time.

   Prevent: Take counter-measures.

111 *Sir Actaeon*: Actaeon, in classical mythology, while out hunting, accidentally came upon Diana, the goddess of chastity, as she was bathing. To revenge this intrusion on her privacy, the goddess turned him into a stag and had him torn to pieces by his own hounds. Actaeon thus became identified with the horned man, the cuckold.

   he: This superfluous pronoun is added for emphasis.

   Ringwood: A traditional name for a hound in England.

112 *the name*: The name 'Actaeon', signifying 'cuckold'.

114 *horn*: Mark of the cuckold.

115 *foot*: Walk.

116 *cuckoo-birds do sing*: The song of the cuckoo, which lays its eggs in the nests of other birds, was thought of as a warning to the cuckold or potential cuckold.

117 *Away*: Come away.

119 *find out*: Inquire into.

121–2 *should have borne*: Was expected to bear; was ordered to bear.

123 *it shall bite upon my necessity*: It will cut when I need it to.

127–8 *and there's the humour of it*: These words, which are not found in F, have been added from Q. Their inclusion seems necessary so that Page can pick them up and comment on them in his speech after Nym has made his exit.

129 *'a*: He (colloquial).

130 *his*: Its.

132 *affecting*: Affected.

135 *Cataian*: Scoundrel; sharper (literally, a native of

Cathay, the old name for China).

144 *crotchets*: Strange notions; queer ideas.

146 *Have with you*: I'm coming.

151 *fit it*: Fit the part; be the right person for the job.

162 *offer it*: Try to do such a thing.

163 *yoke*: Pair.

167 *I like it never the better for that*: I don't like it any
     better, knowing that.
     lie: Lodge.

169 *voyage*: As a metaphor for his seduction.

170 *turn her loose to him*: Leave her free to do as she
     likes with him (a farmyard reference to the turning
     loose of a cow and a bull in the same pasture).

171–2 *lie on my head*: (1) Be my responsibility; (2) appear
     on my head (in the form of the cuckold's horns).

173 *misdoubt*: Have doubts about the character of.

174 *turn them together*: Carries on the farmyard allusion
     of *turn her loose to him*.
     confident: Trusting.

181 *Cavaliero justice*: Gallant justice (from Spanish
     '*caballero*', meaning 'gentleman trained in arms').

182–3 *Good even and twenty*: Good day and twenty such
     greetings. 'Even' was used in Elizabethan English
     for any time after noon. Nevertheless, there would
     seem to be a mistake here, because Mistress Page's
     remark *You'll come to dinner, George?* (146–7) makes
     it plain that the time is morning, since dinner, the
     main meal of the day, was eaten about eleven a.m.

191 *had the measuring of their weapons*: Been made umpire
     in their duel.

192 *contrary*: Different.

197–9 *None, I protest . . . for a jest*: In F this speech is
     allotted to Shallow; but Q, while printing a garbled
     version of it, rightly gives it to Ford.

197 *protest*: Declare; assure you.
     pottle: Two-quart tankard.

197–8 *burnt sack*: Mulled sack; white wine heated over a
     fire.

198 *recourse*: Access.

199 *Brook*: This, though misprinted as *Rrooke* on this
occasion, is the reading of Q here and on all subsequent occasions when the name is used. F has *Broome*
throughout; but it is evident that *Brook* is the original name. See An Account of the Text.

202 *Ameers*: Emirs. F reads *An-heires*, which makes no
sense. *Ameers* has been adopted in this edition because
it is in keeping with the Host's fondness for high-
flown titles such as *Caesar, Keisar, and Pheazar* (I.3.9),
but the emendation 'mynheers' (Dutch for 'sirs') is
equally plausible.

207 *you . . . your*: Used indefinitely, not with reference
to persons present.
stand on: Make much of; attach great importance to.
distance: Regulation space that had to be kept between
two fencers.
passes: Lunges.
stoccadoes: Thrusts.

209–10 *long sword*: This heavy weapon had gone out of
fashion by the time the play was written, having
been ousted by the lighter and more deadly rapier.

210 *made you four tall fellows skip*: Made four lusty fellows
skip, I can tell you. The *you* here, meaning 'for you',
gives extra emphasis to the boast.

212 *wag*: Go.

213 *Have with you*: I'll go along with you.

215 *secure*: Over-confident.

215–16 *stands so firmly on his wife's frailty*: Trusts so firmly
in what may really be frailty in his wife.

218 *made*: Did; got up to.

219 *sound*: Measure the depth of; search into.

220 *honest*: Chaste.
lose: Waste.

II.2

4 *I will retort the sum in equipage*: This line, stamped
with Pistol's characteristic idiom, is only to be found
in Q, where it appears as line 2 in response to Falstaff's
Ile not lend thee a penny. It is included in this edition
because it completes the dramatic effect of Pistol's

speech. Pistol begins with a brag, proclaiming his
independence, but then changes his tune, offering to
pay back.

4 *retort*: Repay (in Pistol's inflated jargon).

in equipage: The normal meaning of this term is 'in
military array'; but Pistol seems to think it means
'in equal payments' on the instalment plan.

6 *lay my countenance to pawn*: Borrow money on the
strength of my patronage of you.

grated upon: Pestered; importuned.

8 *coach-fellow*: Companion; yoke-fellow.

9 *grate*: Prison bars.

geminy of: Pair of; twin.

11 *tall*: Brave.

12 *the handle of her fan*: Fans at the time when the play
was written often had very long handles made of
gold, silver or ivory.

took't: Swore; took an oath.

15 *Reason*: With good reason.

17 *short knife*: The cutpurse's tool.

18 *throng*: Cutpurses prefer to operate where there is a
crowd.

Pickt-hatch: A disreputable district of London.

19 *stand upon*: Become punctilious over; quibble about.

20 *unconfinable*: Limitless; infinite.

21–2 *terms of my honour precise*: My honour unstained.

22 *I, I, I*: This is the reading of F. Most editors emend
to 'Ay, ay, I', because 'I' is the normal spelling of
'Ay', as well as of 'I', in F. In this case, however,
the change seems unnecessary, since Falstaff is making
the most of the contrast between himself and Pistol.

22–3 *leaving . . . on the left hand*: Disregarding.

24 *fain*: Obliged; compelled.

shuffle: Resort to shifts.

hedge: Prevaricate; become evasive.

lurch: Steal.

25 *yet you, you rogue*: F reads *yet, you Rogue*, which
editors render as 'yet you, rogue', assuming that the
comma is misplaced. To the present editor it seems

far more likely that the compositor, confronted by two consecutive 'you's, overlooked the first one. Falstaff has already called Pistol *you rogue* twice in this speech.

ensconce: Hide; find protective covering for.

25–6 *cat-a-mountain*: Wildcat; ferocious.

26 *red-lattice*: Ale-house. Lattices painted red were the sign of an ale-house.

27 *beating*: Battering (like blows).

29 *relent*: Comply; give way.

34 *an't*: If it.

39 *vouchsafe*: This word, as Falstaff points out in his answer, is used improperly by Mistress Quickly, since it implies the granting of something to an inferior in rank by a superior.

46 *on*: Say on; continue.

59 *canaries*: Precisely what Mistress Quickly means by this word is not known, though something like 'state of excitement' must be intended. She appears to be confusing 'quandary' with 'canary', the name of a lively Spanish dance and of a light sweet wine from the Canary Islands.

65 *rushling*: Rustling.

66 *alligant*: Mistress Quickly seems to be muddling 'eloquent' and possibly 'elegant' with 'alicant', a Spanish wine made at Alicante.

70 *angels*: Gold coins bearing the figure of the archangel Michael.

defy: Despise; reject.

71 *sort*: Manner.

74 *pensioners*: Gentlemen of the royal bodyguard.

77 *she-Mercury*: Messenger (Mercury being the messenger of the gods in classical mythology).

80 *gives you to notify*: Bids you take notice.

81 *absence*: Mistress Quickly's version of 'absent'.

84 *wot*: Know.

87 *frampold*: Disagreeable.

92 *messenger*: For 'message'.

94 *fartuous*: for 'virtuous'.

100 *charms*: Spells; magic powers.

103 *part*: Personal qualities of mind and body.

104 *for't*: For it (colloquial).

111 *of all loves*: For love's sake (a phrase of strong entreaty).

112 *infection*: For 'affection'.

115 *list*: Pleases.

118 *no remedy*: Beyond all question.

122 *nay-word*: Password; watchword.
     that: So that; in order that.

128 *yet*: Still.

131 *punk*: Harlot; strumpet.
     Cupid's carriers: Cupid's messengers (Cupid being the god of love in classical mythology).

132 *fights*: Screens used to conceal and protect the crew of a vessel during a naval engagement.

133 *ocean whelm*: Let the ocean overwhelm; let the ocean drown.

136 *look after*: Look lovingly on.

138 *grossly*: (1) Clumsily, obviously; (2) by a fat man.
     so: So long as; provided that.
     fairly: Successfully.

141 *would fain*: Much desires to.

142–3 *draught of sack*: Cup of Spanish wine.

149 *encompassed*: Got round; outwitted.
     via: Go on (a word of encouragement to a horse or soldiers).

152 *make bold*: Presume; venture.
     so little preparation: So unexpectedly and with so little ceremony.

154 *What's your will*: What do you want?

155 *Give us leave*: Leave us alone.
     drawer: Person who draws beer – the tapster or barman.

160–61 *charge you*: Cause you expense.

163 *unseasoned*: Ill-timed; unseasonable.

164 *if money go before, all ways do lie open*: A common proverb.

165 *on*: Go forward; march ahead.

168 *carriage*: Burden.

177 *discover*: Reveal; disclose.

181 *register*: Record; list; catalogue.

182 *sith*: Since.

189–90 *observance*: Reverence; deference; dutiful attention.

190 *engrossed opportunities*: Seized every opportunity.
fee'd: Purchased.

193–4 *would have given*: Would like to be given; would like
as a present.

197 *meed*: Reward.

201–2 *Love like a shadow . . . what pursues*: An adaptation
of the proverb 'Love, like a shadow, flies one following and pursues one fleeing'.

201 *substance*: (1) True affection; (2) money, wealth.

208 *quality*: Nature; kind.

209–11 *Like a fair house . . . I erected it*: A building
erected on another man's land belonged legally to
him.

214 *honest*: Chaste.

215 *enlargeth her mirth so far*: Gives such free scope to
her sense of fun.

215–16 *there is shrewd construction made of her*: Her behaviour is open to malicious interpretation; she has a
bad reputation.

218–19 *of great admittance*: Admitted freely into the best of
company.

219 *authentic*: Entitled to respect.

220 *allowed*: Approved of; praised.

221 *preparations*: Accomplishments.

225 *of it*: For it.

226 *amiable*: Amorous.
honesty: Chastity.

229 *apply well to*: Fit in with; be consistent with.

232 *dwells so securely*: Stands so confidently.

233 *folly*: Wantonness.

235 *against*: Directly at (like the sun).
detection: Evidence of infidelity.

236 *had*: Would have (subjunctive).
instance: Evidence, precedent.

238 *ward*: Guard; defence.

239 *other her defences*: Other defences she has.

247 *Want*: Lack; go short of.

254 *speed*: Succeed; fare.

259 *wittolly*: Cuckoldy.

259–60 *for the which*: On account of which.

260 *well-favoured*: Good-looking; attractive.

262 *harvest-home*: Profit gathered.

265 *mechanical*: Base; vulgar (originally 'one engaged in manual labour').

    salt-butter: Cheap-living; cheese-paring (salt-butter, imported from Flanders, being cheaper than English butter).

267 *meteor*: Regarded as an ominous portent in Shakespeare's day.

268 *predominate*: Be in the ascendancy (an astrological term, developing the idea already present in *meteor*).

270 *soon at night*: This very night.

270–71 *aggravate his style*: Add to his title (by turning him from a knave into a cuckold).

273 *Epicurean*: Lecherous; sensual.

275 *improvident*: Rash and baseless.

280–81 *stand under the adoption of abominable terms*: Suffer being called detestable names.

282–3 *Amaimon . . . Lucifer . . . Barbason*: Names of devils. Amaimon and Lucifer are coupled together by Falstaff in *Henry IV, Part I* (II.4.329–30).

283 *additions*: Titles.

284 *Wittol*: Contented cuckold.

285 *secure*: Over-confident.

287–8 *a Fleming . . . Parson Hugh . . . an Irishman*: Flemings were proverbially fond of butter, Welshmen of cheese, and the Irish of strong liquor.

289 *aqua-vitae*: Spirits such as brandy and whisky.

    walk: Lead or ride (a horse) at walking pace.

295 *detect*: Expose.

296 *about*: Set about; go about.

297 *Fie*: An exclamation of disapproval.

II.3

11 *herring*: 'Dead as a herring' was already a stock phrase in Shakespeare's day.

17 *Save*: God save.

21 *foin*: Thrust (in fencing).

22 *traverse*: Move back and forth.

23 *pass*: Employ.
   punto: Thrust with the point of the sword.
   stock: Thrust with the point of the dagger.
   reverse: Backhand blow with the sword.
   distance: Interval of space to be kept between two fencers.

24 *montant*: Upright thrust or blow.

25 *Francisco*: Frenchman.
   Aesculapius: God of medicine in classical mythology.

26 *Galen*: Ancient Greek physician still regarded as an authority on medicine in Shakespeare's day.
   heart of elder: Coward. The Host is taking advantage of Caius's ignorance of English idiom in order to insult him with a seeming compliment. Unlike 'heart of oak' which is hard, *heart of elder* is very soft.

27 *stale*: (1) Dupe, laughing-stock; (2) urine of horses (referring to the use of urine for diagnostic purposes).

28 *Jack*: Base; common.

30 *Castalion-King-Urinal*: This is another string of insults thinly veiled as a compliment. The Castilian king was Philip II of Spain, who died in 1598 and was not regarded with favour in England. The spelling of F (*Castalion*) is retained in this edition, because it indicates a further pun on *stale* and, possibly, on 'stallion'.

30–31 *Hector of Greece*: The Host betrays his own ignorance here. Hector was, of course, the Trojan hero who fought the Greeks, and who was, for the Elizabethans, the very type of the true soldier.

36 *against the hair*: Contrary to the natural tendency; against the grain.

40 *Bodykins*: A mild oath meaning God's dear body.

42 *make one*: Join in; take part.

43 *salt*: Vigour.

52–3 *Mockwater*: This invented name seems to combine mockery of the physician's pretensions to be able to diagnose diseases from an examination of the urine with a reference to 'making water' as a manifestation of fear or cowardice. It would be tempting to read 'Make-water', were it not for the fact that F (*Mockewater*) and Q (*mockwater*) are in complete agreement.

57 *jack-dog*: Mongrel.

59 *clapper-claw*: Maul; thrash.
   tightly: Soundly; thoroughly.

64 *wag*: Go on his way.

68 *Frogmore*: A place to the south-east of Windsor.

75–6 *speak for a jackanape*: That is, on behalf of Slender, an idiot.

81 *Cried game*: Isn't the game afoot? (The image is that of hounds giving cry upon sight of their quarry.)

85 *adversary*: The Host's mistake for 'emissary'.

III.I

5 *the pittie-ward*: Towards Windsor Little Park.
   the park-ward: Towards Windsor Great Park.

6 *Old Windsor*: A village south of Frogmore.

11 *chollors*: Evans's version of 'cholers' – angry passions.

13 *urinals*: Glass vessels in which urine was kept for medical inspection.

14 *costard*: Head (originally a large kind of apple).

16–25 *To shallow rivers . . . To shallow, etc.*: These lines are a garbled version of part of the most famous of all Elizabethan lyrics, Christopher Marlowe's 'The Passionate Shepherd to His Love'. The first three stanzas run thus:

> Come live with me, and be my love,
> And we will all the pleasures prove
> That valleys, groves, hills and fields,
> Woods, or steepy mountain yields.
>
> And we will sit upon the rocks,
> Seeing the shepherds feed their flocks

By shallow rivers, to whose falls
Melodious birds sing madrigals.

And I will make thee beds of roses,
And a thousand fragrant posies,
A cap of flowers, and a kirtle,
Embroidered all with leaves of myrtle.

An instrumental version of the tune to which
Marlowe's poem was sung appeared in William
Corkine's *The Second Book of Ayres* (1612). It is
reproduced, along with another version, in *The
British Broadside Ballad and Its Music*, by Claude
M. Simpson (1966). The tune is also given by John
H. Long in his *Shakespeare's Use of Music: The Final
Comedies* (1961). But, while the tune has survived,
it is impossible to say whether Shakespeare meant
Evans to use it, because the metrical version of
Psalm 137 (see note to 23) is also running through
the parson's mind. The best comic effect can prob-
ably be achieved by having the love song sung to
the psalm tune.

19 *posies*: Bunches of flowers.

23 *Whenas I sat in Pabylon*: These words are an intrusion. They come from the first line of Psalm 137 in
the Sternhold and Hopkins hymnal (1562), where
the opening verse takes the following form:

Whenas we sat in Babylon, the rivers round about,
And in remembrance of Sion the tears for grief burst out,
We hanged our harps and instruments the willow trees
    upon,
For in that place men for their use had planted many a
    one.

The psalm tune is printed by Claude M. Simpson
and by John H. Long in the works cited in the note
to 16–25 (above).

24 *vagram*: Confusion of 'fragrant' and 'vagrant'.

25 *etc.*: This word suggests that Evans continues with the song until Simple enters and speaks.

41 *the word*: The Bible.

43 *in your doublet and hose*: Without a cloak.
   doublet: Close-fitting upper garment.
   hose: Close-fitting breeches like tights.

49 *belike*: It would seem.

50 *at most odds*: At the greatest variance.

54 *wide of his own respect*: Indifferent to his own reputation.

58–9 *had as lief*: Would as gladly.

61 *Hibocrates*: Hippocrates, ancient Greek physician.

62 *Galen*: See note on II.3.26.

67 *offer*: Attempt; prepare.

70 *question*: Debate; discuss.

75 *In good time*: Indeed! what a question!

81 *cogscombs*: Evans's pronunciation of 'coxcomb', meaning 'head'.

81–2 *for missing your meetings and appointments*: This is the reading of Q; the words, which seem essential for the completion of the sentence, are omitted from F.

89 *Gallia and Gaul*: Wales and France.

93 *politic*: Cunning; diplomatic.
   Machiavel: Follower of Machiavelli. Niccolò Machiavelli, the great Italian political theorist of the early sixteenth century, was commonly seen in Elizabethan England as the exponent of an immoral statecraft, largely on the evidence of his best-known work, *Il Principe* (1532).

95 *motions*: Evacuations of the bowels.

96 *no-verbs*: Non-existent words (a coinage of the Host's to describe Evans's misuse of English).

97–8 *Give me thy hand, terrestrial; so. Give me thy hand, celestial; so*: This reading is adopted from Q. F merely has *Giue me thy hand (Celestiall) so*, which destroys the carefully balanced symmetry of the Host's speech. See An Account of the Text.

98 *art*: Learning.

100 *burnt sack*: Mulled wine.
  issue: Outcome; conclusion.
101 *to pawn*: As a pledge; as a security.
103 *Trust*: Believe.
106 *sot*: Fool.
108 *vlouting-stog*: Evans means 'flouting-stock; laughing-stock'.
110 *scald*: Scabby; mean.
111 *cogging companion*: Cheating rogue.

III.2

  1 *keep your way*: Go on; don't stop.
  2 *follower*: (1) Servant; (2) one who goes behind another.
  3 *Whether had you rather*: Which of the two would you prefer.
 12 *as idle as she may hang together*: As bored as she can be without falling completely to pieces.
    want: Lack.
 16 *had you*: Did you get.
    weathercock: Indicates that Robin is wearing a feather in his hat.
 17 *what the dickens*: This is the earliest recorded use of this phrase, in which *dickens* is probably a form of 'devil'.
 18 *had him of*: Got him from.
 22 *on's*: On his (colloquial).
 23 *league*: Friendship; alliance.
 30 *point-blank*: Straight; horizontally.
    twelve score: At a distance of twelve score (240) yards.
30–31 *pieces out*: Encourages.
 31 *folly*: Wantonness.
    motion: Prompting; encouragement.
 32 *advantage*: Favourable opportunity.
33–4 *hear this shower sing in the wind*: Divine that trouble is brewing.
 35 *revolted*: Faithless; disloyal.
 36 *take him*: Take him by surprise; catch him out.
 38 *divulge*: Proclaim; reveal.

39 *secure*: Over-confident.

Actaeon: Cuckold. See note on II.1.111.

40 *cry aim*: Shout applause; give approval. Spectators encouraged archers by crying 'Aim!' when they were about to shoot.

46 *knot*: Company; band.

cheer: Fare.

50 *break with*: Break my word to.

56 *stand wholly for*: Entirely support.

58–9 *my nursh-a Quickly*: His housekeeper, Quickly.

62 *speaks holiday*: Uses choice language; talks gaily.

smells April and May: Smells fresh like the springtime.

63 *carry't*: Win the day; succeed.

'Tis in his buttons: The meaning is uncertain, but 'it is predestined' seems likely. The phrase is unknown outside this passage, and the F reading, *buttons*, is probably a compositor's error for some other word – 'browes' perhaps. Q is of no assistance here, since it has *betmes*, which is not a word at all.

66 *is of no having*: Has no property; is of no substance.

66–7 *the wild Prince and Poins*: Prince Hal and his companion Poins in *Henry IV*, *Parts I* and *II*. The remark also associates Fenton with Falstaff as another companion of theirs, and thereby with his lack of ready money.

67 *region*: Rank; social standing.

68 *knit a knot in*: Strengthen; augment.

70 *simply*: As she is; without a dowry.

waits on: Is subject to.

80 *canary*: (1) Sweet wine from the Canaries (which is what the Host means); (2) a lively Spanish dance (referred to by Ford when he says *I'll make him dance*).

81 *pipe-wine*: (1) Wine from the pipe (a cask holding four barrels); (2) whine of the pipe (in the sense of a musical instrument used for the dance). Ford is using elaborate puns to convey his intention of beating Falstaff, the pipe of wine, until he howls and dances.

82 *gentles*: Gentlemen.

III.3

2 *buck-basket*: Dirty-linen basket.

3 *Robert*: F reads *Robin*, but as the little page does not enter until 18 the emendation seems obvious.

6 *charge*: (1) Order; (2) load.

13 *whitsters*: Bleachers of linen.

Datchet Mead: A meadow between Windsor and the Thames.

16 *ha'*: Have (colloquial).

20 *eyas-musket*: Young male sparrow-hawk.

24 *Jack-a-Lent*: Puppet (literally the figure of a man dressed in bright clothes that was set up in the season of Lent for boys to throw stones at).

28–9 *turn me away*: Discard me; dismiss me.

38 *pumpion*: Pumpkin.

39 *turtles*: Turtle-doves (proverbially faithful to their mates).

jays: Light women (because the jay has a gaudy plumage and is given to chatter).

40 *Have I caught thee, my heavenly jewel*: Falstaff is quoting, not quite accurately, for the word *thee* is not in the original, the opening line of the Second Song in Sir Philip Sidney's *Astrophil and Stella* (1591).

42 *period*: Goal; conclusion.

44 *cog*: Tell smooth lies; flatter.

52 *becomes*: Suits; goes well with.

53 *ship-tire*: Elaborate woman's head-dress shaped like a ship.

tire-valiant: Fanciful head-dress.

53–4 *tire of Venetian admittance*: Head-dress fashionable in Venice.

55 *kerchief*: Cloth used to cover the head, female head-dress of an unpretentious kind.

56 *become*: Fit.

58 *absolute*: Perfect; accomplished.

fixture: Placing.

60 *semi-circled farthingale*: Skirt with hoops of whalebone

which made it extend behind but not in front of the
body.

60–61 *I see what thou wert if Fortune, thy foe, were – not
Nature – thy friend*: I can imagine how celebrated
you would be if Fortune, now your enemy since it
has placed you in the middle class, had been your
friend, and not merely Nature, which has given you
beauty but not the rank that should go with it.
'Fortune my foe' was a popular tune.

67 *hawthorn-buds*: Fops; young dandies.

68 *Bucklersbury*: London street where herbalists had their
shops.

68–9 *simple-time*: Midsummer (the time when apothecaries
were supplied with herbs or 'simples', as they were
called).

74 *Counter-gate*: The Counter was the debtors' prison,
and prisons were notorious for the bad smells that
emanated from them.
reek: Smoke; vapour.

83 *presently*: Immediately.

84 *ensconce me*: Hide myself.

85 *arras*: Hanging screen of tapestry placed round the
walls of rooms.

90 *overthrown*: Ruined.

93 *well-a-day*: Alas.

97–8 *Out upon you*: An exclamation of reproach.

109 *clear*: Innocent; clear of guilt.
friend: Lover.

110 *convey him out*: Get him away secretly.
amazed: Confused; bewildered.

112 *good life*: Respectable position in society.

117 *stand*: Waste time over.

123 *bucking*: Washing.
whiting-time: Bleaching-time.

131–2 *and none but thee*: These words, which are not found
in F, are taken from Q. They are included in the
present text because they add force to Falstaff's efforts
to reassure Mistress Page of his love for her.

139 *cowl-staff*: Stout pole used for carrying a basket slung

between two men.

drumble: Dawdle.

141 *come near*: Come in; enter.

146 *what have you to do*: What is it to do with you; what concern of yours is it.

147 *buck-washing*: Process of washing dirty linen by soaking it in an alkaline lye and then beating and rinsing it in clear water.

148–9 *Buck? . . . I warrant you, buck*: Three senses of the word 'buck' are involved here: (1) clothes for washing; (2) male deer (symbolizing cuckoldry); (3) to copulate.

150 *of the season*: In the rutting season.

151 *tonight*: Last night.

153–4 *unkennel the fox*: Dislodge the fox from its hole.

155 *escape*: F reads *vncape*; but there is no known example of this word elsewhere. Assuming that it is addressed to Page and the rest, some editors gloss it as 'uncouple the hounds', while others emend to 'uncope' or 'uncase'. The present editor takes the view that the word is addressed to Falstaff, who, Ford thinks, is now imprisoned in the house. He therefore emends *uncape* to *escape*, meaning 'escape if you can'.

156 *be contented*: Restrain yourself.

156–7 *wrong yourself*: Put yourself in the wrong.

163 *issue*: Outcome; result.

168 *taking*: Fright; state of alarm.

170–71 *I am half afraid he will have need of washing*: Mistress Ford is implying that Falstaff's terror may have made him befoul himself.

174 *strain*: Nature; disposition.

178 *try*: Test.

180 *obey*: Yield to; respond to.

181 *carrion*: Used as a term of contempt.

187 *that*: That which.

188 *compass*: Bring about; accomplish.

190 *use*: Treat. Her question and Ford's reply are both ironic, revolving around their different senses of appropriate behaviour; see Introduction, pp. xlv–xlvii.

195 *wrong*: Discredit; disgrace.

199 *presses*: Cupboards; clothes presses.

203 *suggest*: Prompts you to; tempts you to.
   imagination: Mad idea; baseless suspicion.

204 *distemper*: Disturbance of mind; deranged condition.
   in this kind: Of this sort; of this species.

206 *fault*: Misfortune; weakness.

209 *and five hundred too*: Funny because the lower number makes her less precious.

218 *a-birding*: Hawking with a sparrow-hawk at small birds, which were driven into a bush and then shot.

219 *for the bush*: For driving birds into the bush.

III.4

2 *turn*: Direct; refer.

5 *state*: Estate.
   galled: Chafed away; injured; much reduced.
   expense: Extravagant spending; squandering.

6 *only*: As my sole purpose (in asking for your hand).

7 *bars*: Objections to my claim.

8 *wild societies*: Association with wild companions.

10 *property*: Means to an end.

12 *heaven so speed*: As heaven may prosper.

16 *stamps in gold*: Golden coins.

17 *very*: True.

22 *Break*: Break off; interrupt.

24 *make a shaft or a bolt on't*: Try it one way or the other. (Shafts and bolts were two kinds of arrows.)
   'Slid: By God's eyelid.

32 *ill-favoured*: Ugly.

36 *To*: Go to.
   coz: Kinsman.

42 *cousin*: Kinsman.

46 *come cut and long-tail*: No matter who comes; let them all come (a common proverbial expression, used originally of dogs and horses, to express a whole category).

46–7 *under the degree of*: In the rank of.

49 *jointure*: The part of a husband's estate which he settled on his wife in the marriage contract, in order

to provide for her widowhood in case he died before her.

56 *'Od's heartlings*: Euphemism for the oath 'God's heart'.

62 *motions*: Proposals.

62–3 *happy man be his dole*: Good luck to the man who wins you (a proverbial expression meaning literally 'may his lot be that of a happy man').

76 *for that*: Because.

78 *checks*: Reproofs.

79 *advance the colours*: Raise the standard (as a preliminary to battle).

82 *mean*: Intend.

84 *quick*: Alive.

89 *affected*: Inclined.

96 *once*: At some time.

105 *speciously*: Mistress Quickly's version of 'specially'.

106 *must of*: Must go on. Verbs of motion are often omitted after 'must'.

108 *slack it*: Put it off; be so remiss about it.

III.5

3 *toast*: Piece of hot toast (to warm the drink).

4 *barrow*: Barrow-load.

7–8 *new-year's gift*: In Elizabethan England New Year was the traditional time for the giving of presents.

8 *slighted me*: Slid me slightingly. Q reads *slided me*. It looks very much as though Shakespeare has created a portmanteau word here combining the senses of 'to slide' and 'to slight'.

9 *remorse*: Pity; compunction.

13 *shore*: Bank.
   shelvy: Made of sandbanks; shelving.

16 *mummy*: Dead flesh; mass of pulp.

21 *reins*: Loins; kidneys.

23 *cry you mercy*: Beg your pardon.

25 *chalices*: Drinking cups; small goblets.

25–6 *a pottle*: Two quarts.

28 *Simple of itself*: Unmixed with anything else.
   I'll: I'll have.

29 *brewage*: Concocted drink.

36 *take on with*: Scold.

37 *erection*: Mistress Quickly's mistake for 'direction'.

40 *that*: So that.

41 *yearn*: Grieve.

51 *miss*: Fail.

62 *sped you*: Were you successful.

63 *ill-favouredly*: Badly.

64 *determination*: Mind; decision.

65 *peaking cornuto*: Sneaking cuckold (*cornuto* meaning literally 'the horned one').

66 *dwelling*: Existing.

67 *'larum*: Perturbation; fear.
   me: Ethic dative.

68 *encounter*: Amatory meeting.

70 *rabble*: Pack.

71 *distemper*: Bad temper.

82 *smocks*: slips; linen undergarments.

83 *that*: So that.

90 *knaves*: Menials.
   hinds: Servants.

100 *with*: By.
    bell-wether: Ram with a bell on its neck that leads the flock. Ford made a lot of noise, led the pack, and was, in Falstaff's eyes, a horned man, a cuckold.

101 *compassed*: Bent in the form of a circle.
    bilbo: Sword from Bilbao (noted for the temper and elasticity of its blade).

102 *peck*: Round vessel used as a peck measure.

103 *stopped in*: Fastened in; stoppered in.

104 *fretted*: Rotted; fermented.

105 *kidney*: Constitution.

106 *dissolution*: Melting; liquefaction.

107 *in the height*: At the highest pitch.

109 *Dutch dish*: Dutch cooking was thought of as greasy.

113 *good sadness*: All seriousness.

114 *desperate*: Hopeless.

115 *undertake*: Have to do with.

119 *embassy*: Message.

122 *address me*: Betake myself.

130 *There's a hole made in your best coat*: A proverbial phrase meaning 'your reputation is badly flawed'.

135 *halfpenny purse*: Diminutive purse for holding small silver halfpence.

140 *horn-mad*: Furious with rage at being a cuckold.

IV.1

There is nothing whatever in Q to correspond to this scene. The obvious reason for its complete omission from that text is that it is a self-contained episode, totally unrelated to the rest of the action. What it offers is an amusing picture of the Elizabethan schoolboy and of the kind of education he was subjected to, together with a lot of bawdy innuendo. It has been suggested that Shakespeare wrote it as a sophisticated titbit for a courtly audience, the only audience, it is argued, that would have the knowledge of Latin necessary for a proper appreciation of the blunders and of the improprieties they give rise to. The answer to this view is in the scene itself. Little William, the son of a citizen, already has enough Latin for the purpose. All that is required is an elementary acquaintance with Lily's *Latin Grammar*, the standard authority in schools at the time. It is not William's defective Latin that lets him down, leaving him in a state of innocent ignorance, but the fact that he has hitherto, it would seem, been shielded from contact with some of the grosser and more indecent terms in the English language. Clearly this is a deficiency that will soon be remedied. A citizen audience of grown-up Williams would have no difficulties with the scene.

4 *courageous*: Probably associated in Mistress Quickly's mind with 'raging'.

6 *suddenly*: At once.

7–8 *but bring*: Merely accompany.

12 *let the boys leave to play*: Asked that the boys be given a holiday.

15 *profits nothing in the world at his book*: Makes no

progress at all in his studies.

16 *accidence*: Rudiments of Latin grammar.

23 *'Od's nouns*: God's wounds (an oath).

24 *Peace your tattlings*: Silence your idle prattle.

26 *Polecats*: A slang term for 'prostitutes'.

43 *hung, hang, hog*: Evans's pronunciation of *hunc, hanc, hoc*.

44 *'Hang-hog' is Latin for bacon*: An allusion to an old saying: 'Hog is not bacon until it be hanged'.

49 *caret*: Is lacking (Latin). Mistress Quickly confuses this word with the English word 'carrot'.

57 *Vengeance of Jenny's case*: Fie on Jenny's situation. Some complicated misunderstandings, with very bawdy implications, are going on here. Mistress Quickly takes *Genitive case* as a reference to the occupation of Jenny, the local prostitute, and to the female genital organs; thinks *horum* means 'whore'; and finds yet another sexual allusion in *harum*, 'hare' being a slang term for 'harlot'.

61 *to hick and to hack*: The precise meaning of these words is not known, but 'to drink (causing hiccups) and to wench' seems likely. For *hack*, cf. *These knights will hack* (II.1.47-8).

73 *preeches*: Evans's version of 'breeched', meaning 'flogged on the bare buttocks'.

77 *sprag*: For 'sprack', meaning 'lively, alert'.

IV.2

2 *sufferance*: Suffering; pain.
    obsequious: Devoted; zealous.

3 *to a hair's breadth*: Exactly; precisely.

4-5 *accoutrement*: Suitable formalities (literally 'equipment').

5 *complement*: Accompaniment; external shows.

12 *people*: Servants; household.

20 *lines*: Role; part (a theatrical allusion). Many editors, not recognizing the reference to an actor's part, emend to 'lunes', meaning 'fits of lunacy', but the Q reading, *in his old vaine againe*, shows that *lines* is correct.

22 *complexion*: Appearance; colour of the skin.

23 *Peer out*: A reference to the budding horns of the cuckold.

32 *experiment*: Trial; test.

42 *should*: Can.

43 *bestow*: Dispose of.

47 *that*: So that.

49 *make you*: Are you doing.

52–3 *use to discharge their birding pieces*: Are in the habit of firing off the guns they use for shooting birds. This method of chimney-sweeping is put to good dramatic use in Thomas Middleton's play *The Changeling* (1622).

54 *Creep into the kiln-hole*: F gives these words to Mistress Ford, but in view of what she says at 56–60 Mistress Page seems the likelier speaker.
kiln-hole: Oven.

57 *press*: Clothes cupboard.

58 *abstract*: List; register.

62–3 *If you go . . . go out disguised*: F allots this speech to Mistress Ford, thus giving two consecutive speeches to the same character, which is plainly wrong.

67 *muffler*: Kind of scarf or wrapper worn by women in Shakespeare's day to cover part of the face and the neck.

68 *extremity*: Extravagance.

69 *mischief*: Calamity.

70–71 *the fat woman of Brainford*: Q reads *Gillian of Brainford*, thus giving the fat woman's identity. Gillian of Brainford (the modern Brentford, twelve miles east of Windsor) is the central figure in *Jyl of Breyntfords Testament*, by Robert Copland, a ribald piece of work published about 1560 but probably written twenty years earlier.

73 *thrummed hat*: Hat made of, or perhaps fringed with, 'thrums', the soft waste ends of the weaver's warp.

76 *look*: Look for; search for.

78 *straight*: Immediately.

86 *good sadness*: All seriousness.

88 *try*: Test; make an experiment on.

96 *dishonest*: Lewd; unchaste.

99 *honest*: Chaste.

100 *act*: Commit adultery; fornicate.

101 *Still swine eats all the draff*: The quiet pig eats all the swill (a proverbial expression to describe the demure hypocrite).

103 *hard at*: Close to.

109 *unfool me*: Take the reproach of folly away from me.

110 *Youth in a basket*: Fortunate lover (proverbial).

111 *panderly*: Pimping; procuring.
    knot: Band.
    ging: Old form of 'gang'.
    pack: Plotting confederacy.

112 *Now shall the devil be shamed*: An allusion to the proverb 'Speak the truth and shame the devil'.

115 *passes*: Goes beyond all bounds; beats everything.

126 *Hold it out*: Keep it up.

132–3 *take up your wife's clothes*: Evans blunders again. He means 'pick up your wife's dirty clothes', but what he says is 'lift up your wife's dress', the preliminary to sexual intercourse.

139 *intelligence*: Information.

140 *Pluck me out*: Pluck out for me.

144 *By my fidelity*: On my word of honour.

145 *wrongs*: Disgraces.

146 *pray*: In order to drive out the devil by whom Ford is, Evans thinks, possessed.

151 *show no colour for my extremity*: Admit no excuse for my extravagant behaviour.

152 *table sport*: Laughing-stock of the company.

154 *leman*: Lover; paramour (with a pun on 'lemon').

161 *quean*: Jade; woman of questionable reputation.
    cozening: Cheating; deceiving.

162 *of errands*: Ford suspects the fat woman is a bawd.

165 *by th' figure*: Either by using astrological diagrams or by making effigies in wax for the purpose of enchantment.

daubery: Specious methods; false shows; trickery.

166 *beyond our element*: Out of our sphere; beyond our comprehension.

169 *not strike*: F omits *not*; but it is clearly demanded by the sense, and was inserted in the second Folio (1632).

172 *prat her*: Beat her buttocks ('prats' being a slang word for 'buttocks').

173 *rag*: Worthless creature *Ragge* is the reading of F. Many editors prefer *hag*, the reading of the third Quarto (1630), which is based on F, and of the third Folio (1664).

174 *polecat*: Whore.
     ronyon: An abusive term for a woman, probably meaning 'scabby old wretch'.
     conjure: Charm; bewitch.

178–9 *'Tis a goodly credit for you*: It does you great credit (ironical).

185 *issue*: Final outcome.
     cry out: Bark (like a hound in full cry).

186 *trail*: Track; scent.
     open: Give tongue (hunting language).

187 *obey his humour*: Give way to his whim.

197 *wantonness*: Lust.

198–9 *in fee simple, with fine and recovery*: In complete possession, under the fullest legal sanction (legal terminology).

199–200 *in the way of waste*: As mere objects to be exploited. Mistress Page is carrying on the legal terminology in suggesting that Falstaff has been treating them both as though they were a piece of common land. There is probably a quibble on 'waist'.

204 *figures*: Idle fancies; phantasms.

206 *ministers*: Agents.

208 *period*: Limit; fitting conclusion.

IV.3

This scene introduces the horse-stealing episode, which is never properly worked out or fully integrated into the structure of the play. Its most significant addition to the plots is as part of the focus on revenge. See Introduction, pp. xxv–xxviii.

9 *sauce them*: Make them pay dearly; make it hot for them.

9–10 *at command*: Reserved.

11 *come off*: Pay up.

IV.4

1 *'Tis*: She is.
best discretions of a 'oman: Most discreet women.

3 *at an instant*: At the same time.

6 *with*: Of.

10 *submission*: Four syllables.

24 *use*: Treat; deal with.

26 *old tale*: The legend seems to be invented. *Herne* is a dialect form of 'heron', a water bird, but the type of story Shakespeare has in mind is linked to the attention of the 'green man' or 'wild man of the woods' of pagan folklore.

27 *Sometime*: Once; formerly.

29 *ragg'd*: Rugged; jagged.

30 *blasts*: Blights; withers.
takes: Bewitches.

31 *milch-kine*: Dairy cattle.

34 *eld*: People of olden times.

35 *Received*: Accepted (from the past).

37 *want not*: Are not lacking.

39 *device*: Plan; contrivance.

41 *Disguised like Herne . . . head*: Omitted from F, this line preserved in Q is essential, for without it Page's words *And in this shape* (43) make no sense.

47 *growth*: Size; stature.

48 *urchins*: Goblins.
ouphes: Elves.

49 *rounds*: Circlets.

52 *sawpit*: Pit used for sawing timber.

53 *diffusèd*: Confused; disorderly.

56 *pinch*: Pinching was the traditional way in which fairies punished those who incurred their displeasure.

59 *MISTRESS FORD*: F gives this speech to Ford.

60 *sound*: Soundly.

66 *jackanapes*: Properly 'tame monkey', but Evans must mean 'satyr', since this is the form he actually takes.

67 *taber*: Evans's version of 'taper'.

68 *vizards*: Masks.

73 *Eton*: Across the river from Windsor.

76 *properties*: In the theatrical sense.

77 *tricking*: Costumes; ornaments.

85 *affects*: Likes.

IV.5

2 *discuss*: Declare; make known.

6 *truckle-bed*: Small bed on castors, which could be pushed under the larger *standing-bed* when not in use.

7 *Prodigal*: The Prodigal Son in the Bible.

8 *Anthropophaginian*: Man-eater; cannibal.

11 *be so bold as stay*: Venture so far as to wait.

16 *Ephesian*: Boon companion.

18 *Bohemian-Tartar*: Barbarian; wild man.
   tarries: Waits for.

23 *wise woman*: Witch and fortune-teller.

25 *mussel-shell*: Empty-headed useless fool.

28 *thorough*: Through.

29 *beguiled him of*: Cheated him out of; robbed him of.

34 *cozened*: Cheated.

35 SIMPLE: F, mistakenly, allots this speech to Falstaff.

40 *conceal*: Simple's mistake for 'reveal'.

50 *like who more bold*: As bold as the boldest.

53 *clerkly*: Scholarly; a man of learning.

57 *was paid*: Suffered; was beaten.

59 *mere*: Absolute; nothing but.

60 *varletto*: Rascal (the Host's attempt to turn 'varlet' into Italian).

64 *Doctor Faustuses*: An allusion to the hero of Marlowe's play *Doctor Faustus*, who practised black magic.

69 *Have a care of your entertainments*: Evans means 'beware of your guests, keep a sharp eye on the people you entertain'.

71 *cozen-germans*: (1) First cousins; (2) cozening

Germans, German cheats. The reading of Q is *cosen garmombles*, which has led to much learned speculation. It has been seen as a reference to Frederick, Count of Mömpelgart, who visited England in 1592 and became very desirous of being made a member of the Order of the Garter. He was finally elected to the Order in 1597, by which time he had become the Duke of Würtemberg, but the investiture took place in his absence, and Queen Elizabeth did not bother to send on the insignia of the Order to him. There may be something in this; but Q is so inaccurate that *garmombles* could well be nothing more than the reporter's version of 'German nobles' or something of that kind.

Readins: Evan's version of 'Reading'.

72 *Colebrook*: Modern Colnbrook, a village not far from Windsor.

73 *for good will*: Out of friendship (ironical).

74 *vlouting-stocks*: Evans means 'flouting-stocks; laughing-stocks'.

convenient: right; proper; fitting (ironical).

77 *doubtful*: Apprehensive.

81 *that the court is know to come*: Caius's attempt at 'whose coming the court knows of'.

83 *Hue and cry*: Shout calling for general pursuit of a felon or felons.

villain: Addressed to Bardolph.

90 *liquor*: Grease; oil.

91–2 *crestfallen as a dried pear*: A defeated cock is crestfallen and a dried pear is shrivelled; the two are joined together into a ridiculous image of Falstaff's reduced (phallic) state.

92 *forswore myself*: Lied (about my cards).

93 *primero*: A card game.

93–4 *to say my prayers*: Omitted from F, these words, which are essential to the sense, have been preserved in Q.

102 *speciously*: For 'specially'.

103 *that*: So that.

109 *action*: Movements and behaviour.
117 *crossed*: Thwarted.

IV.6

2 *I will give over all*: I will give up.
10 *answered*: Responded to; requited.
11 *far forth*: Far.
12 *to*: According to.
13 *contents*: Stress on the second syllable.
14 *larded with my matter*: Intermixed with the matter that concerns me.
17 *image*: Main idea.
18 *at large*: As a whole.
20 *present*: Represent; play the part of.
22 *something rank on foot*: Going forward in some profusion.
29 *shuffle*: Spirit; use trickery to get.
30 *tasking of*: Occupying; making demands on.
31 *attends*: Awaits.
34 *it rests*: Matters stand.
36 *habit*: Dress.
38 *intended*: Planned; arranged.
40 *vizarded*: Disguised.
41 *quaint*: Elaborately; elegantly.
42 *flaring*: Streaming loose.
43 *vantage*: Opportunity.
44 *token*: Sign; signal.
48 *here it rests*: This remains to be done.
51 *united ceremony*: The union of the marriage rite.
52 *husband your device*: Manage your plan prudently.
54 *bound*: Indebted; under obligation.
55 *present recompense*: Immediate reward.

V.1

1 *hold*: Keep my word; keep the appointment.
2 *third time*: Alluding to the proverb 'The third time pays for all'.
3 *divinity*: Oracular power; divination.
7 *wears*: Wears on; passes.
8 *mince*: Walk off in an affected manner.
12 *yesterday*: Shakespeare has nodded here; the beating

of Falstaff took place on the morning of this same
day.

20–21 *Goliath with a weaver's beam*: An allusion to 1 Samuel
17:7: 'And the shaft of his [Goliath's] spear was like
a weaver's beam . . .'

21 *life is a shuttle*: Falstaff, whose knowledge of the
Bible is impressive, is here quoting from the Book
of Job 7:6: 'My days pass over more speedily than
a weaver's shuttle . . . '

23–4 *pluncked geese, played truant and whipped top*: Three
mischievous activities seen as typical of boyhood.

V.2

1 *couch*: Lie hidden.

5 *nay-word*: Password; watchword.

6 *mum . . . budget*: The two words together form
'mumbudget', meaning 'silence'.

9 *decipher*: Indicate; distinguish.

11 *become*: Suit, fit.

V.3

7 *abuse*: Ill-usage.

12 *the Welsh devil Hugh*: The F reading is *the Welch-
deuill Herne*, but Herne is not a Welsh devil, and
the emendation is accepted by most editors.

13 *couched*: Hidden.

17 *cannot choose but amaƺe*: Is bound to frighten.

20 *betray*: Deceive.

21 *lewdsters*: Lascivious persons; lechers.

V.5

0 *Enter Falstaff . . . upon him*: This direction is adapted
from that in Q, which reads *Enter sir Iohn with a
Bucks head vpon him*.

2 *hot-blooded*: Amorous; lecherous.

3 *Jove, thou wast a bull for thy Europa*: In classical myth
Jove, the king of the gods, abducted Europa by
appearing to her in the form of a milk-white bull.
He seemed so gentle that after garlanding his horns
with flowers she climbed on to his back. Thereupon
he dashed into the sea and swam away with her.

6–7 *Jupiter, a swan for the love of Leda*: Referring to

another of Jove's amorous exploits: his seduction of
Leda by appearing to her in the guise of a swan.

8 *complexion*: Appearance.

11 *hot backs*: Carnal desires; strong sexual urges.

13 *rut-time*: season of the year in which the male deer
become sexually excited.

14 *to piss my tallow*: If I urinate my fat away (alluding
to the fact that stags grow thin in the rutting season).

18 *scut*: Short tail of a deer or rabbit.

19 *potatoes*: Yams; sweet potatoes (regarded as an aphrodisiac in Elizabethan times).

19 *Greensleeves*: See note on II.1.59.

20 *kissing-comfits*: Perfumed sugar-plums (used to sweet-
en the breath).
eringoes: Sweetmeats made from the candied root of
sea holly (thought to be an aphrodisiac).

21 *provocation*: Erotic stimulation.

24 *bribed*: Stolen.

25–6 *the fellow of this walk*: The keeper in charge of this
part of the forest. Falstaff is quibbling; he means
(1) that his shoulders are the perquisite of the keeper;
(2) that he will use them to shoulder off the keeper,
should he turn up.

27 *woodman*: (1) Hunter, one skilled in woodcraft; (2)
woman-hunter; (3) wild man of the woods, like Herne.

28 *Cupid*: God of love in classical mythology.
of conscience: Who is conscientious; who keeps his
word.

36 *cross*: Thwart.

38 *shades*: Phantoms; spirits.

39 *orphan*: Probably an allusion to the belief that fairies
had no fathers.

40 *Attend your office and your quality*: Apply yourselves
to your proper function and business.

41 *oyes*: Hear ye (call of the public crier, from the
French *oyez*).

42 *list*: Listen for.
toys: trifles; things of no substance.

44 *unraked*: where the embers have not been covered with

ashes so as to keep the fire going all night.

46 *sluttery*: Sluttishness.

48 *wink*: Close my eyes.

couch: Lie hidden.

51 *Raise up the organs of her fantasy*: Stimulate her imagination (so that she has pleasant dreams).

52 *Sleep she*: May she sleep; let her sleep.

careless: Free from cares; untroubled by anxieties.

53 *as*: Who.

55 *About*: Get to work; bestir yourselves.

57 *ouphes*: Elves.

58 *perpetual doom*: Day of Judgement.

59 *wholesome*: Sound.

60 *Worthy the owner and the owner it*: As suitable to its owner (Queen Elizabeth) as she is to such dignity.

61 *The several chairs of order*: Each of the chairs of the order.

order: Order of knighthood (in this case the Order of the Garter).

62 *balm*: Fragrant, aromatic substance.

look: Make sure; take care that.

63 *instalment*: Place or seat wherein a person is installed; stall.

coat: Coat of arms.

several crest: Separate heraldic device.

64 *blazon*: Armorial bearings.

65–73 *And nightly, meadow-fairies . . . charactery*: They are to make 'fairy rings' in the grass which will resemble the blue ribbon worn below the knee of the Garter knights, their flowers imitating its jewelled inscription.

66 *compass*: Circle.

67 *expressure*: Impression; picture.

69 *Honi soit qui mal y pense*: Shamed be he who thinks evil of it (French – the motto of the Order of the Garter).

70 *tufts*: Bunches.

73 *charactery*: Writing (pronounced to rhyme with 'refractory').

75 *dance of custom*: Customary dance.

79 *measure*: Dance.

80 *man of middle earth*: Mortal (*middle earth* being the earth seen as midway between heaven and hell).

82 *a piece of cheese*: The Welshman's fondness for cheese was the subject of a number of 'merry tales' in the sixteenth century, a stock joke. Cf. II.2.287–8.

83 *o'erlooked*: Looked upon with the evil eye; bewitched.

84 *trial-fire*: Testing fire (as in the trial by ordeal).

86 *turn*: Put.

92 *still*: Continually.

The Song: The original music for this song has not survived.

94 *luxury*: Lechery; lasciviousness.

95 *bloody fire*: Fire in the blood.

99 *mutually*: Jointly; all together.

102 *During this song . . . Mistress Ford*. There is, as usual, no stage direction in F at this point. Q, from which the direction in this edition is adapted, reads as follows: *Here they pinch him, and sing about him, & the Doctor comes one way & steales away a boy in red. And Slender another way he takes a boy in greene: And Fenton steales misteris Anne, being in white. And a noyse of hunting is made within: and all the Fairies runne away. Falstaffe pulles of his bucks head, and rises vp. And enters M. Page, M. Ford, and their wiues, M. Shallow, Sir Hugh*. The reference to Shallow is particularly interesting, because in F he has no lines to speak in this scene, and there is therefore no warrant for bringing him on, though in keeping with Shakespeare's general practice in comedy one would expect him to be present at the denouement, especially as his 'wise cousin' is so intimately involved in it. Q, on the other hand, gives him a speech as well as an entrance. He is the first of the company to address Falstaff, saying to him *God saue you sir Iohn Falstaffe*. It seems highly probable that these words, or something like them, were part of the text, but were omitted from F.

103 *watched you*: Caught you in the act.
105 *hold up*: Prolong; continue.
    higher: Further; longer.
107 *yokes*: Mistress Page means Falstaff's horns, of course, but also the idea of the cuckold's horns which has so obsessed Ford.
114 *arrested*: Seized on a legal warrant.
120 *ox*: Fool. 'To make an ox of one' was to make a fool of him.
    proofs: Horns.
    extant: (1) In existence; (2) conspicuous, standing out to view, protuberant.
124 *power*: Intellectual faculties.
    foppery: Deceit; dupery.
125 *received belief*: Article of faith; absolute conviction.
    in despite of the teeth of: Contrary to; in spite of.
126 *wit*: Inventiveness of mind.
127 *Jack-a-Lent*: See note on III.3.24.
135 *wants matter*: Lacks the capacity; has no means.
136 *ridden with*: Harassed by; tyrannized over by.
    Welsh goat: For the Elizabethan English the important place which the goat had in the rural economy of Wales was an indication of the poverty of that country. Cf. Glendower's remark: 'The goats ran from the mountains' (*Henry IV, Part I*, III.1.36).
137 *coxcomb of frieʒe*: Fool's cap of coarse woollen cloth (of the kind made in Wales).
142 *makes fritters*: Makes a hash.
143 *decay*: ruin; cause of destruction.
    late-walking: Staying out late (to keep assignations with women).
146–7 *by the head and shoulders*: Violently; headlong.
150 *hodge-pudding*: Large sausage made of numerous ingredients.
    bag of flax: Sackful of flax for weaving; both images are of receptacles stuffed full of their contents.
151 *puffed*: Inflated; blown up.
152 *intolerable*: Excessive.
154–5 *Job*: The biblical figure. See Job 1:9–11, where Satan

slanders him, and Job 2:9, where his wife tempts him to curse God.

157 *metheglins*: Welsh mead.

158 *starings*: Swaggerings; efforts to stare one out of countenance.

pribbles and prabbles: Empty chatter and petty quarrels.

159 *start*: Advantage.

160 *dejected*: Cast down; humbled.

161 *is a plummet o'er me*: Has sounded me; has got to the bottom of me.

plummet: (1) Woollen fabric (quibbling on *flannel*); (2) plummet-line (used for sounding depths at sea).

165 *should*: Were to.

that: That which.

168 *posset*: Drink made of hot milk curdled with ale, wine, or the like.

172 *Doctors doubt that*: A traditional phrase expressing disbelief.

175–6 *dispatched*: Settled the business.

178 *on't*: Of it (colloquial).

181 *lubberly*: Clumsy; loutish.

182 *swinged*: Beaten; thrashed (pronounced to rhyme with 'fringed').

184–5 *postmaster's boy*: Boy working for the man who has charge of the post horses.

200 *un paysan*: A yokel; a peasant (French).

212 *amaze*: Perplex; bewilder.

215 *contracted*: Betrothed.

216 *sure*: Firmly united (in marriage).

219 *unduteous title*: Name of undutifulness.

220 *evitate*: Avoid.

227 *stand*: Station taken up by a hunter.

glanced: Missed its mark.

231 *muse*: Grumble.

PENGUIN SHAKESPEARE

ALL'S WELL THAT ENDS WELL
WILLIAM SHAKESPEARE

A poor physician's daughter cures the King of France, and in return is promised the hand of any nobleman she wishes. But the man she chooses, the proud young Count of Rosillion, refuses to consummate the forced marriage and flees to Florence. Depicting the triumph of trickery over youthful arrogance, *All's Well that Ends Well* is among Shakespeare's darkest romantic comedies, yet it remains a powerful tribute to the strength of love.

This book includes a general introduction to Shakespeare's life and the Elizabethan theatre, a separate introduction to *All's Well That Ends Well*, a chronology of his works, suggestions for further reading, an essay discussing performance options on both stage and screen, and a commentary.

Edited by Barbara Everett

With an introduction by Janette Dillon

General Editor: Stanley Wells

Penguin Shakespeare

TWELFTH NIGHT
WILLIAM SHAKESPEARE

Separated from her twin brother Sebastian after a shipwreck, Viola disguises herself as a boy to serve the Duke of Illyria. Wooing a countess on his behalf, she is stunned to find herself the object of his beloved's affections. With the arrival of Viola's brother, and a trick played upon the countess's steward, confusion reigns in this romantic comedy of mistaken identity.

This book includes a general introduction to Shakespeare's life and the Elizabethan theatre, a separate introduction to *Twelfth Night*, a chronology of his works, suggestions for further reading, an essay discussing performance options on both stage and screen, and a commentary.

Edited by M. M. Mahood

With an introduction by Michael Dobson

General Editor: Stanley Wells

PENGUIN SHAKESPEARE

OTHELLO
WILLIAM SHAKESPEARE

A popular soldier and newly married man, Othello seems to be in an enviable position. And yet, when his supposed friend sows doubts in his mind about his wife's fidelity, he is gradually consumed by suspicion. In this powerful tragedy, innocence is corrupted and trust is eroded as every relationship is drawn into a tangled web of jealousies.

This book includes a general introduction to Shakespeare's life and the Elizabethan theatre, a separate introduction to *Othello*, a chronology of his works, suggestions for further reading, an essay discussing performance options on both stage and screen, and a commentary.

Edited by Kenneth Muir

With an introduction by Tom McAlindon

General Editor: Stanley Wells

PENGUIN SHAKESPEARE

JULIUS CAESAR
WILLIAM SHAKESPEARE

When it seems that Julius Caesar may assume supreme power, a plot to destroy him is hatched by those determined to preserve the threatened republic. But the different motives of the conspirators soon become apparent when high principles clash with malice and political realism. As the nation plunges into bloody civil war, this taut drama explores the violent consequences of betrayal and murder.

This book includes a general introduction to Shakespeare's life and the Elizabethan theatre, a separate introduction to *Julius Caesar*, a chronology of his works, suggestions for further reading, an essay discussing performance options on both stage and screen, and a commentary.

Edited by Norman Sanders

With an introduction by Martin Wiggins

General editor: Stanley Wells

PENGUIN SHAKESPEARE

MEASURE FOR MEASURE
WILLIAM SHAKESPEARE

In the Duke's absence from Vienna, his strict deputy Angelo revives an ancient law forbidding sex outside marriage. The young Claudio, whose fiancée is pregnant, is condemned to death by the law. His sister Isabella, soon to become a nun, pleads with Lord Angelo for her brother's life. But her purity so excites Angelo that he offers her a monstrous bargain – he will save Claudio if Isabella will visit him that night.

This book includes a general introduction to Shakespeare's life and the Elizabethan theatre, a separate introduction to *Measure for Measure*, a chronology of his works, suggestions for further reading, an essay discussing performance options on both stage and screen by Nicholas Arnold, and a commentary.

Edited by J. M. Nosworthy

With an introduction by Julia Briggs

General Editor: Stanley Wells

PENGUIN SHAKESPEARE

HAMLET
WILLIAM SHAKESPEARE

A young Prince meets with his father's ghost, who alleges that his own brother, now married to his widow, murdered him. The Prince devises a scheme to test the truth of the ghost's accusation, feigning wild madness while plotting a brutal revenge. But his apparent insanity soon begins to wreak havoc on innocent and guilty alike.

This book includes a general introduction to Shakespeare's life and the Elizabethan theatre, a separate introduction to *Hamlet*, a chronology of his works, suggestions for further reading, an essay discussing performance options on both stage and screen by Paul Prescott, and a commentary.

Edited by T. J. B. Spencer

With an introduction by Alan Sinfield

General Editor: Stanley Wells

PENGUIN SHAKESPEARE

A MIDSUMMER NIGHT'S DREAM
WILLIAM SHAKESPEARE

A young woman flees Athens with her lover, only to be pursued by her would-be husband and by her best friend. Unwittingly, all four find themselves in an enchanted forest where fairies and sprites soon take an interest in human affairs, dispensing magical love potions and casting mischievous spells. In this dazzling comedy, confusion ends in harmony, as love is transformed, misplaced, and – ultimately – restored.

This book includes a general introduction to Shakespeare's life and the Elizabethan theatre, a separate introduction to *A Midsummer Night's Dream*, a chronology of his works, suggestions for further reading, an essay discussing performance options on both stage and screen, and a commentary.

Edited by Stanley Wells

With an introduction by Helen Hackett

General Editor: Stanley Wells

PENGUIN SHAKESPEARE